THE INNOVATION MINDSET

THE INNOVATION MINDSET

Eight Essential Steps to Transform Any Industry

LORRAINE H. MARCHAND

WITH JOHN HANC

 Columbia Business School
Publishing

Columbia University Press
Publishers Since 1893
New York   Chichester, West Sussex
cup.columbia.edu

Copyright © 2022 Columbia University Press

Library of Congress Cataloging-in-Publication Data
Names: Marchand, Lorraine Hudson, author. | Hanc, John, author.
Title: The innovation mindset : eight essential steps to transform
 any industry / Lorraine Hudson Marchand with John Hanc.
Description: New York : Columbia University Press, [2022] | Includes index.
Identifiers: LCCN 2021053902 | ISBN 9780231203081 (hardback) |
 ISBN 9780231554862 (ebook)
Subjects: LCSH: Product design. | Product management. |
 Technological innovations—Economic aspects.
Classification: LCC HF5415.153 .M3378 2022 |
 DDC 658.5/75—dc23/eng/20211109
LC record available at https://lccn.loc.gov/2021053902

Cover design: Noah Arlow

TO DAD, AN ORIGINAL THINKER, WHO SHOWED ME HOW
PROBLEMS ARE OPPORTUNITIES WAITING TO BE CREATED.

TO MY SONS, JOE, NICK, AND MATT,

YOU POSSESS INNOVATOR DNA—CURIOSITY, CREATIVITY,
AND RESILIENCE. STAY ALERT AND YOUR HEART AND
HEAD WILL REVEAL OPPORTUNITIES TO PUT IT TO USE
FOR GOOD.

CONTENTS

FOREWORD

Spencer Rascoff

What Lorraine Marchand has written in this book is nothing short of, well, innovative. The detailed road map that follows, packed with engaging anecdotes and practical planning processes from companies of every size and scale, will provide any individual or team the tools needed to create the perfect environment for innovation. Discussing notables and novices alike, Lorraine's examples and commentaries are relevant and fascinating.

Lorraine is a dynamic force, writing on a subject that she not only espouses but embodies herself. As the GM of Life Sciences for IBM's Watson Health, a strategist for big pharma, a repeat start-up founder, a director at NIH, and a professor at Columbia Business School, she has a breadth of experience and insights that have empowered her to innovate and pivot throughout her career, just as she guides businesses to do.

She will equip readers to ideate unique start-ups, learn comprehensive steps for customer research and advancement, and be inspired to foster innovation throughout every stage of a company's growth. The examples and actionable techniques laid out in the following pages will set up innovators of any age for success—and would have been a welcome tool in my own arsenal when I began my professional career.

I've had the good fortune to be involved in a number of inventive companies—companies such as Hotwire, Zillow, and Pacaso—that successfully disrupted massive sectors of the economy, including travel, real estate, and the vacation-home market. I'm also an angel investor and have invested in more than one hundred start-ups.

Lorraine's Laws of Innovation are right on. In fact, I give similar advice to my portfolio companies and use some of her laws to determine where to invest.

First, Lorraine says that a successful innovation must offer a solution. I agree with this completely. This was the case for my three successful companies. Hotwire, founded in 2000, changed the way people booked travel. Internet-assisted travel booking was still new, and hotels and airlines were changing the way they thought about inventory and distribution. Consumers, too, had few options for booking at that time. We created Hotwire to solve both those problems—and twenty-two years later, the brand is still going strong.

I agree with this law of innovation so much that it is one of my criteria for investment. If a company can't easily define a problem for me—and show me they are solving it—I won't invest.

I've also had deep experience with Law 4 (one hundred customers can't be wrong) and Law 5 (be ready to pivot at any point in the process).

At Zillow, a key to our success was always listening to customers. Lorraine is a proponent of one hundred interviews—talking to people of different demographics but all prospective customers. This is critical, and such practices formed the brand and foundation of all of my companies. At Zillow, this practice was continual. We talked to customers constantly—in an annual survey of thousands of home buyers, sellers, renters, and owners; in one-on-one interviews and small focus groups; and on social media. Those insights formed the basis for ongoing product and marketing decisions and are a key to any company's success—big or small.

I've also seen the pivot, or "3-P," law in action—and this can be the toughest one for a start-up founder or a leader of a mature company. When we launched Zillow in 2006 it was merely a voyeuristic toy, a way to bring information transparency to real estate. But through product innovation and acquisitions, we expanded Zillow into new businesses such as rentals, mortgages, and title and escrow. We also morphed from a media business that was dependent upon advertising into a transactional business that helped people complete real estate transactions. There were pivots, and unpivots, and repivots along the way. But as we navigated these advances, we followed consumer preferences and grew the company enormously.

It wasn't easy, by any means. Lorraine's book gives guidance for how to know when it's time to pivot—and how to do it well.

The Innovation Mindset is an excellent insider's guide, complete with planning templates and Lorraine's "innovation must-haves." Whether founding a start-up or creatively problem-solving within a large corporation, seize the moment. Be curious, be creative, be adaptable—and always be so. I wish you well on your own journey to innovation.

Spencer Rascoff
Cofounder and former CEO, Zillow
Cofounder and executive chairman, dot.LA
Angel investor in more than one hundred companies

FOREWORD

Laura Maness

A s the first female CEO of the North American flagship agency of Havas Group, I've spent the majority of my career fostering a culture of continuous innovation and creating deeper meaning for some of the most recognized companies in the world—all the while breaking the tired old *Mad Men*-era traditions that no longer serve the advertising (or any other) business.

Over the past three decades, I have often found myself one of the few females in the room—be it in meetings with staff and clients, in the boardroom as a director, or in the start-up world, where I consult, advise, and invest in what I believe can be world-changing ideas.

I know Lorraine Marchand has had the same feeling of being outnumbered. And I also know that despite the challenges that women have been facing in the workplace since the days of Don Draper, Lorraine has risen in her industry as a new-products development specialist, a consultant, an educator—all the way to her current role as a general manager of IBM Watson Health, where she is helping develop new ideas for no less an innovator than Big Blue.

An innovation mindset, much like the one that Lorraine helps you cultivate in this book, is what fuels us at Havas, perhaps best known for creating one of the most iconic and celebrated ad campaigns of all time, "The Most Interesting Man in the World" for Dos Equis.

As one of the world's largest integrated communications agencies (home to 19,000 people across more than sixty village offices in one hundred countries), Havas uses that kind of creativity to help our clients create breakthrough work and unlock new sources of growth. That approach has also helped us develop pioneering accelerator programs that open access for marginalized talent and advance women and people of color at a faster pace. Through these initiatives, we are helping to reinvent parental leave and mental-wellness benefits and achieve pay equity across race and gender. Simply put, we will stop at nothing less than radically transforming the culture and the employee experience for the better.

So far, the results of these innovative approaches to cultivating an inclusive growth culture are staggering, yielding a retention rate of more than twice the norm for the ad industry.

That all started with a mindset—yes, an innovation mindset, which, as Lorraine explains in these pages, is the starting point for all meaningful change in your business and career, no matter what industry or field you are in. Lorraine's book offers a wealth of practical advice and a tested-and-true, step-by-step approach on how to make your brainstorm a reality—whether it's a business, a service, or a game-changing idea.

Women can lead that change. I'm seeing it happen from the front lines. Females are now the majority in Havas's group globally, a concept that would have seemed like a pipe dream nearly a decade ago. And I believe a similar transformation is happening in many sectors of our society. New-product development, innovation, and entrepreneurship—predominantly male preserves in the past—are now opening up to a diverse group of underestimated people. And that's of course what we'd all like: a world where all innovators, where people with great ideas of any gender identity and any race or background, are welcome and encouraged.

A charming and illustrative anecdote that Lorraine relates early in her book—about how her father encouraged her to create her first innovation at a diner she and her family used to frequent when she was a child—particularly resonated with me. I recently found my own "sugar packet solution" in leading the development of a breakthrough innovation for Havas by becoming—along with such forward-thinking and concerned companies as Patagonia, Allbirds, and Athleta—a certified B Corporation that places equal emphasis on people, planet, and profit and uses business as a measurable force for good.

If achieving such lofty goals sounds like an unreachable dream to you, then you most assuredly need this book. For innovators, there are no limits. If you want to soar to new heights, if you're interested in innovating around the highest priorities and needs of our world today, if you're curious about what led to some of the greatest inventions of our time, or if you're simply looking to unlock your own business-building, new-product-developing potential, follow Lorraine's practical guide to mobilize your own innovation mindset.

Word of caution as you dive in . . . you just might change the world.

Laura Maness
Chief Executive Officer, Havas, New York
ny.havas.com; annex88.com
Most Innovative Culture (*Digiday* 2018); Best Places to Work (*Ad Age* 2019 & 2021); Best Collaborative Agency Team (*Adexchanger* 2020); CEO of the Year Finalist & Network Agency of the Year (*The Drum* 2021)

THE INNOVATION MINDSET

INTRODUCTION

How Sweet It Is: The Spark of a Great Idea

Several years ago, I found myself standing in front of a group of ninety-six executives from a Fortune 100 corporation. We were in one of those cavernous conference rooms at a corporate meeting center, dimly lit to accommodate the parade of slide presentations that preceded my talk, which was after the morning break. The executives were sitting at round tables to facilitate group discussion, but most were intent on their mobile screens, seemingly oblivious to the presence of the colleagues around them.

They didn't seem like an energized, forward-looking group, and that might have been part of the reason for bringing them together that day. Like so many others, this corporation, a major player in the pharmaceutical industry, was acquiring most of its intellectual property, products, and services from academia, small companies, and codevelopment collaborations with peers. The CEO believed his executives could be trained in the science and art of generating new ideas. He wanted to create a culture of innovation, one that would flow down like a waterfall from him to the executives to their teams.

My job was to show them what that looked like: a culture that would embrace new ideas and encourage creativity; an organization that, when properly tapped, could produce a torrent of free-flowing, fresh ideas worthy of satisfying customers and making it to market. It's what I called the Innovation Mindset.

The name of my session that morning, "How to Innovate Without Fail," promised a process that could be followed from inception to market. I suspected the executives were expecting a formula they could execute after lunch and without too much effort. Some were probably hoping the CEO's latest obsession with innovative cultures would blow over.

But I knew that he was on to something, regardless of whether his management team was on board.

And before I could get them excited—before I could show them that, in my opinion, their CEO was absolutely right in pointing this ship in the direction of change—I needed to know more about them.

I started out by asking the distracted executives to rate, on a scale of 1–10 with 10 as the highest, their level of general curiosity. Most raised their hands at 4 or 5; no one was higher than a 7.

So, not that curious.

I then asked them to think back to when they were twelve or thirteen years old. "What were you dreaming about?" I asked. "How curious were you then? What were you doing in your free time?"

That question seemed to stir something in this incurious bunch. I saw a few brows wrinkle and a few eyes gaze off, conjuring up images of long ago.

"My friends and I hung out at the local firehouse; I wanted to be a fireman," one man volunteered. "I guess I still do spend most of my day putting out fires other people make." A few people chuckled.

"Well, I know one thing, I wasn't dreaming about sitting in meetings twelve hours a day," a woman in a crisp white blouse said. Some heads nodded in agreement.

Point taken. I wanted to say, "Don't worry, I'm not going to waste your time," but now others had raised a hand, wanting to speak.

The head of engineering, wearing a white polo with the corporate insignia, grabbed the mic. "My uncle helped me make glue for my science fair project in sixth grade and that experience stayed with me," he said. "I ended up in chemical engineering. I like figuring out how things work."

A couple of others spoke up. One guy, fascinated with robots as a kid and working in logistics, said he'd love to see the company invest in drone technology.

A woman, about fifty years old, raised her hand and made eye contact with me. I nodded for her to speak. "My mom died from breast cancer when I was fourteen. I decided to go into cancer research as a result. I'm a breast cancer survivor with a sixteen-year-old daughter. I'm doing this for my family and all the patients and families affected by cancer."

She had shared a deeply personal testimony in front of a large group of colleagues. I thanked her for her courage.

I sensed the mood had suddenly shifted. This room of extremely accomplished professionals, nominated (whether they liked it or not) by the executive team to participate in a two-day retreat on innovation, seemed to have been shaken out of their torpor. A handful seemed tuned into their passion and willing to talk about it. The rest now seemed less interested in their text messages and more attentive to what I might have to say.

"That's great, thanks," I continued. "We've all taken circuitous routes to get where we are today. But often, the spark that led us to what we really wanted to do was lit long ago, as some of you just shared. That's what happened to me. Except I'd forgotten about that spark and had to rekindle it several years ago, when I was stuck in a job that had lost its meaning."

I paused. "I guess we've all been in that kind of situation."

A few nods. I imagined that one or two naysayers in this room were still wondering why they were being forced to listen to another consultant telling them something they thought they already knew. But I could see that the audience, having heard some of their colleagues offer up formative childhood memories, now seemed more intent, perhaps even eager, to hear if the innovation consultant had something new to offer.

I started by doing just what I'd asked them to do. I shared a story from my own childhood.

"It's really a story about my father," I said.

My dad, Garland Hudson, was an inventor, innovator, and serial entrepreneur. He dreamed, talked, and obsessed about inventions from as far back as I can remember until he took his last breath in 2006. He solved big problems like industrial sanitation and little frustrations like how to transfer gasoline from the car to the lawn mower. (His solution to the latter? He developed a portable, handheld pump, called the Porta-Pump). Growing up, whenever my dad observed a problem, he would challenge my brother and me to devise at least three solutions. We then had to defend the pros and cons of each.

Dad brought that lesson about product innovation home one morning at the Hot Shoppes Cafeteria in Wheaton, Maryland. I was thirteen and my little brother, Greg, was ten.

As I related the anecdote to the audience, my mind went back to that summer day long ago, when—whether I knew it or not—the seeds of my own innovation mindset were first planted.

HOLD THE SUGAR: RECIPE FOR
A SUCCESSFUL INNOVATION

As we settled into the big red vinyl booth, my dad addressed Greg and me as if we were having a team meeting. "Now, I brought you here for a reason."

"Would that reason be breakfast?" my brother asked.

"All in due time," Dad replied. "We're here to figure out how to solve a problem."

"What kind of problem?" I asked, craning my neck over the booth at the bustling restaurant. "Things look like they're running pretty well."

"Ah," said Dad. "But looks can be deceiving . . ."

For three mornings in a row during that sweltering hot week in August we sat in the booth, eating a breakfast of scrambled eggs and orange juice, enjoying the air conditioning—a bit of a luxury in those days—and watching the breakfast traffic. Our assignment? Observe how long it took to clear a table for the next customer. We jotted down notes in our marble composition books and used our four-color pens to draw stick-figure pictures and diagrams. We concluded that the biggest impediment to speedy cleanup was the trash created by the sugar packets kept on the table. We'd noticed that people crumpled the wrappers and threw them on the tables, spewing granules everywhere. Others threw the half-empty packets in the booths or even on the floor, where they had to be swept up.

"What a mess," Greg said.

"Seriously?" I questioned. "There are Cool-Pop wrappers all over your room." Greg frowned. Dad clinked his spoon on the white coffee cup. He loved using sounds to get our attention.

"Let's focus on the problem," he said. "Cleanup is taking too much time, and now we may know why. What's next?"

Under Dad's guidance, we spent the next week brainstorming solutions. We considered eliminating the sugar packets and replacing them with a sugar dispenser, putting a trash can at each table so cleanup could be faster, putting bottled liquid sugar on the lazy Susan alongside the maple syrup and ketchup. We had about half a dozen solutions. With Dad's encouragement—"It's always important to talk to those closest to the problem," he advised—we talked to the manager and to a couple of waitresses to get their input.

They were amused at first. "Mr. Hudson, why are you and your kids so interested in sugar packets?" asked the manager, Esther, who was stout with blonde hair in a neat bun, after I'd fired some questions at her.

"We're trying to solve your problem," I cut in, as assuredly as if I were already a paid Hot Shoppes consultant.

"What problem?" The manager looked suspicious.

My dad assuaged any fears the manager might have had. "The food is great, and we love coming here," he said. "But I'm teaching the kids a lesson about how to solve problems and create new solutions. And we have an idea that might help you. See that line of people outside in the heat waiting to get in here for breakfast?"

The manager looked out the window and nodded. "I can't keep busboys more than a week since the new Friendly's ice cream parlor opened in the mall; the waitresses are complaining about having to bus their own tables." We now had the manager's attention. Her customers were unhappy about waiting lines, but her waitresses were even more unhappy about added work. To this day, I remember thinking my dad was the smartest person in the world at that moment. He had observed the manager's problem and talked to her about it with genuine interest and concern. But even better, we had some ideas about how to help fix things.

Our interaction with our client, the manager, gave us renewed enthusiasm for our project. We kept generating ideas. When one idea didn't make sense—sugar in a dispenser was too tempting for bored kids—my dad showed us how to pivot and move in a different direction. The idea we took to prototype (and yes, my dad actually introduced us to that term) was a small, plastic, cube-shaped receptacle that sat on the table. We called it the Sugar Cube, and to ensure it had value beyond just holding filled packets and empty wrappers, we designed it to display advertising, adding a new potential revenue stream for Hot Shoppes.

My dad scheduled a meeting with the manager right before school started in September so we could demonstrate how the Sugar Cube with the Hot Shoppes logo worked. My role was to review our research, showing our diagrams and charts with timings of table turnover. And, of course, we simulated the process of using the Sugar Cube. My mom, Polly, joined us for the sales pitch. Dad called her the "closer," and she lived up to the title. Wearing the smart navy dress she saved for special occasions, she pointed out the features and benefits of the product while we demonstrated it: Dad with a cup of coffee and Greg and I with unsweetened iced tea. The manager loved it. The Sugar Cube hadn't solved all her problems, but it was a start. Not only did we put it in her store but in several others in the area, too.

With Dad's guidance, we had taken our first product to market. Dad was proud. Looking back now, I realize I had found my calling.

INTRODUCING THE INNOVATION MINDSET

Most of the audience seemed to have been listening keenly to my story. Some were even smiling. Maybe they knew Hot Shoppes or had a kid brother named Greg or remembered what it was like to be thirteen and in awe of your dad. But this was a tough audience. One woman scowled. It was as if I could read her mind. "She thinks we're supposed to be impressed that she invented a product when she was a kid?"

My intention, of course, was not to impress but to instruct—specifically, to instruct about problem solving, which is at the heart of the innovation process.

"So, what did I learn from that experience?" I asked the audience, rhetorically. "Problem solving was a good skill to have, and it was fun. Problems are all around us, and we can find ways to make things better if we put our minds to it. Solutions that meet a customer's need, one they're willing to pay for, have the highest chance of commercial success. I've spent my life, my career, and my personal time helping to bring new treatments and services to patients. If I ever find myself getting off track, I remind myself of that story. I encourage you to jot down some of your earliest memories of being creative, feeling inspired. It will help spark your creativity and fuel your inspiration as you develop new ideas and new solutions."

I then introduced a tabletop exercise designed to practice problem solving. I gave each table a problem to solve and a collection of gadgets (Legos for adults) with instructions to add, subtract, and combine the parts to come up with different solutions. To make the exercise more engaging, I introduced a competition for the best ideas in different categories. Heads started nodding and people started examining the pieces on the table. Someone turned the lights up and the slide projector off. I noticed that mobile devices were facedown on the table.

That talk and the exercises we did that day were an introduction to what I call the Innovation Mindset, the state of mind I first learned in the Hot Shoppes and have adopted in my work as a pharmaceutical and technology executive, a consultant, and an academician who studies and teaches the art and science of innovation.

To create meaningful change, to be innovative, we have to first adopt the right posture, the right attitude. An Innovation Mindset emanates from a problem-solving culture coupled with personal curiosity, passion, and natural talents. From there, you have a springboard to explore an area where you can understand and empathize with customers' needs and develop solutions they want. It all comes together once you understand what you're good at, what the customer needs, and the impact you want to have. Consider these stories that led to marketed products and services. You'll also notice that each was a response to frustration with the status quo.

An engineer with a grandmother who had severe arthritis in her hands and couldn't hold a needle to inject herself with insulin decided to experiment with an insulin-delivering skin patch. A self-employed businessman frustrated by the high cost of booking flights at the last minute created software that lets customers bid for seats on flights of their choice. A public-health worker who was an asymptomatic carrier of COVID-19 and unintentionally infected his entire family developed a patient registry to examine what other asymptomatic carriers have in common. These are stories about passion and focus—people who cared about the customer and the problem they set out to solve.

By the way, there is no magic time for opening the floodgates so innovation can flow. Ralph Lauren was twenty-nine when he created Polo. Actress Hedy Lamarr was thirty-seven when she invented the signal system that led to the creation of WiFi and GPS. (Yes, she did invent such a system.) Henry Ford was fifty when he started his first manufacturing assembly line. Ray Kroc was fifty-two and a milkshake salesman when he established McDonald's. Benjamin Franklin was seventy-nine when he invented bifocal eyeglasses. And if you're still not convinced it's never too late to achieve your dream: Dimitrion Yordanidis was ninety-eight when he ran a marathon in Athens, Greece, in seven hours and thirty-three minutes.

Whether you're sixteen or sixty, your whole life is ahead of you. You can choose your area of focus and start generating new ideas today. Your time is now.

INVENTION AND INNOVATION

The word *invention* dates to the thirteenth century and is defined as "finding or discovering something." It had its earliest home in research and development (R&D) labs and the patents that ensued. In the 1950s, use of the term started to decline as companies focused on the external and economic benefits of research and patents—getting an invention to market became the goal. Out of that context, a new term started showing up in the lexicon, one synonymous with the need not only to conceptualize an invention but also to market it.

That word *innovation* also traces back to the thirteenth century. It was originally a derogatory term, referring to a revolt, rebellion, or heresy at a time when change, no matter how small, was deemed politically disruptive. Over the centuries its meaning has evolved; it's now used to describe new ideas, creative thoughts, and the application of new solutions that meet unmet market needs. A Google search produces two billion references to innovation.

Some experts these days complain that its thirteenth-century use is more appropriate. These critics argue that innovation is an overused buzzword. Maybe so, but it remains a high priority on the agenda of the chief executive officer (CEO). In 2019, 55 percent of the company leaders participating in the Twenty-Second Annual Global CEO Survey by the accounting firm known as PWC (Price, Waterhouse, Cooper) claimed they were not able to innovate effectively. They put that talent gap at the top of their list of concerns—meaning, we need innovators more than ever!

Of course, the critics might be right on one point. The term is used loosely. Those of us who teach and research in this area have developed a typology of innovation. Here are the principal ones:

1. *Incremental innovations* are new features or process changes to existing products or services. Think of Gillette razors' evolution from a one-track blade to three for a closer shave or Tylenol® PM, which added a sleep aid to its pain reliever, or improvements to processes and work flows like creating greater efficiency among supply-chain partners to get a product to market faster.

2. *Breakthrough innovations* are new ways of doing things that start inside a company, usually with a multidisciplinary team, and push it to the next level of performance; they may create a new market for a product or service, or change the way the customer interacts with the market or an industry. No list of breakthrough innovations is complete without a mention of Dyson. The world's first bagless vacuum cleaner was based on the existing business model, but the company harnessed new technology to improve the market offering. They used this approach to develop their bladeless fan, the Dyson Cool™.

I led development of a breakthrough innovation for a biopharmaceutical company struggling to get its drugs to market faster. You can find this case study at the end of this chapter.

3. *Disruptive innovations* change the world forever. Much has been written about these kinds of innovations, defined in 1995 by Harvard professor Clay Christensen as creating a new market and value network that disrupts or displaces established market-leading firms, products, and alliances. It's widely cited as one of the most influential business ideas of the twenty-first century and led the *Economist* to term Christensen "the most influential management thinker of his time." Uber is a current-day example of disruption. Uber moved the ability to afford a car service down-market and enabled anyone with a smartphone and a bank account to order a personal ride to their destination. It has displaced taxis, car services, and even rental cars on the supply side and created a new job category for people looking for temporary and part-time work.

Airbnb started as a service renting out air mattresses for the night and eventually climbed up-market to compete with hotels, effectively changing how we make decisions about and experience overnight stays. The company used clever marketing to switch the initial consumer reaction from "staying at a stranger's place sounds creepy" to "wow, my host is personalizing my visit and gave me great tips on restaurants and fun things to do in the neighborhood." Today, Airbnb is a $31 billion company and was one of the top three initial public offerings (IPOs) in 2020, raising more than $3 billion.

The COVID-19 pandemic has caused renewed discussion on the topic of innovation. According to McKinsey & Company, the minimum economic value that has been vaporized by the pandemic is somewhere in the range of $9 trillion. It's no wonder business leaders worldwide are seeking to understand how their businesses are changing and how they need to respond. Software developer Bill Gates, in an article published by the *Washington Post*, likened COVID-19's impact to that of World War II, saying that things would be changed forever. He outlined numerous opportunities to innovate to stem the pandemic and its recurrence but also pointed out how society will require new ways of thinking and doing things forever. Whether it's kids going to school, people eating in a restaurant, or a hospital ordering supplies, nothing will be the same.

Many misconceptions exist about what is and what isn't an innovation. I have some further thoughts on this, which I'll share with you in a moment.

HOW TO USE THIS BOOK TO FOSTER YOUR INNOVATION MINDSET

This book is for general, educated readers and business students interested in fomenting change or who want to better understand the process of innovation. In it you'll learn a process I've developed and used with clients and students, as well as to guide my own process of taking new ideas to market. It involves an evidence-based, stepwise approach, and many of its components are used by many leaders of innovation and entrepreneurship.

I've organized chapters in this book according to the stages of the innovation process—which I call the Laws of Innovation—and each is infused with real-life case studies, examples, and tools. Here's an at-a-glance summary of those laws, which you'll learn more about in each of their respective chapters.

PROF. LORRAINE MARCHAND'S LAWS OF INNOVATION

The process starts with the right mindset, what we call the Innovation Mindset. This is an attitude that welcomes change and that is biased toward asking questions and solving problems.

It's the starting point for meaningful change. From there you must then lay down the law—the eight laws of successful innovation.

Law 1. **A successful innovation must offer a solution.** Ask yourself, "What's the problem I'm trying to solve?"

Law 2. **One great innovation starts with at least three good ideas.** You need to explore multiple solutions before you narrow it down to three, and then one.

Law 3. **Innovators are dreamers, but they're also realists.** Keep your idea as simple as possible and identify your MVP—minimum viable product.

Law 4. **One hundred customers can't be wrong.** That's why you need to ask them—all of them—about their needs and whether your idea can meet them.

Law 5. **Because conditions are constantly changing, follow the 3-P law.** Be ready to Pivot at any Point in the Process!

Law 6. **A successful innovation flows from a sound business model and plan.** Write it down.

Law 7. **The odds are against you, but you can improve the odds.** Take the steps needed to de-risk your business model.

Law 8. **There is no innovation without persuasion.** So, your pitch must be perfect!

We'll also cover raising capital and include templates and tools you can use to jump-start your own innovative ideas, and we'll discuss some relevant case studies and the views of great innovators.

In the Innovator in Focus section of chapters 1 through 8, you'll meet interesting innovators we interviewed.

DRILLING DOWN ON THE MOST EFFECTIVE
TYPES OF INNOVATION

Since the time of inventor Thomas Edison, the stereotypic picture of the invention process has been the "aha" moment—the burst of inspiration from the brilliant mind of the inventor when the lightbulb literally or figuratively flashes on. Edison himself made it clear that inventing is a disciplined process involving patience and hard work. "None of my inventions came by accident," he said. "I see a worthwhile need to be met and I make trial after trial until it comes. What it boils down to is 1 percent inspiration and 99 percent perspiration." Although he became an individual icon as an inventor, the key to Edison's productivity was his development of a multidisciplinary team of innovators in his Menlo Park laboratory. Today we credit him with creating a culture for innovation to flourish, fostering an Innovation Mindset. He knew that the quantity of ideas was important and that the failure of many potential solutions was inevitable. He tried several thousand filaments before finding a stable material for his first successful lightbulb.

What does innovation look like? It can take many forms, a few of which I listed earlier in this chapter.

Let's look at a couple of examples. This first example requires a short background on oxidative stress, a by-product of just about every disease known—from congestive heart failure to Parkinson's and many diseases in between. In the early days of my journey as an innovator, a colleague asked me to help him develop the marketing strategy for a diagnostic test that could measure oxidative stress levels in blood. I knew it was risky trying to market a product that was looking for a problem to solve, but he was excited about the technology and the impact it could have on the medical field, so I agreed to lend a hand. We assembled a who's who of oxidative stress experts across various diseases. In my colleague's eagerness to get a product to market with limited funds, we ran into some problems. We had a broad-based technology—a solution—with no clear target. What would doctors do with this information? What problem were we solving? The choices were so vast we couldn't narrow them down efficiently. My colleague ended up licensing the technology to a research lab.

This type of innovation is common but not effective. I call it the *Field of Dreams* innovation. In that 1989 film, starring Kevin Costner, a mysterious voice implores Costner's character, Ray Kinsella, to build a baseball diamond in his Iowa cornfield. "If you build it, he will come" are the exact words Kinsella hears as he walks through his field. But that line is commonly repeated as "If you build it, *they* will come." And later in the movie, they do—the ghosts of former major leaguers, led by the legendary Shoeless Joe Jackson.

That was Hollywood. In the world of corporate innovations, "they" means customers—and profits.

The impact of one *Field of Dreams* innovation changed society but not very efficiently, initially. In 1968, Dr. Spencer Silver, a scientist at 3M, discovered an acrylic that had high stickiness but low adhesion, making it the perfect fix when you needed a lightweight sticky adhesive that wouldn't damage a surface, like paper, when removed. For five years he tried to find the right problem to solve with his adhesive, with no luck. It wasn't until coworker Art Fry decided to use the adhesive to paste notes in his church hymnal that Post-It Notes were born—becoming one of the most popular product innovations of all time. Do you think companies like Google, Amazon, IBM, and even 3M could wait five years for a return on their investment now? Unlikely. This type of innovation may work a small percentage of the time, eventually, but it's the wrong kind of innovation if getting to market efficiently is your goal. You might as well wait for the ghost of Babe Ruth to show up in your backyard.

Let's try another example. Did you know that the top-selling pill for male pattern baldness was originally developed to treat high blood pressure? The clinical studies for the drug that we know as Rogaine included middle-aged men with hypertension, many of whom just happened to be bald. During the study, these men experienced hair regrowth. Although this was unanticipated, the Upjohn company nimbly pivoted and launched its drug earlier than expected—as a treatment for male pattern baldness. Most people think this is how new ideas should work: there is a "Eureka!" moment and behold, the cure for baldness is revealed. But this type of innovation, while attractive, is also rare. It's like winning the lottery—the reward is huge, but the odds of reaping that reward are slim to none. We can be seduced into thinking we might be the one to buy the winning ticket, but chances are we won't be. This type of innovation is known as serendipity. While a serendipitous innovation is exciting and occasionally successful, most of us are unlikely to be involved in one.

So, if a *Field of Dreams* or serendipity innovation can't be counted on to produce the best results, what does a path to more predictable success look like?

Let's consider an example of innovation that was successful because it followed the problem-solving process. A twenty-five-year-old engineer named Willis Carrier was working in a printing plant when he tried to solve the problem of controlling the humidity that was causing the ink to clot. He told a friend about his vision for drying air by passing it through water to create fog. Carrier designed a mechanical prototype that forced air through water-cooled coils, effectively reducing humidity in the plant. His innovation in 1902 not only improved ink quality but also had the added benefit of improving the comfort of the workers in the plant, leading to modern air conditioning and making Carrier a name that even today is synonymous with cool. Carrier had a clear problem statement and worked to solve it. His solution had far-reaching implications.

Finally, new ideas that change an industry or the way customers do something forever are called disruptive innovations. A current-day disruptive innovation is how Amazon completely transformed the shopping experience. Another is how Netflix reimagined the way we watch movies. A third is PayPal, which changed how we pay for things.

Instead of a disruptive innovation, difficult to plan for, you can start by making incremental changes or process improvements. I learned to innovate by focusing on small things I could change. That Sugar Cube I told you about—the idea we hatched on a summer morning at the Hot Shoppes when I was thirteen—was my first successful innovation, but not my last.

What do sugar packets and Carrier have in common? They illustrate how a results-driven approach to innovation works. Innovation that starts with a problem defined with customer input and then uses a process that systematically evaluates potential solutions for best fit has the highest hit rate.

It's not serendipity, it's not disruption, and it's not having a cool solution that's searching for a problem. It's identifying a customer's problem and coming up with the best solution. It takes focus and hard work, as Edison said. Innovators must be passionate for a reason: it takes a lot of energy to work this hard.

So how do you create an Innovation Mindset for your company, your team, yourself?

First, find your sugar packet—the problem you're going to tackle. Make sure it's a problem worth solving, one a customer is willing to pay for. Then examine it, breaking it down into its parts. Look at it from every angle and from multiple points of view. Your goal is to capture a concise problem description.

Next, evaluate and test solutions, choosing the best fit to take to prototype. Devise several solutions, realizing you'll have to go through one or several options before you find your best one. Remember, options that aren't the best fit are not failures. They're just not your best options.

After we'd shared our stories, after I'd presented the overview of the Laws of Innovation, after we'd completed our hands-on exercises, I polled the group for feedback on the session. Most said the Innovation Mindset had struck a chord and they were eager to put it into practice. A few had ideas for pilot projects. Corporations love the idea of piloting a new idea. Why? As one executive told me confidentially, "If we're going to fail, let's do it discreetly and safely so no one's career is hurt."

As a result of our work together that day, several leaders in the room introduced ideas for products and services to their managers. One ambitious information technology (IT) leader got approval to design and implement a digital tool to improve communication with physicians. An engineer created a customer-focused version of Siri to help triage customer questions earlier and more efficiently. The company's customer satisfaction scores increased by 14 percent in one quarter.

Six months later, I got this note from a woman on the product development team: "Lorraine, I just wanted to let you know how inspired I was by your talk last June. I did what you recommended: I got a notebook and started recording my observations and new ideas. I then shared a couple of project ideas with my team and manager. We got approval to move ahead on a new approach to managing our supply chain that promises to get one of our consumer products to the store shelves faster. Our pharmacy customers are thrilled! In our own way, we are changing the culture, and it feels great."

CHAPTER TAKEAWAYS

- Make problem solving a way of thinking, and reward it when you see it.
- Find your sugar packet—a problem area you're passionate about.
- Make the customer your number one priority.
- Strike *failure* from your lexicon and replace it with *pivot*. Pivot as often as you need to until you succeed. Make sure you learn every step of the way.
- Remember that the innovation with the highest rate of success is based on a problem-solving approach that meets the customer's needs.
- Don't forget to enjoy the journey. While arduous at times, it should leave you feeling energized and liberated.

Case Study: An Award-Winning Innovation in Clinical Trials

Several years ago, I was working for a large pharmaceutical corporation that was increasingly struggling to get its products to market efficiently, costing millions of dollars a day in lost revenues. A main reason for the delay was inaccurate forecasting and management of clinical trials. We ran 250 studies a year, and approximately 90 percent were missing deadlines for completion, a critical step for submitting a drug for approval to regulatory authorities such as the Food and Drug Administration (FDA). This meant therapies weren't getting to patients in need quickly. I was recruited to help improve clinical trial performance and get drugs to market safely and faster. I recognized this challenge as a great opportunity to create a new solution to an old problem.

After examining and discussing the problem with management, teams, and partners, I determined that the rate at which we were recruiting patients into our trials was one of the biggest impediments to finishing our studies on time. So, what did we do?

First, I assembled a team of experts and stakeholders. We interviewed internal and external customers and stakeholders, observing how they were recruiting patients and what was and wasn't working.

We defined the problem. It turns out we lacked the data needed to make good business decisions about where to run our trials and with which doctors, globally. This lack of data and of a vigorous process led to inaccurate forecasts about trial completion and affected how the team managed the trial.

Next, we brainstormed solutions. We realized that we needed a way of gathering more data on the situation to help guide better decision-making. We learned how teams were choosing study sites and realized it was based on relationships. No performance data or benchmarks were part of the process.

We selected a couple of solutions to test and ultimately designed a suite of six data-based tools informed by actual data available in different departments inside and outside the company.

The prototype we designed was piloted with two teams on two different programs. We designed it with the clinical teams to ensure that we achieved their critical goals and objectives.

The clinical teams (our internal customers) appreciated having data to help inform decision-making about their trials. One manager said, "The data the Study Strategy and Planning Department provided [have] been invaluable as we've planned our diabetes study, including where to deploy our $50 million budget globally. This is going to be like the 'Good Housekeeping Seal' of approval for future study planning."

But it's results that count. A major global diabetes study with more than a thousand patients was finished nine months early, a time frame unheard of in the company. A study for rheumatoid arthritis was completed three months ahead of forecast, enabling the company not only to save money but also to realize revenues sooner and get the drug to patients faster. This drug was launched ahead of the closest competitor, and patients reported symptom relief unmatched by other therapies at the time.

Once the prototypes and pilots were finished, we evaluated them, got more customer input, and refined our solutions. We made the tool easier to use and improved the accuracy of results.

Ultimately, after working with management to secure more resources, we built the new model to scale. The chief of R&D mandated that every study be planned with our model and tools as part of the study approval process. The team and I won the company's Innovation Award that year. While we were all proud of the recognition, and the fact that what we had developed became the forerunner of the R&D protocol being used to this day, it wasn't a testament to us as much as it was to the attitude and the mindset our team embodied: the Innovation Mindset.

1

THE FIRST LAW OF INNOVATION

A Successful Innovation Must Solve a Problem

Easter Sunday, April, in the late 1970s. My family was hosting the annual Hudson family Easter egg hunt at 2 p.m., a favorite for more than a decade. Only problem was that the grass, which had sprung up following several days of early spring rain, was sorely in need of cutting. At breakfast my mother reminded my dad of the chore at hand, probably the third time she had brought the topic up that weekend. After church, Dad, my brother Greg, and I headed to the shed to ready the lawn mower and get trash bags. Greg and I were to pick up sticks so dad could mow. I had the extra chore of weeding, which I loathed.

Dad took the gas cap off the push mower and let out a low whistle.

"What's wrong?" Greg asked.

"There's no gas in the mower," Dad responded shaking his head. "I had the gas can in the car yesterday but forgot to get it filled. Your mother isn't going to be happy."

"What should we do?" I asked. I knew my mom was anxious whenever we had company, especially on an important holiday like Easter, so I didn't want to be the one to break the news to her. This was also a time when "blue laws" were in effect in Maryland, so gas stations, along with most other stores, were closed.

We were going to have to improvise—or should I say innovate?

"Should we use the hedge trimmer?" Greg asked only half-jokingly—we both knew our dad, the teacher and inventor, would be pressing us for three solutions, just as he had done at the Hot Shoppes.

"We can hide the eggs in the house," I offered.

"We could ask Mr. Cassady if we could borrow his mower. I saw him mowing his grass yesterday," Greg piped up. Mr. Cassady, who lived next door, was a retired federal government worker, according to Dad, and "very nosy," according to Mom. I was pretty sure my dad wasn't going to let him in on our little Easter Sunday secret.

"Well, before we jump to solutions, let's look at the problem."

Even in the midst of a minor family crisis, Dad never missed an opportunity for a teachable moment.

"So, what's the problem here, guys?" he continued.

"We have to cut the grass for the Easter egg hunt, but there's no gas in the mower and the gas stations are closed," I answered promptly.

"Let's look at the problem of the mower needing gas," Dad said. "It's true we need gasoline, but is it true that we have no available gasoline?"

I looked at my mom's 1972 Chevy sitting in the driveway. Mom was always prepared. She never let the gas in her car get below half a tank. On the other hand, I was pretty sure my dad's station wagon was running on fumes.

"How can we get the gas out of your mom's Chevy and into the mower?" Dad asked.

I ran into the house and returned with the turkey baster, relieved we were having ham for dinner. In the house I had successfully avoided Mom, who was vacuuming the dining room. We would tell her after dinner, I resolved. After all, I knew she would notice the missing gas when she went to work Monday morning.

Dad removed the gas cap quietly so as not to make any noise that would attract Mr. Cassady's attention. Carefully inserting the turkey baster into the gas tank and depressing the suction cup, he determines that the Chevy's gas tank was actually full—he pulled the gas into the baster easily. "I knew it," I said to myself, proud of my mom's Girl Scout–like preparedness.

"But Dad, you have to keep the baster suction cup squeezed to keep the gas in the tube and then put that little bit in the lawn mower," I observed. "This is going to take too long," I added under my breath, listening for the hum of the vacuum.

"Well, now that we know we have a source of gas, this is just the prototype device," Dad said.

"Wait here." My dad manufactured and distributed plastic containers through his company, Sandell Sales and Manufacturing. He had a big cardboard box of spare plastic pieces in the shed.

I heard the sound of boxes sliding and shelves creaking as Dad went through his spare parts in the shed. He returned with a clear plastic hose about three feet long, a suction cup the size of his hand, and a makeshift pump he had rigged to draw standing water out of the gutters last fall. He laid it on the ground as an example of what he was about to design.

I watched as Dad cut the hose in half, made two holes in the suction cup, and then used the hose and tubing to insert the suction cup in between the two pieces of hose. He sealed the edges with a half-used tube of caulking we found in the shed.

We gave our new gas pump a try. I snaked one end of the hose into the Chevy's gas tank while Greg guided the other end into the lawn mower. Dad started to squeeze and release the suction cup. I smelled the amber fluid before I saw it, but as it started flowing through the hose, I felt like we had struck oil.

Dad pumped. Greg cheered. "Sssh!" I said, reminding him that this was a clandestine innovation operation. When the lawn mower's gas reservoir was full, Dad motioned with his hand.

We finished the lawn just as Mom came outside to rush us inside to change into our spring outfits so we could hide the Easter eggs, which she had filled with coins and Hershey kisses.

As the egg hunt got under way with my younger cousins, Dad winked at me and squeezed Greg's shoulder. "Good work" was all he said.

Later that evening I overheard Mom telling Dad that she had enjoyed watching our gas-stealing escapade from the kitchen window. Dad gave a good-natured laugh. "We got the job done and the kids learned a little something, too."

This story from my childhood has a lesson: The Innovation Mindset starts with the right approach to problem solving. The best perspective is inquiry based, requiring you to put yourself into the problem to understand the environment and the problem's impact. It sounds easy, but it's not. It takes discipline to think about the problem and avoid jumping to solutions.

"If I had sixty minutes to solve a problem, I'd spend fifty-five minutes thinking about the problem and five minutes thinking about the solution." That quote, often (and inaccurately) attributed to physicist Albert Einstein, is nonetheless a wonderful reminder about the importance of thinking before we act impulsively.[1]

The experiential inquiry process is like a bicycle for the mind—speeding things up and getting you to a problem statement and solution faster. In 1990, Apple cofounder Steve Jobs used this analogy when looking at a diagram showing how fast animals can travel and how slowly humans move. "What a computer is to me is it's the most remarkable tool that we've ever come up with," Jobs said, "and it's the equivalent of a bicycle for our minds."[2]

Think about that next time you whip out your smartphone to look up a fact or get directions—tasks that not too long ago would have involved going to a library or opening up a map. Jobs saw the phone, a device hitherto designed for people to speak to one another, as something much more—something that could solve many problems.

CONSTRAINTS IMPROVE PROBLEM SOLVING

The lawn mower story is also an example of Plato's famous quote about innovation, "Necessity is the mother of invention," from the dialogue *Republic*.

Nothing demonstrates the benefits of the constraint-based approach to problem solving better than COVID-19. The pandemic, while devastating to global public health and economic stability, has also been a catalyst for some of the most significant and probably longest-lasting innovations in modern times, such as new ways of shopping, socializing, seeing the doctor, going to school, and even going to work.

While some innovations existed, several languished until COVID-19 created the tipping point for growth and adoption. Others were created during the pandemic. Let's look at a few examples.

Problem: How to develop vaccines to address global demand. Before the pandemic, only three pharmaceutical companies were in the business of developing vaccines.

Solution: As a result of the need for vaccine technology and government incentives, a dozen companies are now working on multiple vaccine candidates, and companies that had never launched a drug, including Moderna and BioNTech (working with big pharma partner Pfizer), were the first to bring vaccines to market.

Problem: Limited hospital capacity for large ventilators for COVID-19 patients with respiratory distress.

Solution: Tesla and Medtronic took over a factory in Buffalo, New York, and developed the first mobile, battery-operated ventilators that could be used in an outpatient setting.

Problem: How to run business meetings and hold classes when the pandemic had eliminated social contact.

Solution: Videoconferencing company Zoom's stock increased exponentially as a result of COVID-19, and the growth of videoconferencing for business and education is at record levels. No longer is in-person communication essential. A new way of working and communicating has emerged, and it has its share of benefits.

Problem: How to provide health care when people couldn't visit a doctor's office.

Solution: Telehealth companies like Teledoc were growing but below expectations. During and even after the pandemic, people from all walks—from parents of kids with the sniffles to elderly people who need medical monitoring—actually prefer to use online services for access to medical care. The growth in telehealth visits during the peak of COVID-19, as reported by the Centers for

Disease Control in 2021, has leveled out. But telehealth is now recognized as an efficient and effective way of providing health care for millions of people in the United States.

These problems and solutions seem obvious now, but each required innovators who observed a problem in its natural environment, found proof or evidence to support the problem, conducted customer research and secured investor interest, and created products, services, and new ways of doing things—fast and with limited resources. Layering on constraints when you don't know what the problem is, however, can have negative results, as corporate executives can attest.

First, you have to diagnose the right problem.

As noted in the introduction, early in my journey as an innovator, a colleague asked me to help him launch a new product. He had licensed a technology from an Israeli research lab for a diagnostic test that could measure oxidative stress, a by-product of most diseases. The technology was exciting, and we assembled a who's who of oxidative stress experts across various diseases to help us identify a focus area. In my colleague's eagerness to get a product to market with limited funds and aggressive timelines from the investors, we ran into some problems. We had a broad-based technology—a solution—with no clear target. What would doctors do with this information? What problem were we solving? The choices were so vast that we couldn't narrow them down efficiently. He ended up in a research collaboration and licensed the product but never commercialized it. We lacked a well-defined problem and failed to articulate a problem statement the market cared about. I had cautioned him that it was risky to work backward—developing a technology that was looking for a problem to solve. That example—how *not* to innovate for commercial success—has always stayed with me.

My colleague and I weren't alone in our experience. Corporations launch new products without sufficient market and customer input on the problem statement all too frequently. In a survey of 106 C-suite executives at ninety-one private and public companies from seventeen countries, 85 percent agreed that their companies were bad at problem diagnosis and 87 percent said the gap produced serious financial implications.[3] Spurred by a penchant for action, managers tend to switch to solution mode without checking if they understand a problem. Many companies hire consultants to train their teams on root-cause analysis, asking the right questions, reframing the problem, and other techniques, usually with mixed results.

How do you avoid this "ready-fire-aim" approach to problem solving? By asking yourself some specific questions before springing into action.

Questions to ask during problem identification

1. *When and where was the problem first observed?* Observation is a one-time event and should take place in the natural habitat.
2. *What is its level of recurrence?* A problem must recur with some frequency to be a problem.
3. *What is the need?* How significant is the problem? How many people are affected? What is the cost?
4. *What are your assumptions about the problem?* Have you challenged those assumptions?
5. *Can you deconstruct the problem?* When Elon Musk was told by auto-manufacturing experts that he could not make an affordable battery-operated car, he broke down the problem of making a battery into its component parts—nickel, chromium, cobalt—and sourced each element on the commodity market where each was affordable. But he didn't stop there. He figured out a way to eliminate cobalt, the most expensive of the elements. He cut the price by two-thirds.
6. *Can you verify that the problem is real and worth solving?* Direct verification ensures you are addressing the problem that the target audience is experiencing and that it is sufficiently important to guarantee that a solution will be well received by customers.

Now that you know the right questions to ask, let's look at several approaches for identifying the right problem to be solved.

APPROACHES TO EFFECTIVE PROBLEM IDENTIFICATION

Below are examples of ways to help your team diagnose the right problem. They aren't mutually exclusive, and you can blend or sequence techniques based on your team's situation.

Technique 1. Ask better questions!

What's the best way to unlock a problem and find a better answer? You can start by asking better questions. This technique works especially well in corporate environments where there can be pressure to have the right answers to impress one's colleagues, direct reports, and the boss. Problem solving actually gets worse in proportion to the level and number of executives in the room as they try to outdo each other with brilliant answers!

I tried this technique once in a brainstorm with my team when putting solutions on sticky notes on the wall was leading to nothing but a wall of yellow and pink notes and obvious frustration among my team. We were trying to create new and better ways of recruiting patients for clinical trials, and the solutions were getting pretty ridiculous.

"Let's forget about solutions for the rest of the day," I said. "Let's get back to basics. Let's look at the problem that we wrote on the board this morning—what questions do you have about the problem?" I gave them five minutes to write down as many questions as they could think of. We then went around the room. The energy level increased, and everyone was building off of the questions—we had a question flow that started taking us in some really interesting directions. Everyone had questions, including one usually quiet person who asked, "Is the problem really the right problem?" "You know," I said, "Eric is actually onto something. Let's focus more on our customers' problems and less on ours. Our problem is that physicians aren't recruiting enough patients for our diabetes clinical trial in the time needed, but what do we know about the challenges the physicians are facing?"

Those adjustments did the trick. We took a step back and organized our questions around the customer instead of ourselves, a technique called reframing, which I'll introduce in a minute. What's more, we stayed focused on diagnosing the right problem, instead of jumping to possible solutions. We ended up with a promising set of insights and opportunities to improve our customers' experience. Ever since, I've made asking the right questions the focus of my problem-solving approach. Fresh questions beget new insights and perspectives, can turn a negative into a positive, and can help reframe the problem from the perspective of different stakeholders including, importantly, the customer!

Problem-oriented questions might include:

- How can we describe the problem?
- What facts do we know about the problem?
- What assumptions do we have about the problem?
- What is our hypothesis about why the problem exists?
- Who is affected and how? (Come up with examples of how each stakeholder, including the customer, is affected.)
- How is the problem currently being addressed by each stakeholder?
- What gaps exist with current solutions?

Technique 2. Frame the problem wearing different hats

Another approach for making sure you and your team are solving the right problems is called reframing. As mentioned in the example above, this involves looking at the problem from the perspective of different stakeholders—customer, supplier, manufacturer.

To help spark the reframing process among your team, you can share a case study. A simple but universally understood example is the problem of people complaining about the long wait time to get into a building or event; it could be for a concert, a movie, a sporting event, or a store opening. One approach is to analyze the duration of the wait time and try to reduce it, if possible, but another approach is to examine how people are spending their time waiting and why they are getting frustrating and bored. This reframing of the problem can produce different insights and new and creative ways of addressing the problem. For example, a Broadway theater in New York sends actors dressed as different characters to mingle with the crowds. The actors tell stories, make jokes, and take pictures with the audience, helping them forget they are even waiting in line. One multistory office building installed a mirror at the entrance to the building. Apparently, time passes more quickly and pleasantly when you're checking yourself out.

Steps in the reframing process include:

- Bringing outsiders (stakeholders wearing different hats) into the discussion to get multiple perspectives on the problem.
- Getting problem definitions in writing, written clearly and crisply.
- Asking what's missing from the problem statement; examining various angles.
- Considering multiple categories of the problem. Are there times or situations when the problem is more acute than others? In the waiting line example above, tolerance of the problem and willingness to be distracted are more likely when the weather is nice and people are out with friends for an evening of entertainment.
- Analyzing positive exceptions to the problem. Are there times and situations when the problem is not a problem?
- Challenging assumptions, often and vigorously, to eliminate mental models and biases.

Technique 3. Analogize: "This problem is like . . ."

Bill Gates is a fan of using analogies to solve problems. He says the best way to solve a problem or achieve a goal is to find people who have solved that problem or achieved that goal. In a recent GatesNotes blog he writes: "Ever since I was a teenager, I've tackled every big problem the same way: by starting off with two questions. I used this technique at Microsoft, and I still use it today. I ask these questions literally every week about COVID-19. Here they are: *Who has dealt with this problem well? And what can we learn from them?*"[4]

Corporations like analogy-based problem solving because it's low risk and requires little creativity. When the automotive industry wanted to create a virtual model of a connected vehicle, they conceived the "digital twin." They copied a concept coined by a University of Michigan researcher in 2003 that had been in use since 1960s when NASA created physical duplicate systems for its various space missions at ground level to test its equipment in a virtual environment.

Digital twins are virtual replicas of physical entities, giving innovators an in-depth look at data and the ability to monitor systems to mitigate risks, manage issues, and use simulations to test future solutions. They can help technicians with root-cause analysis and accelerate problem solving.

They are now being used more broadly in artificial intelligence applications to improve supply chain planning and management, particularly in the wake of COVID-19, when supply chain challenges led to stockouts of PPE, ventilators, respirators, and other equipment and supplies. Companies such as Johnson Controls and Microsoft are using digital twins to create smart, environmentally sustainable buildings.

Technique 4. Tear the problem apart

The deconstruction approach to problem solving is counter to the analogy-based approach in that it involves creating completely new knowledge about a problem. This technique is embraced by entrepreneur Elon Musk. He calls it "first principles,"[5] and it involves the following steps:

Principle 1. **Identify and define the problem.**

Principle 2. **Challenge your current assumptions.** Write down your assumptions and then systematically question each one.

Principle 3. **Break the problem down into fundamental principles, its basic elements.** Think of it like examining a tree. You look first at the trunk, then the large branches. Examine these in order, first, before getting to the leaves of the tree—the details.

Principle 4. **Create new solutions from scratch.** After you've broken down the problem, tackled your assumptions, and broken the problem into basic elements, only then should you begin to create new insightful solutions from scratch.

Principle 5. **Don't forget the customer.**

What do all these examples and approaches to problem solving have in common? They share the same fundamental approach to *problem identification.* Before new solutions can occur, innovators must first identify and understand problems facing their customers, using observational skills and finding new ways of looking at processes, procedures, and events. The well-observed problem—whether it's a lawn mower that won't start or a worldwide epidemic that might seemingly never end—in turn, provides the basis for describing a customer need: the fundamental building block of the innovation process.

Case Study: The COVID-19 Vaccines: Innovation for the Ages

When COVID-19 first surfaced in early 2020, health-care executives said that, based on the current process for drug and vaccine development, it would optimistically take two to three years to get a vaccine developed, approved, and distributed in the United States. Given the spiraling rates of infection and death around the world, not to mention the economic devastation, this proposition was unacceptable.

The fastest any vaccine had been developed before COVID-19, from viral sampling to approval, was four years (a mumps vaccine in the 1960s).[6] Hopes for a vaccine even by summer 2021 seemed highly optimistic. Yet by the beginning of December 2020, developers of several vaccines had announced excellent results in large human trials. On December 2, a vaccine developed by the U.S. drugmaker Pfizer and the German biotech company BioNTech became the first fully tested immunization to be approved for emergency use.

How did that happen? How were researchers and developers at these huge corporations—not always known for acting nimbly and swiftly—able to shatter the speed record for proven, safe vaccine development?

It started, as we've pointed out, with good questions:

The small biotech firm BioNTech (partnered with Pfizer) and Moderna asked the questions: Why does it need to take two to three years? What if our approach to COVID-19 could change the way vaccines are developed, forever? Could we safely execute the entire process in under a year? Using deconstruction, they asked, what are the component parts of vaccine development?

The answers: the steps are human testing, regulatory approval, manufacture, and distribution.

They then broke each step down, asking what is the longest part of the process? The most complex? The riskiest? Why? They took advantage of years of previous research on related viruses and created RNA sequences for COVID-19 in January 2020. This allowed the technology to be ready for acceleration in the testing part of the process. They also looked at faster ways to manufacture vaccines. Enormous government funding allowed firms to run multiple trials at once, even risking manufacturing vaccine candidates that might not work out. Regulators did their part too, learning how to quickly review and approve data for safety. Under the program known as Operation Warp Speed, the U.S. government poured more than $10 billion into vaccine development by pharmaceutical companies.[7]

The result was the fastest development and approval of a vaccine ever. At this writing, it's chilling to imagine what might have happened—indeed, whether the world as we know it would have survived—if the development of those vaccines had taken two more years. *That's* the power of the Innovation Mindset.

INNOVATOR IN FOCUS

Phil McKinney, president and CEO, CableLabs; former CTO, Hewlett-Packard

INNOVATOR CREDENTIALS The former chief technology officer (CTO) for Hewlett-Packard (HP), Phil McKinney founded the HP Innovation Program Office, which developed new products and services for the computer giant. His department produced several innovative products, including video-sharing platforms; 3-D display technology; the award-winning Blackbird 002, a high-end gaming PC; Firebird, a gaming PC using laptop technology; and the Envy 133, the world's thinnest carbon fiber laptop, which won a design award in 2009. These and other innovations earned HP a place on *Fast Company*'s list of the fifty most innovative companies three years in a row.

McKinney is currently CEO of CableLabs, an innovation research lab funded by sixty of the largest cable companies in thirty-five countries. CableLabs exists to keep people connected by making broadband faster and more responsive, reliable, and secure, cementing the cable network as the platform of choice for entertainment and connectivity. McKinney serves on the advisory board for Hacking Autism and is chair of the board for the Techtrend Group, which invests in entrepreneurs in developing countries to create jobs that fuel economic growth. He is the author of *Beyond the Obvious* as well as host of the podcast *Killer Innovations*. Most recently, McKinney was named one of the top influencers transforming media production and distribution on MultiChannel News's 2020 Industry Watch List, and he received the 2021 Broadcasting and Cable Technology Leadership Award.

Innovation claim to fame

McKinney's first innovation, which he developed in 1988, is one that has had widespread implications: the ThumbScan, a device that allows only authorized users to log into encrypted data on a computer. It's the technology in the fingerprint scanner now used in police stations, by security industries, and even on smartphones.

Lessons learned

During McKinney's time at HP, not everything he touched was a success. The company entered the tablet market and competed with the iPad by releasing its own device called the HP TouchPad. Despite having some software advantages over the iPad, it had limited success and was sold in retail stores for only one month before being taken off the market.

But as a lifelong learner, McKinney knew he could turn this into a lesson. He says bias can occur when people mistakenly attribute success to the process that produced that success. They think that making that process into a routine will yield further success. He compares it to a group of adults praising a children's dance performance—giving them praise because they were in the dance as opposed to how well they performed. "It's OK to praise your kid's dance performance but it's not OK to believe your assumptions that past success begets future success in business."

As CTO for HP, McKinney says he spent much of his time identifying and fixing problems for everything from PCs to tablets to gaming devices. He got his clues to problems by observing and even talking to customers while they were shopping for these devices.

You can't make this up (fun fact)

Despite his many innovation credits, the proudest achievement for this Cincinnati native is the fact that he earned the rank of Eagle Scout.

Insights for innovators

"Ask yourself Killer Questions every day, and never believe that your past success guarantees future success."

McKinney's favorite Killer Questions are:

- How can you make a customer's life easier, better, or more interesting?
- Why should the customer buy my product over the competitor's?
- What does the customer *dislike* about interacting with the product, with my company?

Learn more about McKinney at philmckinney.com.
Check out his products and books at the following links:
https://www.cnet.com/reviews/hp-blackbird-002-dedication-edition-review/
https://www.wired.com/2008/11/pr-voodoo-envy-133/
https://beyondtheobvious.com/
https://killerinnovations.com/

LAY DOWN THE LAW

Prof. Marchand helps you put the principle of problem identification into action

In this chapter, we've discussed the importance of identifying the problem properly—asking the right questions and finding approaches to doing just that—all parts of what we call the First Law of the Innovation Mindset. So, where do you go from here? Where are the problems you're going to solve? You don't have to solve world hunger. Even incremental changes can make a big difference in your company's bottom line. I guarantee that if you talk to the chief financial officer, you'll learn a ton about where the pain points are. That's where you'll innovate. If you talk to business unit leaders and learn which objectives they are falling behind on, that's where you'll innovate. If you talk to the loading dock foreman, the call center manager, the distribution manager, you'll uncover problems. That's where you'll innovate.

Let's say you've talked to the chief financial officer, and maybe he or she told you about how they're trying to solve the problem of cutting the cost of getting a product to market in half. Or maybe you learned from your visit to the call center that a key problem facing your company is cost efficiency: how to ensure the customer has a fully satisfying experience while reducing the time spent per call by a third. Or it could be that from your talk with the loading dock foreman you've learned that a top priority is reusing shipping supplies to reduce costs and meet your objectives around being environmentally conscious.

Once you find the problem, you'll learn all you can. You'll talk to the right people, of course, but you'll do more than that. You'll look for data—facts and information that will add dimension and perspective to the problem.

I recommend getting yourself a notebook. Observe the problems you see, when you see them, as often as you see them. Write them down, and draw diagrams and pictures to add the necessary dimension. Talk to your customers, your chief marketing officer, the head of product innovation, the head of IT, and business and functional leads in your company. Come up with lots of questions. Test them. Layer on constraints. Develop multiple solutions. Choose one or two solutions and test the fit with customers and stakeholders. Learn, adjust your strategy, and if something needs tweaking or a change in direction is called for, be bold. Pivot. If you exhaust all solutions and have to move on, then move on, and don't look back. Just make sure you took away some new learning.

In upcoming chapters, we will examine some of these steps in greater depth. But as we move forward in the process, remember this: an Innovation Mindset emanates from curiosity, knowing what makes you tick, and using that as a springboard to explore your passion and purpose. From there, you can move on to identifying an area to focus on, an area where you can find problems worth solving, ones that you're passionate about and that align with your values.

2

IT'S THE LAW!
ONE GREAT INNOVATION STARTS
WITH AT LEAST THREE GOOD IDEAS

Here's How to Find Them

Randy motioned for me to join him outside the conference room, where his team had just finished our Day 1 morning workshop with mixed results. "You need to push them harder," he said evenly. "The ideas I just heard don't move the needle. We need some big solutions to achieve our growth goals in the sector. Do you need me to give them a pep talk?"

I looked through the glass wall at the mechanical engineers and account leaders sitting around the open square, surrounded by flip charts, sticky notes, colored markers, empty coffee cups, and candy wrappers. A few were talking quietly among themselves; a couple were answering text messages; and several were at the whiteboard earnestly rearranging the Post-It notes from the morning brainstorm in response to Randy's feedback. They were a likable group, smart mechanical and electrical engineers who were in my workshop to learn how to think like their customers—in this case the world's largest medical device manufacturers—and how to expand their business of designing and developing the critical components that were part of the medical devices sold to the end user. They had worked hard all morning, reviewing industry trends; assessing their customers' competition, business goals, and strategic initiatives; and bubbling up problems they thought their customers were facing. But several had struggled to articulate the difference between a customer goal, a strategic initiative, and a problem statement; all were eager to brainstorm technical solutions without fully understanding the customers' challenges, risks, and problems. We had started with an exercise called Big Idea Vignettes, a popular method of generating new ideas, but I stopped it after thirty minutes because I could tell they weren't ready. This method requires a good understanding of your product's end user, and it was clear that this group was not familiar enough with the needs of people with diabetes to generate useful ideas.

I knew I had a challenge on my hands when Randy arrived at lunch, unannounced. He was the general manager of the healthcare division of this $20 billion manufacturing company, specializing in plastics and electronics components and based in Tampa, Florida. Randy reviewed the flip charts and the whiteboard, interrogating his team with questions like "Where's the Big Idea?"; "I've taken you out of the field for two days; now where are the results?"; and "Our competition is beating us; how are we going to respond?"

A couple of the guys were pink with embarrassment.

I let Randy know he was seeing the results of our early-stage brainstorming. I assured him the Big Ideas were coming and he had to trust the process. Now, looking at him wringing his hands, clearly anxious about the company's end-of-quarter results, I was certain what he had termed a "pep talk" wasn't going to improve the situation. "I appreciate the offer," I said with a sympathetic smile, "but give me the afternoon with them. We have more work to do. Let's stay with the original plan of meeting with you late morning tomorrow."

Randy looked relieved and nodded in agreement. I slipped back into the conference room and announced they had fifteen minutes until we reconvened. I walked to the glass wall at the back of the room and looked out over the lake where ducks were floating gracefully on the water. Small groups of employees were laughing as they enjoyed lunch at the wooden picnic tables around the lake. Under the May noontime sun, the company's campus was serene and welcoming. One would never imagine the storm brewing inside as a result of missing the financials for the past two quarters. I was thinking hard about how to bolster the group's confidence after Randy's visit and what we could do to produce some truly Big Ideas that could translate into new products and solutions.

I knew I had a secret weapon waiting in the wings and hoped it would be enough to help spark the kind of creative thinking Randy expected—and to justify my consultant's fee.

"OK," I said bringing the group back to attention. "Let's start this afternoon with a fresh approach. I want to reframe our discussion and look at diabetes through the eyes of your customers' customer—the person with diabetes and the doctors and family members who care for them. We're going to examine the experience of being a person with diabetes."

My "storytelling" methodology, based on gaining a deeper understanding of customer personas, was always a big hit and usually produced good results. Technical professionals in particular liked it. The group sat up in their chairs, nodding. "I don't know much about the patient perspective, as I'm new to diabetes," admitted Avik, the head of engineering. "I like that idea."

On my laptop, I pulled up the diabetes patient journey map I had created based on interviews with patients, caregivers, and physicians. The map is a visual flow describing what the patient experiences, from diagnosis through treatment.

Now it was time to deploy my secret weapon, on cue—my colleague Jan, a diabetes nurse educator, mom of a daughter with diabetes, and the quintessential nurse. I had texted Jan just before we resumed the session to make sure she was nearby. She entered the room, dressed in gray slacks and a white blouse and carrying her tan cardigan on her arm. "Conference room temperatures are so unpredictable," she said as she put her things on a vacant chair. She strode purposefully to the head of the room and turned to face the audience.

"Hi, everyone," she greeted the group with a big smile. "Lorraine tells me you're the folks who help make the blood glucose meters, insulin pens, and monitors we use to measure blood sugar and administer insulin. Well, guess what? *I'm* your customer. Nice to meet you."

I quickly gauged the reaction of the audience. A few sat forward in their seats, and yes, I did see a few jaws drop at this unexpected development, as if some of these engineers were trying to process something truly unexpected. "A customer . . . *here?*"

Jan walked the group through different patient stories—child, adult, pregnant woman—explaining each patient persona's typical experience on the patient journey map I was shining from my laptop to the front of the room. She answered questions and explained the issues, challenges, and decisions patients and their families face at each step of their experience. She shared her own experience when her daughter was diagnosed with diabetes as a young child, demonstrating the classic symptoms of thirst and weight loss, and described the fear and anxiety she and her husband felt when Amy started kindergarten. "We packed her insulin pen and blood sugar meter in a special bag she took to school," Jan said. "Come to think of it . . . maybe that was one of *your* meters that helped keep Amy safe."

One of the participants in the seminar, Dave, was really moved by this, and raised his hand when Jan had finished her introduction. "Jan," he said, fumbling for words, "I just have to say, this is really amazing. It really makes me feel good about what we're doing here. Thank you so much."

It was indeed a moving interaction and, as I hoped, one that would provoke the group into thinking a little differently. Now it was time to use Jan's appearance to achieve our objectives. I broke the group of twenty-five into five teams, a mix of product engineering and account leads, and gave them their afternoon assignment. "I want you to draw this patient journey map on your flip chart and at each stage, from diagnosis through treatment to end of life, I want you to identify problems and ask questions." I waved a pad of Post-It notes at them. "Write your problems and questions on the sticky notes." Jan and I made our way to each team, pushing them to think harder about the problems and the questions that needed answering.

At the break, Eric, a product designer, approached me. "Thank you for this exercise—I try to read what I can about diabetes care, but I never really thought about the patient in this way. I'm learning a lot."

When the session resumed, we went around the room and did a readout of each group's insights.

Ray, an account lead new to diabetes, had listened to Jan tell stories of how at night it was sometimes hard for Amy to read the meter and avoid giving herself too much or too little insulin. "I had no idea that the numbers on the glucose meter were too small," he said. "Yeah, and I didn't realize that the glucose-sensing patch patients wear on their arms could tear and had to be replaced so often," Cheryl, the marketing lead, added. "What a pain, especially for little kids." "I'm wondering what these parents need to make their lives easier," Jay piped up, "so that when their kids go to school and play sports, they don't have to worry."

By the end of the day the group was still bubbling with creative energy and had brainstormed a solid group of problems and related questions. "How many of you are game to reconvene after the dinner break?" I asked. I knew they were tired.

Every hand shot up. "Let's keep going while we're on a roll," Sabrina exclaimed. "We've got to meet with Randy tomorrow, and this time we need to be ready with some Big Ideas."

We worked until 10:30 that night, crystallizing problem statements, outlining key questions that still needed answering, and selecting three problems to take to solution brainstorming.

At 7:30 sharp the next morning, we reconvened, and even before they'd had their coffee, the group was buzzing with energy. It was now time to conclude our session by brainstorming solutions. I used the end-user experience method, in which we focused on matching the problem to the solution, completing sentences such as "This problem causes our user to struggle with . . ." and "With our solution, our user can now . . . ." The group decided on solving two problems: the difficulty of reading the glucose meter at night and the wear and tear on the glucose patch. We selected three solutions to each problem and decided on the one that was the best fit for what we call the minimum viable product, or MVP.

For the glucose meter, it meant a new design that would include a backlight that operated by sensing the ambient light in the room. The light would come on automatically when the room was dark and the meter was activated, making it easy to read. The wear and tear on the glucose patch was solved by designing a small plastic cap over the patch. And in the spirit of anticipating what it must be like to be a kid wearing the patch, they designed waterproof stickers of superheroes and Disney characters.

Randy showed up later that morning, and the grim look on his face suggested that he had low expectations for this group and was wondering if this whole exercise had been a waste of time and money. But what he heard inspired a 180-degree turnaround in his mood and confidence. The group was beaming proudly as they reviewed their research into the problem and explained their solutions. "A glucose meter with a nightlight?" he said. "Damn, that's a good idea!"

I checked in with Randy a month later. Those solutions plus a couple of others that had resulted from our workshop had moved to prototype and MVP testing. "We've already got the finance team working on this," he said. "That's how confident I am that this is going to fly." Perhaps most gratifying, Randy told me they had held a user experience workshop with a key customer, one of the world's largest manufacturers of diabetes devices, and they were excited about the new ideas. "I'm not sure we would have done that in the past," Randy admitted. "Meeting your friend and what we learned from you really changed our perspective on how we interact with the people who buy and use our products." The change in attitude was reflected in the company's relationship with this manufacturer. "Our customer satisfaction score with this client has improved by several points. The team is really stoked!"

No doubt Jan's surprise appearance was a turning point for the team that day. But I think what it really shows is how important it is to consider the end user as you generate new ideas. In fact, you could say that the creative process can't succeed without the customer's perspective, which is critical for generating ideas and relevant new solutions.

GENERATING NEW IDEAS

Where do new ideas come from? Do they just pop into our minds through divine intervention, in dreams, after a long run when our brains are flooded by endorphins, or with a glass of wine? Of course, the nature of the muse—the source of inspiration and creativity—has been speculated upon for centuries. But in the organizational context, we can't sit around and wait for someone's muse to strike (literally or figuratively). The most innovative organizations have a system, a process for fostering new ideas, and it includes some basic tools and principles. Here are a few examples of methods commonly used (some of which I referenced in the case study above).

Method 1. Big Idea vignettes

WHAT IT IS Think of a Big Idea as a single frame of a storyboard. We sketch a visual depiction of what the idea might look like. You're generating ideas here, not features of a solution. A Big Idea describes how a user might experience the solution. Features describe implementation of the solution. For example, a Big Idea is "our customer needs to be able to book the best affordable flight at the last minute." A feature might be "flight status needs to update in real time on the app."

WHY WE DO IT In this approach we rapidly produce a wide range of possible solutions to meet the users' needs.

HOW WE DO IT This activity starts with a good prompt, such as a needs statement, a user story, or a pain point. A sample question might be "Developers need a way to interact with their design teams so they can prototype faster." Without talking, the group sketches ideas on sticky notes. During the discussion, the main points are summarized and posted to the wall. A key thing to keep in mind is that—as with our case study on the diabetes equipment manufacturer—you want to stay focused on your end users. Tell stories about them during the discussion to keep them at the center of attention. At the outset, welcome all ideas; later, you'll come back together to cluster, seek patterns, and then select the strongest ideas. In this simple example, ideas in response to the problem "Developers need a way to interact with their design teams so they can prototype faster" might include "a direct line to get what you need," "a hotline to the design team," and "a common workspace to iterate ideas in real time." When you cluster or converge the ideas, you'll create useful categories. In this case, we had communication-related solutions to improve productivity between the developers and the designers.

Method 2. Storyboards

WHY WE USE THIS APPROACH Storytelling helps people intuitively understand how your idea fits into the users' world. It gives visual form to those ideas and helps others understand them more clearly. In our diabetes example, we looked at the problem of checking your blood sugar at night when you couldn't see the screen clearly or make out the numbers on the blood sugar monitor.

WHEN YOU SHOULD USE THIS METHOD Storyboards work well when you know the problem you're trying to solve and for whom. Draw a storyboard anytime you need to share an idea about your user's needs quickly and visually.

HOW TO GET STARTED Begin with a story. Identify a character, a setting, and a plot. In our diabetes example above, we analyzed the patient experience of a child being diagnosed with diabetes after the teacher picked up on changes in the child's energy level throughout the day. Then pick scenes that show the plot from start to finish. Make sure to include major events, shifts in setting, twists in the plot, or the emergence of a new character. Think of your storyboard as a comic strip. Combine quick sketches with speech and thought bubbles, actions, captions, and narration.

Method 3. User experience road map

WHY YOU SHOULD USE THIS ACTIVITY To explore what long-term experience you want your users to have, what you want them to be able to do, and when.

WHEN YOU SHOULD USE THIS ACTIVITY This method works best once you have identified your users' problems and needs and established ideas for how to address them.

HOW TO GET STARTED Write the statement "Our user can / will be able to . . ." on the whiteboard. Label short-term on the left side and long-term on the right side. This method is also helpful in setting up the MVP that we will examine in the next chapter.

THE BEST PROCESS OF GENERATING IDEAS

- Define your purpose.
- Brainstorm spontaneously, copiously.
- Remember there are no bad ideas, no critics, no negativity
- Record ideas in full view (use a whiteboard, virtual or real, to keep track).
- Resist becoming committed to one idea (keep it moving during the initial part of the session).
- After thirty to forty-five minutes, go back and identify the most promising ideas, and build on them.
- Refine and prioritize.
- Recognize everyone for their participation and innovative thinking!

CREATIVITY IS SYNONYMOUS WITH INNOVATION

The word *creativity* is usually associated with artists, musicians, and writers—people who somehow, through their talents and imaginations, originate paintings, films, and symphonies. But I believe that some of the world's most creative individuals are innovators.

The notion that creativity can be learned or enhanced holds important implications for those of us who are seeking to innovate, to *create* change. Most people can spot creative flair. Think about the curiosity and creativity kids possess. Several studies suggest that creativity peaks around the first grade and then declines as the child's life becomes increasingly structured, defined by others and by institutions. Intellectual discipline and rigor become very important when the child enters school, and as the child advances academically, the focus is on logic, reasoning, and analytical thinking. It's no wonder that by the time they're adults, their creativity is at an all-time low. This is why idea generation approaches, like the ones described above, and brainstorming, the process of generating ideas in a group in a set period of time, are important to unlocking the creativity we need to innovate effectively.

A WORD ON BRAINSTORMING:
A GROUP PROCESS FOR GENERATING NEW IDEAS

While the term *brainstorming* is often used loosely, and people claim to be doing it any time they're throwing around some ideas with a colleague, it's actually a more formal, group process, based on a methodology like the ones described above. In brainstorming, participants with different backgrounds leverage their collective knowledge, understanding, and creative power to bring forward a larger number of innovative ideas than an individual could generate. People from varied parts of the organization, such as product design, product management, marketing, sales, and operations, come together as a mixed functional team. With their different perspectives, ideas can cross-pollinate.

Brainstorming allows innovators to open their minds to a creative flow of ideas, set aside preconceived notions, and look beyond the solution they may have been consciously or subconsciously forming during problem identification. It works best when participants suspend their tendency to evaluate and make judgments about new concepts as they arise. This can be difficult for bright businesspeople, engineers, and scientists who have built their careers having the right answers, as the example of my manufacturing client demonstrated.

Brainstorming is appropriate at different times: addressing problems; asking questions; identifying solutions; and examining market segmentation, business models, and tactical challenges. Brainstorming supports an iterative cyclic approach to creative group thinking. The team that makes brainstorming a best practice is never done! New information comes up at each stage in the innovation process, so the team should be prepared to go back to brainstorming mode at different junctures.

I follow five rules for brainstorming. They are based on the model taught by the product design firm Innovation Design Engineering Organization (IDEO), which was founded in 1991 in Palo Alto, California. The model uses *design thinking*, defined as a human-centered approach to innovation that draws from the designer's tool kit to integrate the needs of people, the possibilities of technology, and the requirements for business success. You can learn more at Ideo. com, but here are the basic rules of design thinking.

Rule 1. Think visually

Thinking visually begins with the space in which the brainstorming is occurring. It's useful to have flip charts, whiteboards, sticky notes, colored markers, even toys and gadgets to create an environment where ideas can flow. Everyone needs to be able to see what's being written. It's also helpful to have a scribe or two to take notes. Catchy labels and headlines help the group remember what was said. You can also use cartoons and personas to communicate information. In a brainstorm with an ophthalmology company, to stimulate thinking, we created a character, and a cartoonist sketched out the character's experience having an eye examination. You can also cluster ideas that are related in a section of the room, with arrows diagramming how these clusters relate to one another. Having people write ideas on sticky notes and paste them in categories on the whiteboard or flip chart ensures that everyone's ideas are captured.

During the COVID-19 pandemic, in-person brainstorming has not been possible. Digital brainstorming techniques, such as digital whiteboards, allow people to list their ideas on a virtual board and move them around into different categories so that team members can build off one another. Another way to record notes is through digital forums where people can record thoughts and reactions in real time during the presentations and discussions. I was working at IBM Watson Health during COVID-19, a time when people were required to work from home for more than a year. During that time, we used virtual whiteboards to facilitate brainstorming exercises, collaborate on setting our organization's goals and objectives, and even test ideas with customers. We also used social forums such as Trello Boards to collect feedback in real time while we were engaged in brainstorms and group meetings. And we used Slack to communicate with others during video meetings. Zoom has features such as breakout rooms and whiteboards to facilitate group working sessions, as do Teams, WebEx, and Google Meets. These technologies helped simulate the experience of being in the same room, chatting with each other informally and spurring creative conversations. Learn more at trello.com and slack.com.

Rule 2. Defer judgment

Of all the rules, deferring judgment is probably the most counterintuitive and difficult to follow. The point is to suspend any critical thoughts or commentary until later in the innovation process. The purpose of brainstorming is to open up individual creativity and the group's creative process. One good way to make this happen is to accept any new idea—even suggestions that may seem impractical or silly—and move on to the next concept. Learning to defer judgment can be challenging for many people. If people are new to the process, it's important to explain this rule.

Rule 3. Go for quantity

Successful brainstorming builds a momentum or flow that breaks through the usual group inhibitions. One way to achieve this flow is to set a target for the group to create a large number of concepts without regard to how good the ideas are. A typical brainstorming session lasts sixty minutes. Within this time frame, a team might expect to generate sixty new ideas, with a stretch goal of one hundred. Clearly, moving quickly is key.

Rule 4. Have one conversation at a time

The critical concept underlying this rule is that listening is as important as, if not more important than, talking. The Dalai Lama said, "When you talk, you are only repeating what you already know. But if you listen, you may learn something new." Enforcing this rule falls to the facilitator, but everyone in the group should keep the conversation focused on one discussion. This rule should be established at the outset of the session. The facilitator can use a fun phrase to keep people on track. Once when facilitating a brainstorm with a loquacious colleague, I used the words "Got it" to indicate when it was time to move on. He would instantly smile and stop talking—it started out as humorous, but ultimately his colleagues used that phrase to keep him in check even in staff meetings. He thanked me a few months later— "honestly, I learned something about myself, and I'm applying it at home and work."

Rule 5. Stay focused on the topic

Even the most disciplined participants may tend to let their conversations wander. While these digressions sometimes result in valuable ideas and information, they can have a negative effect on the flow and productivity of the meeting. To keep the group focused, avoid distractions, sidebar conversations, real-time analysis, and idea filtering. One useful strategy for minimizing these distractions is to have a flip chart handy to capture ideas that deserve to be recorded but aren't particularly germane to the discussion. This is called creating a Parking Lot. If the brainstorm stalls, the facilitator should jump to a new area of the topic or reframe the discussion on a new angle or a different stakeholder. At the same time, staying focused shouldn't be confused with encouraging wild ideas—there is a distinction, and learning that comes with practice.

EVALUATING SOLUTIONS—WHY YOU NEED THREE

So, you've followed your preferred method of generating ideas and the brainstorming session has been held. Now, you have a whiteboard or notepad filled with ideas—dozens and dozens of them. How do you sift out the gold?

Evaluating solutions at this stage can feel like a leap of faith, but if the process has been informed by observing the problem in its natural habitat, then evaluating the top three solutions that best fit is less of a leap and more a balance of art with science. In the earlier example of my session with the engineers who manufactured medical devices, the fact that I had interviewed patients and Jan could speak to the patient experience helped build the group's confidence in defining solutions. Narrowing down to three solutions ensures that you have enough variety to test different approaches and create a plan B if needed but not so many solutions that narrowing them down or filtering them is laborious.

At this point, getting to a few solutions for rapid prototyping of the MVP is critical. When my dad told my brother and me that we always had to have at least three solutions—whether it was at the Hot Shoppes or during our Easter "emergency"—I'm not sure if he was working from data or just a gut feeling that three was the right number. Either way, that approach has been a good target for me and for most of my colleagues and clients.

INNOVATOR IN FOCUS

Aris Persidis, PhD, cofounder and president of Biovista

INNOVATOR CREDENTIALS Dr. Persidis was a cofounder of three biotech companies. He wrote the industry trends column for *Nature Biotechnology*, served as the first editor-in-chief of the journal *Drug Repurposing, Rescue, and Repositioning*, and has authored ninety papers and book chapters. Persidis serves on the boards of MBF Therapeutics and GridNews Bureau and was voted one of the Top-50 World Futurists in 2020. He earned his PhD in biochemistry from the University of Cambridge.

Innovation claim to fame

When Persidis and his brother, Andreas, were graduate students at Cambridge, they had a notion that if they could match everything known to humanity about every drug against every disease, they could determine new uses for marketed drugs. And they were right. More than twenty years later, Biovista has helped bring several new drugs to market to treat diseases for which they were not originally intended, including Parkinson's disease, through artificial intelligence (AI). Their method, examining already approved drugs to determine what the disease for which they were approved had in common with other diseases, led to several options.

Lessons learned

As the Persidis brothers developed the concepts that would lead to Biovista, a company that uses artificial intelligence to discover new uses for existing drugs, they used idea-generation approaches and brainstorming to explore and evaluate their options. "For example, we learned that a drug approved for pain had potential benefit in Parkinson's, hypothyroidism, and depression. We then had to determine where to focus based on customer needs; for us that meant the pharmaceutical manufacturers and the end users, patients with the disease."

You can't make this up (fun fact)

As an undergraduate student in London, Persidis entered a contest sponsored by Honeywell in which entrants were asked to write an essay predicting a technological advance in the next twenty-five years. The young Persidis chose AI—specifically, artificial photosynthesis. He won.

Insights for innovators

"I can come up with five ideas in the next five minutes of cool things to make. It's the discipline of following a process for problem identification and solution generation that makes the difference between success and failure. I learned at a young age that the most important thing is the ability to divorce yourself of confirmation bias. It's so easy to be driven by your ego, by your assumptions, and to have a bias toward a solution that is absolutely not supported by your research. The market, the customer will tell you all you need to know about the merit of your problem and solutions, but you have to be listening to those voices and willing to follow what you learn."

Learn more about Persidis at https://www.biovista.com and https://www.linkedin.com/aris-persidis-7761492.

3

WE'RE ROOTING FOR YOUR MVP!

F rom the podium on the stage, I looked out over the dimly lit
hotel conference room, cavernous and cold, as seventy-one
sets of eyes stared at me, expectantly.

A few of my clients, arms crossed tightly across their chests,
tapped their feet, which to me sounded like a thunderous drumbeat
tapping out a rhythm of imminent doom. Others strummed their
fingers on the white-clothed tables, organized classroom style. The
clients in the back row were heads down, typing on their laptops,
clearly trying to make the most of the extra free time my travesty
had bestowed upon them.

As a consultant, it's a situation I'm not unfamiliar with. Money
has been spent and schedules have been disrupted. For what? What
does *she* have to say that could be worth this inconvenience? But
this time, the frostiness of the audience was almost palpable.

I cleared my throat, but my stomach was doing flips and I was
pretty sure the front row could hear my heart beating. I glanced at
my smartwatch and was surprised to see my heart rate was only
75—it felt like 175, my running heart rate.

"I'm really sorry about this unexpected delay," I said in my most
apologetic voice. "I know you've given up your weekends and traveled from all over the country to Indianapolis for the demo of our
minimum viable product (MVP) and user experience workshop.

Our team in India is working diligently to get the network back up and running so we can start the software-testing session this morning."

Why had I agreed to allow the live test environment for this critical MVP workshop with seventy-one clients to be run out of India? I had requested a backup environment, but Partha, our lead software development engineer based in Mumbai, had insisted that the network was stable and his team would be on-site in Mumbai to ensure the MVP user testing was a success. I silently vowed never to do another technology workshop without at least two backup scenarios.

"We're going to start the coffee break early, and we hope to have this resolved within the hour," I offered as I left the stage to murmurs of discontent from the audience and made my way to our lead client, Jackie. She was the executive sponsor of the event, and I knew this made her look bad, too.

"What can I say?" I offered. "We need to get this fixed and fast. It doesn't make any of us look good for such a high-profile event." Jackie raised an eyebrow, a look I had seen before when she was ready to render an admonishment. "I understand, Lorraine," she said supportively, but with an edge of concern on her voice. "Let's just hope they fix it soon."

The executives from seventeen global corporations were members of an industry consortium. We were gathered at the Indianapolis Marriott Hotel for user testing of a new software product my company was developing for the consortium, which each member company was going to deploy at its own company. We had worked together over the past four months on a "sprint." That's a software development methodology that uses short time intervals to create a minimum set of critical features based on user needs. The goal of today's workshop was to have users test the minimum viable product (MVP) in a live environment. The user experience session is a common method for testing the MVP with the users for whom the product is designed.

What does all this mean? The executives were supposed to be able to log into the web-based portal, navigate the several screens, and input data into some forms in the real, live system, which was being hosted on the network in India. Think of trying to host a Zoom meeting in which you can't share your screen, take participants off mute, or create breakout rooms. The executives were staring into frozen laptop screens as Partha and the team in India tried to get the network back online.

The sprint was starting to feel like a marathon. And it didn't take long for some of the more outspoken clients to start complaining. Dave, the VP of IT for one of the medium-sized companies, approached me. "I've looked through the test script you've prepared," he said coldly. "It's lacking. There are too few features to even warrant this meeting." "Yeah," Alan, from a large manufacturer in Chicago, chimed in, "I mean I know it's an MVP test of how to log into and navigate the portal and input some basic data, but I thought we'd have more features to try out by now."

I tried to keep my cool. "Guys, you were in the meetings where the features to be tested in the MVP were agreed to. With seventeen companies accessing this system, we need to make sure logging in, navigating screens, and inputting basic data work first, right? But I'll talk to the design team. We may be able to take a peek at the road map."

Dave and Alan shrugged. "Whatever," said Dave. "But you know, I have a lot of better things I could be doing with my time than looking at a frozen screen in a hotel in Indianapolis." They stomped off to the coffee break.

I quickly made my way to our team's huddle room in the corner of the conference center where the ten-person user testing team, project managers, and product designers were on a conference call with Partha trying to troubleshoot the situation. "OK, we can't wait for Partha to get the network in Mumbai up and running. We need to launch Plan B now," I said.

My team looked at each other quizzically. I expect they were wondering exactly what Plan B was. "This is what we're going to do," I said. "Tom, Jeff, Sid, and Beenu, get your laptops—I know you preloaded the sample demo. I want you each to create a station and get a small group of users together. Walk them through the demo of

55

the web portal experience and then let each of them give it a try." This was risky. The experience we had planned would have allowed the audience to tap into a live environment on their own laptops, giving them the look and feel of being in the actual portal, navigating screens and entering data. Now they would just walk through a static view.

"Chris, Ragan, Amit, I want you to get the user storyboards and set up three stations in the conference room," I said. "Get the rest of the group to give you feedback on the storyboards. Victoria, I want you to break the group into these smaller subgroups and assign each to a station and then rotate them from the MVP user stations to the storyboard discussions."

"Let's make the best of this," I concluded, as my team sprang into action. "We'll get their feedback on a static version of the MVP and a manual version of the storyboards."

Fortunately, with a little prodding from Jackie and me, it worked. Soon people were in small breakouts contributing their ideas and talking with one another. The team was gathering input on flip charts, asking questions, and engaging with the clients. The sound of talking in the room grew louder, and I knew we were on the backside of the crisis.

By midafternoon the India team had the network back up and we could do our live testing. They could even activate a couple of the features we hadn't planned to demo until later in the week, just to get the group's energy and confidence up. Even Dave and Alan seemed appreciative. "Hey," said Dave as we were leaving. "That actually turned out pretty well."

Jackie came over to me, looking around the conference room and listening to the buzz of conversations. "Nice save," she said. "That happened to me last year when I was hosting an MPV user testing workshop at our site in Munich, Germany. I sent everyone out for an afternoon of sightseeing, which made them very happy," she laughed. "Given that we're in Indianapolis in the middle of March, clearly that's not an option, so I'm glad you had a Plan B."

By the end of the weekend, we had learned a lot. We adjusted the MVP based on our customers' experience—we made the navigation more intuitive and added some drop-down menus to make data input easier. We launched the first version of the product later that spring.

WHAT IS AN MVP, AND WHY DO YOU USE IT?

Sports fans know it as the acronym for Most Valuable Player, bestowed annually on the top performer of the year in the NFL, the NBA, or MLB. In the world of innovation, it has a very different meaning, but a good MVP—minimum viable product—in business can be just as critical to success as an MVP on the field.

The term was coined in 2001 by Frank Robinson, not the MVP ballplayer and manager of the 1960s and 1970s but the cofounder and president of product development consulting firm SyncDev. It was popularized as an efficient, customer-focused way to develop products by serial Silicon Valley entrepreneurs Eric Ries, author of *Lean Startup*, and Steve Blank, who wrote *The Startup Owner's Manual*.

In barely twenty years, MVP has become a best practice in innovation. "An MVP turns an idea into something real," writes Ries in his book, "in order to begin the process of iterating and retesting." The MVP creates a two-way street between the customer and the innovator. "While you decide what's minimal, the customer decides what's viable," Ries writes in *Lean Startup*.

You've probably heard of Zappos, a popular online shoe and handbag retailer. Nick Swinmurn founded the company in 1999 when he wanted a pair of Airwalk Desert Chuka boots and couldn't find them at his local San Francisco mall. He had the idea to sell a variety of footwear online through a website. Swinmurn's first MVP was a simple website, called Shoesite.com, where people could order limited types of shoes, such as running shoes and hiking boots. What purchasers didn't know was that, behind the scenes, Tony was physically going to local shoe stores, buying the shoes, and then delivering them. Once he had proof of his MVP and business model—namely, that people were willing to buy shoes online through a website that carried popular brands—he raised capital and invested in automating the supply chain, offering more products, and developing a customer experience that was synonymous with excellence. In 2009, Amazon bought Zappos in a $1.2 billion deal.

The purpose of the MVP is to rapidly refine or test your idea—to create just enough features to test with customers so you can get feedback and refine your product before you go into full production, which is expensive and time consuming. It's one of the best ways to find out if you have a solution a customer is willing to pay for. The goal is to translate a promising concept from a draft idea into a rudimentary design. It allows the innovator to learn about functionality and features, gather feedback from target users, and continually refine product design.

The MVP is a stand-alone product composed of the smallest possible group of features that solve the core problem and demonstrate the product's value. While it grew out of a best-practices approach to software development, the MVP can be used for all types of products and even services with some modifications. It maximizes customer insight while minimizing cost, time, and effort.

In today's marketplace of uncertainty, whoever learns the fastest wins! Innovation cycle time is defined as how much time elapses between having an idea and validating whether the idea is brilliant or crazy, which only a customer can help you do. Teams that accelerate validation cycle times are much more likely to optimize a product's market fit and increase their probability of success. The MVP can allow you to do just that.

WHAT ARE THE BENEFITS OF AN MVP?

First, an MVP allows you to get the product into customers' hands as soon as possible. These early customers can translate into evangelists for your product later.

Second, it's a tool for generating maximum customer learning in the shortest time, allowing you to accelerate your development.

Third, it focuses on a small set of features, reducing unnecessary engineering hours and costs.

Let's look at an example. Three mechanical engineering post-doctoral researchers at Princeton University participated in the innovation lab I was running there at the time. They all had erratic schedules and were frustrated with the lack of healthy, affordable meal options. Eating out was expensive, especially if they wanted to eat healthy and not at Hoagie Haven every day as the under-graduates did. Buying and preparing healthy food was expensive and time consuming, especially when cooking for one person. After conducting interviews with other graduate students and observing their own cooking and eating behaviors, they determined that a big drawback to healthy cooking at home was the time required to cut and chop vegetables and meat.

Their idea? A robot that could be a cooking assistant by slic-ing, dicing, cutting, and chopping raw vegetables and meat, reduc-ing preparation time. They needed an MVP to test with potential customers. Narrowing their MVP to a couple of critical features, they determined that the robot needed to be able to chop two vegetables at a minimum—most of the stir fry dishes they loved included onions and celery and both were unpleasant to chop! They created a mechanical arm with metal, wires, plastic, and a couple of different types of knife blades in the lab in the mechanical engi-neering school. They met with students, the chefs at local restau-rants, and even the food preparation team at Blue Apron, a local fresh food preparation and delivery company. Based on what they learned from these sources, they developed a prototype robotic arm for Blue Apron to test in their kitchen. They timed how long it took the robot to chop compared with a human. They looked at the accuracy of the chopping compared with that of a human. They determined that the robotic arm, once they tweaked it, saved time and was appealing, particularly to Blue Apron, which was having a tough time retaining student employees to do the food prep. The company became the first MVP customer, and the students refined and iterated the robot with Blue Apron, an early evangelist for the product.

From there they worked with customers on how to set up the robot, where in the kitchen it would be positioned, how the vegetables would be prepared for robotic chopping, and even how the robotic arm would be cleaned and stored. Once they got additional prototypes of the robotic arm into a few Blue Apron test markets, they figured out how to price it and started speaking with investors. Eventually they added other features, such as knives that could chop raw chicken and beef and even a component on the arm that could lift the bowl and the cutting board and empty the vegetables into the wok.

Ultimately, the time and capital to fully productize the kitchen robot outstripped the students' capacity and interest, and they went on to esteemed research positions in academia, but they got an "A" in class and, more importantly, a lifetime of learning!

The takeaway from this example is that a true MVP is a full experience, one that works. It's functional, reliable, usable, and even delightful to the customer.

Here are some other well-known MVP examples:

Groupon founder Andrew Mason, after launching his not-so-successful start-up, The Point, without testing an MVP, decided not to make that mistake again. He used a manual MVP strategy when he built Groupon. He created a basic website using self-service website design software by WordPress and posted publicly available deals and coupons daily. After orders started coming in, he generated PDFs of the vouchers and coupons and then embedded them in emails from his personal email to the customers during the MVP stage. Everything was done manually with the help of third-party resources. Only after the product idea had been validated and there was a genuine need and customer willingness to pay for Groupon did he create the automated, digital version of Groupon.

Instacart, the popular grocery delivery app, started out as an iPhone MVP. The app code had basic functionality at the time of launch, and customers could use it to place their grocery order, but behind the scenes there was no automation. As orders came in, the founders did the grocery shopping and delivered the goods to the customers, all in a local geography. After validating the concept with customers and showing that the app worked, the company auto-mated the ordering, shopping, and delivery process and went on to incorporate groundbreaking innovations. The manual approach to the MVP gave the company the speed and flexibility needed to man-age resources and costs while proving the idea was scalable.

Etsy, the now-famous online community for anyone to sell things they make themselves, started as a rudimentary MVP web-site that let people register and sell their self-produced products. Despite the website's rudimentary design, thousands of crafters started using it, almost overnight once word got out. This was at a time when eBay was dominating the market and many other online marketplaces had failed because they ran out of cash before they could get a significant number of users and advertising revenues. By conserving cash and developing a basic website to test their idea first, Etsy was able to survive and thrive.

For digital, service-based solutions like the examples above, a manual MVP is the fastest and most cost-effective way to confirm product-market fit. It lets you focus on solving the customer's prob-lem and moves technology and implementation details to a future stage. "Manual first" means your MVP *appears* to have all the func-tionality of the fully featured product while in reality your team is behind the scenes pulling the strings to deliver the product and the customer experience. It allows you to examine the physical work that needs to be performed to fulfill the customer's need, which in turn lets you simulate work flows and processes, figuring out what will stay manual and what you will automate.

It means more work for you at the beginning—you're fulfilling customer orders, generating the coupons, or doing the shopping as the founders of Groupon and Instacart did—but the result, as in these cases, can be a game- and life-changing idea.

TYPES OF MVP

The type of MVP you use depend on what you're trying to learn. MVPs come in different sizes and flavors and are more a state of mind, a product-testing discipline, than a set process or method. These methods are used at Intuit.

Type 1. Fast-cycle sketch tests

Simulate a real experience using paper, cardboard, or other materials you can draw on. An example: you want to create a website, but before starting to write software code, you first sketch the design and functionality on paper or a whiteboard and test it with a customer.

Type 2. Front-door tests

Present a minimal pitch of the idea until the customer indicates interest in learning more. One of my students at Princeton used this method when he wanted to assess interest in a beverage he was developing to treat hangovers. He created a simple webpage describing the beverage and its benefits and asking people who visited the page to indicate if they wanted to learn more. They were able to enter their contact information and he was able to follow up with them.

Type 3. Back-end tests

Manually simulate the product or service. When Zappos created a website for shoe ordering but Swinmurn bought the shoes from a local store and delivered them to the customer, he was using the back-end test.

Type 4. End-to-end tests

Simulate the full user experience and measure how the customer responds. The original MVP, it combines the front-door and the back-end tests. When the Princeton students developed the robotic chopping arm to test customer interest in a kitchen helper, they created an end-to-end test.

Type 5. Dry wallet

Test payment options and revenue models. The customer goes through the process of paying for the product (online) but doesn't actually complete the transaction. This allows the tester to see how many steps are involved in paying for an item and how long it takes.

Type 6. Judo

Test a competitor's product or service to inform how you can improve it. Phil McKinney, former CTO of Hewlett-Packard, hung out in aisles at Circuit City observing customers interacting with tablets and games, then used what he learned to improve upon HP's products.

Type 7. Analog/retro

Create a physical version of the concept, such as a flyer, booklet, or guide, to get feedback on your idea. One of my students had an idea for displaying advertising on Uber and Lyft vehicles, similar to the way taxis display advertising on top of their cars. He created a flyer to show advertisers where on the car the ad would be placed.

Type 8. Pop-up shop

Create a store, booth, or area to showcase and test your product or service. A new type of pet adoption program set up a stand outside a subway stop at the Freedom Tower in New York to test its concept with tourists.

COMMON MVP TESTING APPROACHES

Just as there are many types of MVPs, there are various testing techniques, too.

Technique 1. Websites and applications

One of the simplest methods to test demand for a product is to create a website for it and then drive traffic to that website. As was the case with the Groupon and Instacart MVPs, the website is not fully functional but rather a mock-up explaining what will be available and inviting customers to click for more information. The number of clicks is compared to visitor numbers to determine level of interest in the product.

Technique 2. Services

If you are going to sell a service, the easiest way to test it is to perform the service and ask the customer how much they are willing to pay for it. When my son and his friend were in high school, they started a gutter-cleaning business over the summer break. For the first couple of jobs, they asked the customers to pay them what they thought the work was worth when they had finished. After a few times, they were able to calculate an hourly rate.

Technique 3. New features

Before developing new features for an existing product, it might be worthwhile to advertise the feature on an existing website and provide a link for more information. The link takes the customer to a page explaining the feature under development. You can count the number of clicks as a proxy for level of interest. Going back to the example of the student who developed the beverage for hangovers, after he launched his bottled concoction he started working on a powdered version that could be made with water. He assessed interest by posting a line—"new powdered version" available soon—on his website, where visitors could click the link to learn more. He counted the number of people who clicked the link as a surrogate for interest.

CHOOSING YOUR MVP FROM AMONG MANY CANDIDATES

The competition for an MVP in sports is usually fierce. Typically chosen by votes from players or media, candidates—athletes who've had terrific seasons—are often numerous. But only one can earn the title of Most Valuable Player.

Same with our MVP. If you've gone through the process correctly, you may have several options. How do you narrow it down to the one that you're going to use to test your innovative product or service? Scott Cook of Intuit uses this technique. He asks each person on the team to consider the project she is working on and to spend five minutes writing down ideas/assumptions about the solution. Then he asks each person to pick an assumption/idea and spend five minutes brainstorming different metrics that could measure whether the assumption is true. Finally, he asks each person to pick a single metric to brainstorm different MVPs that could generate the necessary data.

Let's look at an example from *The Startup Way*. I like this example because of its simplicity. Author Eric Ries's original example was for a new artisanal lemonade in California. I prefer carrot juice, which has grown in popularity as a health beverage, so for my version of the MVP we are launching a hand-crafted carrot juice in New York.

Louise is working on creating a new beverage, hand-crafted carrot juice.

Assumption: People who like carrot juice are unhappy with the limited variety and quality of available beverages.

Hypothesis: If high-quality, hand-crafted carrot juice is available for on-demand delivery, customers will increase carrot juice consumption.

Louise now must ask herself some questions:

Who is the product designed for? Is there a segment of carrot juice drinkers who (a) drink carrot juice at least once a week and (b) are willing to pay more for premium beverages—e.g., people who frequent gourmet coffee and juice bars?

What is the simplest product offering I can make to start learning if my hypothesis is true?

Louise has four MVP choices:

MVP 1: Street-corner carrot juice stand with tables, chairs, signage, and a sample before you buy

MVP 2: Website landing page enabling on-demand ordering and delivery by humans

MVP 3: Website and app enabling on-demand ordering and delivery by a robotic drone in Brooklyn, New York

MVP 4: Website and app enabling on-demand ordering and delivery by a fleet of robotic drones anywhere in the state of New York

Louise then assesses what she will learn from each of these MVPs. She also looks at the cost of running her tests.

Which MVP should she test first, and why? While each has pros and cons, she ultimately chooses MVP 2 because it is the fastest and most cost-efficient way to get feedback on her initial concept of an online carrot juice product.

Like Louise, you need to start the MVP process by defining what needs to be learned and from whom. You can engage a small group of early visionary and passionate customers to guide feature development until you know whether a profitable business model might emerge. The sooner the MVP is in their hands, the sooner you can get feedback.

Rather than asking customers about specific features, the best approach to defining the MVP is to ask what is the smallest or least complicated problem the customer will pay us to solve? In our carrot juice example, it might be "I would try hand-crafted carrot juice if I could order a small quantity online and have it delivered for free." By the way, this approach runs counter to the typical focus on how to beat the competition with more, better, different features, but it's far more effective. You noticed that Louise is not asking whether people want carrot juice with ginger or if they prefer a recyclable cardboard drink box or a plastic bottle.

Remember, it's also important to know what *not* to develop. The MVP provides that discipline, based on *less is more*, to ensure that you have a core set of features that solve the customer's problem and can confirm you have a business model. "No new features until you've confirmed your business model!" is what I tell my students.

Mike, a student at Columbia Business School, sought me out for advice on his clinical trial software start-up. His online platform for helping doctors find clinical trials for their patients was six months from completion when he realized he needed to do more work on his business concept. That realization delayed his MVP, and he was now a year away from having a product to test. He was frustrated because he wanted to reach out to his target market to gauge interest in his solution. He asked me if he should wait to develop his MVP or talk to customers to validate his idea. And, he wondered, if he was going to validate his idea, what would he show potential customers? He had an additional concern as he was in a competitive market with few barriers to entry. "How can I test my idea when my MVP isn't ready, and how can I be assured someone won't steal the idea?"

After talking with Mike, I realized that reexamining his business concept meant he had to also reassess his product. That told me he should stop building the MVP right now and harden the concept before spending any more time or money. Instead, he developed a slide deck describing his product and showing how it worked. He outlined key functionality, features, and benefits. Customers were happy to speak with him and were open with their feedback. "I think I actually got better feedback showing them a slide deck than if I had handed them a physical demo of my MVP. I learned about the problems they needed help solving. We focused on their needs instead of their scrutinizing my product and providing feedback that may or may not be relevant at any early stage in product development."

Mike learned a valuable lesson. An innovator should listen to the customer explain the problem but never let the customer completely dictate what they (the innovator) are building. Customers don't always know what they want. Just ask the team who worked with Steve Jobs on the first iPhone! But customers are experts at telling you what problems they need to solve. In Mike's case, as he built his MVP, he gathered customer feedback along the way, which helped him move faster in the long run.

If you have a start-up venture like Mike's, you may have a similar question: "How do I develop something to test with my customer?" We examined this earlier in the section on types of MVPs, but let's apply it to Mike's case.

One option is to create a sample of the product. This is a commonly used approach in book publishing. The author completes a book proposal template that includes an overview of the proposed book and several sample chapters. Based on that, the editor has to decide if it will be a good product. In a book proposal, you need a visualization and a description of your idea. Mike did the same thing when he created a slide deck of his proposed product.

You can also create an interactive demo, which helps to communicate and validate your idea. Interactivity allows people to use your product and react to core concepts while you're doing the demo together. Helpful software packages like Adobe XD, Sketch, and InVision allow you to create visual assets, turn them into mocked-up screens, and then navigate those screens just like a mobile app or web app. Mike ended up doing this with the help of a software engineer at Columbia. They created a demo to simulate the experience of a doctor searching for clinical trials for Alzheimer's patients.

Creating a mock-up of screenshots is also a good option. You can use Photoshop, Gimp, and even PowerPoint or Google slides to mock up screenshots, a visualization of the user's interface with the app, in this case. Mike mocked up a screenshot of the look and feel of the phone app the doctors would use to search for trials. He included this in his slide deck. Remember, these mock-ups first need to be functional; attractiveness is initially a secondary goal.

Next, you must have someone to show your slides, demo, or mock-up to. If you can, start with the decision maker, the person who will be paying for your solution. You can also start with the champion, the person who will find the most use or value in the product and who can get you to the decision maker, the person willing to write the check and pay for your solution. In Mike's case, he needed to get both to the doctors who would be referring patients to the Alzheimer's clinical trials and to the pharmaceutical companies sponsoring Alzheimer's drug trials to which the patients would be referred.

Once you find the right people with whom to test your idea, you can contact them using LinkedIn, Facebook, or Twitter. Be brief. Mike sent prospective pharmaceutical customers a message on LinkedIn: "I'm building a clinical trials patient referral platform and need your professional input. May I ask you a few questions?" You can also refer interviewees to an online survey that's easy to complete. This process helps you establish contacts and build a network of potential customers that you'll need later. It's an easy—and even fun—way to gather input.

This step of speaking with customers early in the process is important even in corporations. Believe it or not, too often they are so internally focused on getting a product to market that they miss the step of speaking with potential customers about their product and listening to their feedback.

MVP TAKE-AWAYS

The MVP strategy is an ideal design approach for start-ups. It is also used by established corporations, especially on designs that may be considered high risk from an investment standpoint. Its goal is to get a basic product to market in a short time and then to examine the feasibility of the product and determine which features should be added in the next iteration. A user-focused design approach, the MVP gathers valuable feedback constantly to provide an improved product at each iteration.

Finally, remember that success is learning to solve a problem.

INNOVATOR IN FOCUS

Leslie Aisner Novak, Founder, Howda Designz

Inspired by a chairlike contraption she'd discovered when her ninety-three-year-old landlord cleared out an old garage, Novak founded Howda Designz in 1990. After sitting in the ersatz wood-and-canvas chair during an outdoor performance by the Boston Pops, she was amazed at its comfort and back support. With some refinements, she developed, patented, and manufactured what she called the HowdaSeat on her own. It quickly became a best seller in the J. Peterman catalog.

In 2006, Leslie launched the multipatented HowdaHug, a children's version of the seat that cradles and rocks kids in place, improving calmness, focus, and attention. Developed initially for students with a range of classroom challenges, the HowdaHug soon became standard equipment for kids in schools around the world.

Innovation claim to fame

Novak grew up in Des Moines, Iowa, where her father was an inventor who held multiple patents—including one for the first pair of plastic scissors. Moving to Boston for a job in textiles, she resolved to make a business of her next Big Idea by immersing herself in the lectures and audiotapes of entrepreneurs such as Paul Hawken and Anita Roddick—champions of sustainability, local production, and service-based products. Her chance discovery of the original seat-like contraption, she realized, represented the idea she had been looking for. She decided to brand it Howda after the Hindi name for a seat used to ride elephants.

Novak did extensive prototyping and always worked with suppliers who could scale up with the success she anticipated. When the HowdaHug won first prize for product design at the nation's largest educational-supply trade show in 2017, it was a game-changing moment that would quadruple production practically overnight.

Lessons learned

"My failures can all be traced to not listening to my gut," she says. "I started this business with no capital, collateral, or related experience, but I knew it was a winner with every fiber of my being. Now I trust my gut about everything—my ideas, my partners and workers, and my decisions about what to do next."

You can't make this up (fun fact)

When she was first launching HowdaSeats, Novak attended the Chicago Home Show, where she was approached about selling HowdaSeats through an experienced distributor. The sales rep showed Leslie an array of products and said the business had started with nothing more than a pair of plastic scissors. "And there was my father's invention in the display case!" Leslie said. She took it as a sign—and it turned out to be a good one. "We wrote more business at that show than I could have imagined."

Insights for innovators

Novak understands well the importance of the MVP. "I didn't share my Big Ideas until I had proof that they were viable," she says, "and sometimes that took years. It meant keeping a safe distance from doubters and working out each phase with broad-minded people in their own specialty."

Learn more about Novak at www.howda.com.

4

THE LAW OF ONE HUNDRED CUSTOMERS
(THEY CAN'T BE WRONG!)

Jenna Ray, wearing a pale blue sundress with tiny white sail-boats, her long blond hair pulled into a neat chignon, smiled with warmth and confidence as she stood in front of the audience of advisers, classmates, and team members. Her deck was cued to the opening slide, Who Is Our Customer? The Blue Catamaran Clothes Shopping Experience. Blue Catamaran was the name of Jenna's start-up, a women's luxury apparel e-retailer, of which she was the cofounder and chief marketing officer. She was presenting her team's work as part of the innovation accelerator program at Princeton University, where she was a senior. "This is Emma." Jenna opened with a wave of her hand, flashing a slide with a photo of a striking woman with long, straight black hair in round sunglasses wearing a short, white sleeveless linen dress and tangerine-colored leather sandals that strapped up to her knees. She was jeweled with big gold hoop earrings and several variegated metal bracelets on one arm. Standing near an elephant in a tourist scene commonly associated with travelogues of Bangkok, Emma fit right in. "She's an investment banking professional in Manhattan who's traveled throughout Asia and wants to convey an exotic traveler look in her fashion."

Jenna flipped to the next slide. "This is Anisha, a photojournalist who likes to capture wild animals in their natural habitat." Anisha was poised on the back of a seat in a mud-splattered jeep, taking photos of a herd of zebras with a Canon camera with a long zoom lens. "She's inspired by the wildlife she's photographed during her safaris in Africa; she lives in the UK and is hoping to land a job at *National Geographic* in DC this summer."

"And this is Dara," Jenna continued, proudly. "She's a volunteer with a program that's teaching jewelry making to women in Afghanistan. She sells the jewelry on her website and shares 50 percent of the profit with the women, so they have a chance at financial independence." Dara, her brown bangs displayed artfully under a red beret, was clad in orange-and-red-striped bell-bottom pants. She stood in front of a photo of a dozen women sitting on a stone floor, beading necklaces, ostensibly making jewelry that Dara would then sell on her website.

"These women represent the inspiration, the customers of Blue Catamaran. We want to give them an experience that speaks to their inner longings for travel, adventure, and living with purpose."

Jenna was about to move on to her marketing plan when I stopped her. The Princeton University innovation accelerator program was a ten-week summer seminar designed to provide students with an immersive experience developing and launching a start-up from an original idea. It was sponsored by the School of Engineering. Now in its second year, it existed to help budding innovators learn how to develop and commercialize innovation. Princeton, with its long, storied reputation as an Ivy League university in the United States, did not offer professional degrees and offered only select advanced degrees because it wanted to emphasize its commitment to a broad liberal arts educational experience. Many scoffed at the idea that innovation could be "taught," but the program's administrators insisted that the immersive experiential design of the program exposed students to the process of innovation. What they did with that experience was up to their creative energy and investment in the seminar.

Jenna and her cofounder were certainly energetic, determined to launch a luxury brand e-retailer for twenty-something professionals, modeled after famous brands such as Tory Burch, Marc Jacobs, Kate Spade, and Ralph Lauren.

I cleared my throat, preparing to provide constructive feedback in front of the program's six advisers and a room of twenty-five student peers. "Jenna, in week four of the program you are supposed to present your customer research. Per instructions given last week in class, you were to interview a minimum of twenty-five prospective customers this past week with your MVP—in your case, a few pages of a mock website where customers could peruse three examples of your ensembles and determine if they wanted to purchase an outfit. Do you have your customer research to share with us?"

"We're doing things a little bit differently," Jenna responded politely. "This week we created personas—profiles of the real women we will be targeting with our luxury brand fashion designs—sophisticated young women who are educated, love to travel, live with purpose, and want to wear fashion that differentiates them from the crowd. When you buy an outfit, you get the profile of the woman who inspired the design, so it feels like she selected it for you and you share a bond."

Well, okay. As someone teaching innovation, how could I disagree with a decision to be innovative in their approach to my assignment?

"I like the personas," I said. "Are these women you've interviewed? Women interested in buying your clothing?" Of all the students, I thought, Jenna, a senior and very bright, understood the program's purpose and the value of robust customer research.

"Kind of," she offered. "They were inspired by women I know, my friends."

Suddenly I didn't feel so enthused about what I thought was my student's enterprising and creative spirit.

"Jenna, how many customers have you actually spoken with, showed your website to? Per the program's syllabus, you must interview one hundred customers by week six and that's only two weeks away now."

She looked down at her manicured nails.

"Uh, I haven't interviewed any customers yet because I've been working on our website and marketing campaign. I've been talking to the designers at Tory Burch to learn more about the website experience they create and how they market their brand. I know the women who will buy our clothes. They are similar to the women who shop at Tory Burch, Kate Spade, Ralph Lauren, Marc Jacobs."

One of the advisers assigned to Blue Catamaran, Paul, a former marketer for Chanel, piped up. "Jenna and team, the purpose of the customer research is to inform the personas and to confirm that there is a business here. Your website and marketing campaign sound awesome and I'm really impressed that you followed up with my contacts at Tory Burch. But I agree with the professor; it's really important to survey your potential customers to find out how they are buying, and what they don't like about the current luxury brand buying experience, so you can address those gaps. Otherwise, you're a start-up competing with some very entrenched successful brands."

"We're learning a lot from the team at Tory Burch," she replied, referring to the mass market luxury brand retailer listed in the Global Top 1000 Brands with a market cap of 102.2 billion. "The Tory Burch Foundation's proceeds support women entrepreneurs. They are excited about what we're doing and want to help. They even offered to help us with customer research," Jenna's sister and marketing assistant said from the back of the room.

"Team Blue Catamaran," I addressed Jenna's team, which included a designer, an operations lead who we learned was scheduling meetings with fabric suppliers and clothing manufacturers in Latin America, and a marketing assistant. "I want to see your plan for identifying fifty women to interview by next class and a draft of your interview guide." I was concerned that the young team had fallen into the start-up trap already: falling in love with their own idea and dismissing the fact they needed to speak with a lot of customers—one hundred to start—to confirm they were addressing a customer's need and offering a product, or in this case an experience, that people were willing to pay for.

While I liked the fact that Jenna and her teammates had envisioned their customer, vividly and in great detail, it's a lot harder to actually go out and talk to even fifty prospective customers, much less one hundred. But it's not just grad students who are guilty of taking this shortcut. I've seen it many times in my career. We have a product, we have a need, we have an MVP. We talk to ourselves and convince ourselves that it's a great idea and that we have an audience. But often we are our own little echo chambers. Everybody pays lip service to the idea of listening to the customer, but most don't actually listen. Or at least not systematically. And not to one hundred people.

But that's what successful innovators must do.

WHAT IS THE GOAL OF CUSTOMER RESEARCH?

When we talk about customer research, it usually connotes images of focus groups, phone interviews, and the spreadsheets, reports, and data they yield.

But what I'm talking about is a little different. My idea of customer research is to become your customers—to understand their pain points, unmet needs, aspirations, and dreams so deeply that you can think like they do. I'm not saying you need to be a method actor. But I am saying you need to understand your customers well enough that you could pick them out in a crowd.

In that sense, Blue Catamaran was onto the right concept when they created the personas. The problem was that they were based on insufficient research and didn't represent a cross-section of real customers.

An important first step is outlining your research goals: What do you need to learn about your customers to develop a solution that they want to buy from you?

In the case of Blue Catamaran, it was whether the professional young woman who loved fashion was willing to spend upwards of $250 on an outfit that was whimsical and expressive, reflecting the persona she related to. In essence, would she spend a few hundred bucks to have a fashion "experience"? Did she trust an online experience to fulfill her desire to make a fashion statement? How could Blue Catamaran bridge the gap from "Wow, this website is amazing with its exotic travel photos and eclectic layout that makes you feel like you're in Bangkok: I can relate to Emma" to actually clicking the checkout tab and entering their Apple Pay, PayPal, or credit card account number?

If Jenna and team had interviewed twenty-five customers, showing them the website and outfits at various price points, they would have learned that while the target audience loved the Blue Catamaran experience, they were hesitant to spend $250 ($500 if they bought accessories) on an outfit. She eventually learned this when she launched the website and found out how difficult it was to drive buyers to the website and convert their visit into a sale. Only a small subset of her target audience was willing to buy clothes and, even then, only for a special occasion. "After all," as one woman they interviewed said, "I have Manhattan rent to pay and work clothes to buy."

Compare Blue Catamaran to Stitch Fix, which offers women of various walks of life different mix-and-match pants and tops that fit their lifestyle and, importantly, budget. The company is flexible, seeks constant feedback, is highly responsive to customer needs, and is hugely successful.

WHY IS CUSTOMER RESEARCH IMPORTANT TO THE INNOVATION PROCESS?

Customer research is a type of market research; it's called primary market research because it involves gathering input firsthand from customers and other key stakeholders. The other form of market research, called secondary, includes performing market landscape and competitive assessments. Data and information are gathered from published sources such as reports and websites. When asked whether customer research is critical to innovation, Facebook CEO Mark Zuckerberg replied yes and said, "Ultimately we are in business to solve a customer's problem. We don't sell services to make money; we make money to solve clients' problems with our services."[1]

How can we solve customers' problems if we don't understand who they are and what they need? And I mean really understand.

Let's look at some examples of industries and businesses that became extinct because they failed to understand and respond to customer needs.

U.S. railroads haven't declined because the need to move people and freight has changed—in fact, it's only grown. The railroads are outmoded because they saw themselves as railroads and not as modes of consumer and commercial transportation. They failed to solve customers' needs. They failed to recognize that their competitors were not other railroads but emerging new technologies: the automobile, the airplane, and high-speed rail.

Taxis didn't get replaced by Uber and Lyft because they failed to get a person from point A to point B. They were displaced because Uber can pick up a person at their home and get them to their destination at a reasonable cost with someone driving their personal vehicle who puts on the music you want to hear and gives you a bottle of water during the drive. They took the riding experience and went downstream (anyone with a mobile phone and debit card can order a ride) and made being driven to your destination mainstream. They designed their service around the customer and the way the customer lives, works, commutes—and likes to be treated.

How about cable television? Cable hasn't seen its membership decline because people are watching less television; in fact, people are watching more. But they're not doing it on cable—or at least not as much as they used to. Now, customers can stream TV shows and movies anytime they want—and customize what they watch. A Chromecast plug-in combined with Netflix, Amazon, and HBO subscriptions offers entertainment that fits your individual profile. That's something cable can't do. But what cable companies could have done, some would argue, is made the viewer experience more user-friendly and provided more options for customized viewing packages than the ones that force you to take hundreds of channels.

These examples illustrate what can happen when you become complacent with the status quo and fail to listen to the changing needs and interests of your customers. There is always someone out there building a better mousetrap. One of those companies is

Apple, and they have mastered creative forms of Voice of the Customer (VOC) research.

HOW DOES VOC RESEARCH WORK?

VOC is a research method that businesses use to describe the needs and requirements of their customers. Companies use it to visualize the gap between customer needs and expectations and their actual experience with their product and the brand. Reports show that companies that use VOC research experience ten times greater annual company revenue because they connect and engage with the customer at every touch point in the customer journey. It costs organizations more money to attract a new customer than to keep an existing one. Let's look at how it works at Apple.

The iPhone is one of the most famous products of the twenty-first century. Yet, many will attest, Steve Jobs never held a single focus group. That's true. But that doesn't mean that Jobs didn't understand and address customer needs. Same with Henry Ford, who created the automobile assembly line. Heck, they didn't even have focus groups when Ford was turning out his first Model Ts. Both inventors were ahead of their time with technologies so disruptive that taking their idea to customers would have been difficult. They had to market it to customers and then convince them they had to have it.

Jobs said, "Get closer than ever to your customers. So close that you tell them what they need well before they realize it themselves."[2] That's exactly what he did with the iPhone camera. No one ever sat in a focus group and said, "Gee, I wish my phone was a camera too." If Jobs had asked customers if they wanted to take photos with their phones, most would probably have replied, "Well, isn't that what my camera is for?" But Jobs realized that in an increasingly fast-paced, digital, and visual culture, the idea of taking a picture anytime, anywhere—without having had the foresight to bring your camera with you—would be something that customers, particularly the young customers who were the initial drivers of iPhone sales, would love. Even if they didn't realize it yet. So, he had to show them. He enhanced the iPhone based on his customer insight—insight gleaned not through formal customer research. How did he know this? Was it simply part of his genius?

Jobs spent a lot of time studying customers, anticipating their behaviors and needs. He knew his target market wanted technology that was trendy, cool, fun, and creative. But how did he know what those needs were? Two ways: self-ethnography and surveys. If that sounds anthropological, well, it is! Apple surveys its customers while they are using the iPhone, for example, to supplement its own internal data and product strategy. The company uses the data to go even further in delighting the customer and ensuring a great customer experience.

And he perfected the Silicon Valley mantra of fail fast, meaning that you get a prototype into the customers hands. If they like it, you continue to develop it; if they don't, you move on. MVP testing, a critical part of the Innovation Mindset, was popularized by Jobs and his compatriots in the Valley.

Like Apple, you need to know the customers you're pursuing and the things they like to do. In addition to checking your assumptions about the customers' problems, you need to validate your hypothesis about how they spend their time and money and how they get jobs done. Whether the product is for corporate customers, social media, not-for-profit sectors, or retail, you want to understand in detail how your customers do things. How does work get done? What's the process, work flow, and communications?

WHY DO YOU NEED TO SPEAK WITH ONE HUNDRED CUSTOMERS?

First, why one hundred? What's so magical about this number? Why not ten or seventy-five or five hundred? There are a few reasons I insist that students, clients, and my own team conduct one hundred customer interviews when testing a new product, whether they are a start-up or an existing business.

First, the best customer research includes voices from various perspectives. You need a mix of demographic and psychographic characteristics. Getting a good cross-section of perspectives means an ample sample size. If you're doing national or global research, you will need to interview customers in different geographies, and you may need to interview customers of various ages, ethnicities, economic levels, and job roles and responsibilities.

Second, the best customer research includes a mix of methodologies: short surveys and interviews, both individual and small group, and increasingly, social media, where you can hear divergent opinions play off one another. You need a critical mass of customers to ensure the right cross-section of perspectives and mix of information-gathering techniques.

Third, one hundred customers give you a sample that is statistically significant and can verify your results. Most investors I've worked with consider one hundred interviews a good baseline to establish customer interest in your solution. Many may ultimately ask for additional customer feedback before they will invest—I've seen investors request three hundred physician interviews for a medical device and even several thousand for an app.

Fourth, of all the steps in the innovation process, this one is the most challenging and important for the innovator. Why? It's hard to identify people to interview, to hear things you might not like, and ultimately to know what to do with all the information you gather.

Finally, customer research is a combination of science with art and a bit of serendipity. In my own professional experience, I always learned the most important piece of feedback from that hundredth interview. It's like running a marathon and hitting mile 25 and you really want to stop and walk that last 1.2 miles. But you push on because you know that last mile is the one that counts the most because it signals you've finished the race. When I became the CEO of a diagnostics company, I interviewed one hundred potential customers, including physicians, patients, and pharmaceutical partners. It was specifically the hundredth interview—with the head of research at a big pharma company—that provided that "aha moment" and led to an MVP pilot. If I hadn't pursued that interview, which took a long time to arrange, I would have missed a critical opportunity in successfully commercializing our product. Could I have stopped at ninety-nine and still gotten a good idea about our product? Yes. Would I have gotten the insight that produced what turned out to be a *great* idea? Not without going the full distance.

Let me walk through an example of how this mix of customer perspectives and research methodology works.

As a consultant to a start-up biotechnology company, I was hired to test market interest in their gene therapy for a condition called age-related wet macular degeneration (wet AMD), a debilitating eye disease that affects older people, eventually causing blindness. Gene therapy involves replacing a missing or defective gene with one that is functioning normally and can be a powerful therapy in diseases where an errant gene can be targeted. If the company's therapy worked, it could significantly reduce the patient's need for drugs to slow disease progression; in the best-case scenario, it could be a cure. But it was still experimental. We knew we needed robust, well-designed, and accurate information from our customer research to inform the design of the clinical trials, the commercial strategy, and the company's investments in both.

We carefully selected and interviewed retinal surgeons, general ophthalmologists, and optometrists from North America, Europe, China, and Japan to learn everything we could about how they diagnosed and treated Wet AMD and to assess their openness to a new gene therapy. We interviewed one hundred doctors, following my Law of One Hundred Customers. That was the number of interviews required to ensure that we collected information from the relevant cross-section of customers; it ensured a statistically meaningful result that would verify our findings, and it suited the client's budget. The chief marketing officer agreed. "Don't come back to me until you've interviewed one hundred customers" were his words of advice as we left the research kickoff meeting with him and his team.

Our market research was split 40 percent North America, 30 percent Europe, and 15 percent each Japan and China. It included representation from three different types of doctors that treated patients with wet AMD: optometrists, ophthalmologists, and retinal surgeons.

Our questions were organized according to the six best Voice of the Customer questions, as outlined in the section below.

In this case, we needed to understand how ophthalmologists were currently treating different types of patients; what was working and not working with respect to patient outcomes; what challenges they faced while helping their patients avoid blindness; what types of alternatives they had tried; whether they were open to trying gene therapy; what data they needed to convince them our therapy was safe and effective; and, importantly, which type of patients they thought would benefit the most from our gene therapy.

These interviews helped us segment the doctors based on their specialty and treatment behaviors. We learned that while some doctors were aggressive and early adopters of new technologies like gene therapy, adoption depended on age, practices in their country, and pricing and reimbursement of treatment. In the United States, the price of therapy and reimbursement amounts drove decision making about what to prescribe and when. We also learned that some doctors were cautious, taking a wait-and-see attitude about experimental therapies. This was particularly true in China. Ultimately, our research findings indicated that the company should design two types of market entry strategies for further testing: newly diagnosed patients for whom the possibility of a cure would be more meaningful and end-stage patients who had no other options. Once a financial analysis was completed on treating the end-stage patients, the company decided it was too risky to launch a new expensive gene therapy in end-stage patients who might have such advanced disease that even gene replacement couldn't reverse the symptoms; that could make it too difficult to evaluate response and show whether the gene therapy worked. The company decided to focus on early-stage patients. Because of our research, the company could develop a clinical trial that provided the data the doctors needed to feel comfortable prescribing a gene therapy to a newly diagnosed patient. However, that trial didn't turn out as planned, and ultimately the company decided to prioritize a different but similar eye disease, diabetic retinopathy, for which treatments were fewer and doctors said the value of gene therapy was greater.

WHAT ARE THE SIX BEST
VOICE OF THE CUSTOMER QUESTIONS?

Let's look at the six key question areas in VOC research. I call these discussion pods because they can encompass several questions to really get at the heart of what you need to know.

1. Who is the customer, and what work does
the customer do?

Find out everything you can about your customer. For example, with the eye doctor case study presented earlier, we needed to understand the doctors' practices, the demographics and psychographics of their patient populations, and things that influenced how the doctors worked.

2. What is the current state of the customer's business?

Next, you want to understand how the customer currently does work and why they do it that way. In the eye doctor example, we asked how and when patients were diagnosed with wet AMD; what therapy the doctors used first and why; what tests they used to determine if a patient was responding to treatment; and if a patient wasn't showing signs of response, what they would try next?

3. What is the customer's pain point(s)
(also referred to as unmet need)?

Find out what the customer's biggest challenges are. Sometimes people use questions such as "What keeps you up at night?" In our eye doctor case study, we sought to understand the factors that would cause the doctors to change therapies and what they struggled with the most in treating their patients—e.g., access to therapies or cost of therapies?

4. Just how big is the problem?

At this point we need to have a way of measuring the impact of the problem. We need to quantify and qualify it. Why? To make sure it's worth solving. In our example, we probed the eye doctors to find out how many patients had wet AMD; how many were not responding to therapy and progressing toward blindness; how much time and money the doctor was spending on wet AMD and how much money the patient and/or the insurance system was spending; and what the level of frustration was among their patients and their families.

5. What solutions have they tried, and what were the results?

This question helps you understand gaps in current solutions. It also helps you understand the competition. Remember, maintaining the status quo and doing nothing are still a form of competition—sometimes it's easier to take the path of least resistance than to try something new—so you need to know this. You can also probe who influences their decision making. In our eye doctor case, we needed to understand the treatment pathway for patients with wet AMD. If therapy #1 didn't work, what would the doctor try next? This helped us determine where in the pathway our gene therapy might fit, according to how the doctor made decisions about how to treat these patients.

6. What does the customer think about your solution?

Now, for the moment of truth! The most important part of VOC for the innovator: you want to know customers' reactions—likes, dislikes, questions, and concerns—to your potential solution.

Ultimately, you want to know how likely they are to use your solution and in what situation. As discussed above in the gene therapy eye disease example, we wanted to know if doctors would be more likely to prescribe gene therapy to a newly diagnosed or an end-stage patient. That was critical information for our positioning in the market.

SIX WAYS TO FIND ONE HUNDRED CUSTOMERS

A question I get all the time from students, clients, and my own team members when we discuss VOC is "How do we find one hundred customers? That sounds really hard." One important thing to keep in mind is that your research should be a combination of surveys, one-to-one interviews, and small group discussions. Typically you would start with a few small group interviews and one-to-one interviews to verify the problem and your potential solution. Then you'd use that data to inform the design of a survey with a representative sample of customers. The survey may probe your value proposition, pricing and preferred features of the solution. You could then complete your research with a few more one-to-one interviews to confirm your conclusions.

It takes effort, yes, but it must be done—and is eminently doable. Let's start with the best approach if you have the money to spend on professional VOC research and then work our way down from a cost perspective.

Approach 1. Full-service research firms

These firms can identify, recruit, and interview customers based on your research goals. You need to prepare a brief of your research goals and project scope. I recommend getting quotes from three vendors and asking to see samples of the candidates in their database and a case study of their past work. This type of research can run into a couple of hundred thousand dollars depending on the ease or difficulty of the interviews, usually based on roles and geography. For example, the eye doctor case study shared earlier in the chapter cost the client approximately $250,000 because it involved eye doctors and five geographies. Consumer research of the same size but limited to a single geography would be under $100,000. This option works best if you have a lot of research to do in a short period of time, aren't capital constrained, and want to ensure the most accurate results and insights gleaned from market research analyst professionals who know how to both conduct and analyze market research.

Approach 2. Self-service research agencies

These agencies can provide subject matter experts, but you conduct the research. Firms such as Gerson Lehrman Group (GLG), Guidepoint, and Alphasights maintain a bank of consultant professionals across a wide array of industries. You can contract with them to provide access to experts in their database, but from there it's self-service, meaning you need to select and interview the experts yourself, usually in a one-to-one, 45 minute phone call. This option can run from $750 to $2,000 per interview depending on the level of specialization required. This is a good option for a small number of one-to-one interviews to inform the research questions for a survey. It also works well if you have a modest budget and the resources and expertise required to manage the customer research in-house.

Approach 3. Lists

If a self-serve option is for you but you have a tight budget, you can buy lists of types of professionals and consumers in general, based on zip codes, from research houses and then send emails to the contacts. A list will cost you about $5,000 per zip code. This option is good if you want to throw out a wide net and don't mind "cold calling" and taking your chances. The positive side is that you will have a list of customers with whom you can work in various ways over a period of time. The other thing to keep in mind is that these lists are usually updated annually, so some of the information may be out of date as soon as you receive it.

Approach 4. In-house market research

This is an option if you have a marketing expert in your company who can run the process and conduct the research. In this situation, you can use social media to post questions and encourage discussion and even to recruit customers for one-on-one interviews. When working with an online English language training program, we posted questions about ways students learned language on sites such as Facebook groups for study-abroad students and TOEFL students in the United States. Students were eager to network, provide their input, and learn more about our platform, especially if it was easy to access and cheap. From there we were able to secure one-on-one interviews and give them access to our MVP for testing. An added benefit of this research method, if it fits your need, is that it's free.

Approach 5. Crowdsourcing

If you're a start-up, trying to identify customers to interview can be especially daunting if your audience isn't necessarily clustered in a social media community. A team that wanted to conduct consumer research on a laser-based razor posted the prototype on websites such as Kickstarter—a crowdsourcing platform for new innovations. Interested customers peruse the site looking for cool new stuff to try that they can purchase for a really low price in exchange for sharing their feedback. It's an efficient way of doing customer research and selling the first version of your product if you're far enough along with your product development to fill orders within a six-month window.

Approach 6. LinkedIn and Facebook

Another research approach for start-ups is identifying customers on LinkedIn and Facebook. You can use keywords to identify people who fit your customer profile. After ensuring the target candidate meets your needs, you can find others in your network who know them and ask for an introduction. Once the contact has been made, you send them a message to connect, letting them know you're doing market research and would like them to take an online survey or participate in a call. For example, when I was trying to find a community of directors of marketing in manufacturing, on LinkedIn, I got one hundred hits. From there I refined my search strategy to an industry and geographic area. I asked each person I interviewed to recommend two other people. Within ten days, I had a qualified list of potential customers. This option works well if you're not on a tight timeline and have no budget but want to expand your LinkedIn network.

INNOVATOR IN FOCUS

Spencer Rascoff, cofounder and former CEO, Zillow

INNOVATOR CLAIM TO FAME After the sale of the travel site Hotwire to Expedia for $685 million in 2003, cofounder Spencer Rascoff and his team had a new idea for a digital business: a website that "turned on the lights" and provided information transparency about home values, allowing everyone to know what their house was worth.

To make this innovative concept a reality, Rascoff and his colleagues knew what they had to do: talk to the customer. "Customer research," he says, "was critical to us." But after launching Zillow, what the customers eventually told them was something unexpected—an "aha" insight that would lead them to enhance their concept and develop a second form of Zillow, one that would go on to become a phenomenal success.

"The Voice of the Customer (VOC) was taken very seriously," Spencer recalls. "It was this voice that clued us into a strategic shift that the market wanted and needed, and we were there at the right time to deliver it."

Lessons learned

Rascoff's research was based on personas: composite personalities of key customer segments, based on extensive demographic and psychographic research, that included dozens of interviews with actual individuals. The personas Spencer and his team created were imaginary but rooted in real information from real people.

"We had Beth the Buyer, Alan the Agent, Larry the Lender, Susan the Seller," he recalls, with a chuckle. "We even had posters of them up on the walls."

Despite their playful names and cartoon representation, these prototypical characters became an important part of the planning that went into the new business. Their concerns, needs, feelings, and attitudes were studied rigorously and taken seriously. And based on what they were told by Beth, Alan, Larry, and Susan (and the actual people those personas represented), the business model for what would become Zillow changed.

"Zillow started out supporting the selling process and was an aid to realtors," Spencer says. "But what we learned from our research was that customers wanted help with all the things that come along with selling your house. They hated the process . . . fixing up the house, having people tour it, having to pay a realtor commission for selling it. And the most important sticking point, not knowing when it was going to sell and therefore not being able to plan their move into a new property."

In 2017, guided by consumer research, Spencer led Zillow's expansion into a new business segment where Zillow would buy homes directly from consumers, renovate them, and resell them. This business extension was successful during Spencer's tenure, and as Zillow rolled out the service to new cities its stock price continued to climb. In 2019, Spencer retired as CEO of Zillow and turned the CEO reins over to his Zillow co-founder, Rich Barton. Two years later, in an attempt to catch the leader in the space, OpenDoor, Zillow expanded too quickly in this segment and bought too many homes. Saddled with hundreds of millions of dollars in losses, Barton remorsefully shuttered the division and laid off 2,000 employees as the company lost tens of billions in value, a sobering reminder that execution is as important as strategy.

You can't make this up

When Spencer was a boy, his father, Joseph Rascoff, left a Big Eight accounting firm to take on a rather unorthodox new client: the Rolling Stones. In addition to learning many business lessons from his dad's work with the world's greatest rock and roll band, Spencer was afforded a once-in-a-lifetime opportunity. In 1990, the Stones toured Europe. His father traveled with them and took along Spencer—then a teenager. The so-called Urban Jungle Tour of twenty-five cities culminated in shows in what were then Czechoslovakia and East Germany. "We toured countries that had never known civil liberties or rock music," he said. "It was an amazing time."

In mid-August the Stones performed a concert at a stadium in East Berlin, in the shadow of remnants of the Berlin Wall, most of which had been taken down just the previous year. That night, young Spencer got a rare opportunity with one of the Stone's most famous songs: "I got to control the lightboard when the band performed 'Sympathy for the Devil,'" he said. And so, with each of the "woo-woos" in its memorable chorus, and fifty thousand newly liberated fans singing along, the future CEO of Zillow would adjust the lights.

Insight for innovators

"Get multiple perspectives on your idea from different age groups and walks of life. Someone may see things through a lens that can help you reshape it for the better."

"Talk to the customer constantly even when you're a going concern. You will learn things about their changing needs and market dynamics."

"Be fearless in making strategic expansion decisions. Systematically remove roadblocks and remember if you're serving the customer, it will all work out for the best."

Learn more about Rascoff at spencerrascoff.com.

5

LAW-ABIDING INNOVATORS MUST BE READY TO PIVOT AT ANY POINT IN THE PROCESS!

Sylvana Sinha looked as if she were about to convene a board meeting. Dressed professionally in a satin burgundy blouse and wearing gold post earrings, Sinha looked every inch the CEO. What's notable is that Sinha is the founder and CEO of Praava Health, based in Bangladesh, which ranked fifty-seventh out of fifty-eight economies in the Mastercard Index of Women Entrepreneurs, 2019, highlighting the country's poor record in creating enabling environments for female-headed businesses. But while she appeared as if she were seated at the head of a conference table in Dhaka, she was in her kitchen in Manhattan.

It was February 2021, and Sinha was a guest lecturer in my course, "Global Healthcare Strategy," at Columbia Business School. She was joining us by Zoom from her apartment in New York because the pandemic was still raging across the globe and New York was in quarantine. From her Zoom background, Sinha appeared to be sitting in a small office area adjacent to the kitchen. For Sinha, joining my class as a guest speaker was a bit of a homecoming. She received her juris doctor in human rights, conflict, and international law from Columbia Law School and a master's in international development economics and conflict from Harvard, both in 2004. She moved to Bangladesh in 2015, determined to elevate health care in her family's home country after her mother had a life-threatening emergency and she learned firsthand how completely inadequate the private health-care system was.

Sinha launched Praava Health in 2018 as a full-service integrated outpatient clinic; soon after, she added digital health services. Within two years it was the fastest-growing consumer brand in one of the fastest-growing economies in the world, offering private, subscription-based health care to the middle class.

In March 2020, Praava's growth was stopped cold by the COVID-19 pandemic. "COVID-19 was a dark moment," Sinha explained, as my students looked on intently from their Zoom screens. "Patients couldn't come to the clinics and our telehealth wasn't fully ramped up. Being a subscription model where people paid month to month, we faced a real dilemma. How could we bring in revenues when we couldn't provide our products and services?"

Worries also prevailed about debt and cash flow. "Our investors were concerned," she says. "I had arrived in New York in March for investor meetings that got canceled, and it was really scary." Sinha was faced with external pressure to pivot to keep Praava alive. She had to move fast to roll out telehealth in April.

In May, Praava received good news. The Bangladesh government approved the company's COVID test, making Praava the first private lab in Bangladesh to get such approval. And that's when things really began to take off: call volume rose from about two hundred to a thousand per day. The brand began getting recognition. Cash flow improved. The patients who were tested for COVID were converted into patients to whom other services could be offered. "We were cash flow positive, month to month," she said. But Praava was not out of the woods yet. "We were still only staying afloat. We're now at an inflection point with some decisions to make about our future." Sinha paused, "I'd love to hear from the class what you think we should do next."

That was our cue.

I looked into the Zoom camera lens at my students' faces in gallery view on the right-hand panel of my computer screen. "Well, class, what would you do if you were in Sylvana's situation? How might you think about pivoting and taking advantage of the COVID crisis and beyond? What opportunity does she have to rethink her business strategy, offerings, and business model and funding going forward?"

One student, a financial professional joining the class from her Manhattan apartment, turned on her mic and spoke up. "Thanks for sharing your story and being with us today, Sylvana. Your work is really exciting. My question or suggestion is How can Praava continue to grow the telehealth business? Does creating a good customer experience help with customer adoption of telehealth, or do other factors matter equally?"

A student joining from his home in New Jersey who was a pharmaceutical professional piped in: "Hi, Sylvana. Thanks for being with us today. My question is Can you expand your lab services, building off the COVID testing success?"

"Yes," Sinha agreed. "Both good ideas. I'd like to use technology to drive patients into the lab services and expand our patient app. I also need to enhance marketing."

I interjected. "Sylvana, you described your pivot at the beginning of COVID, and the students offered good ideas about how you could continue to adjust your strategy and expand your offerings to address patient needs during the pandemic. How realistic are these suggestions, and what kind of timetable and resources would they require? And importantly, since this is a case study discussion, maybe you can share with us what you have done over the past eight months and how it's working."

Sinha smiled and nodded her head. "The students have made some really helpful suggestions." She then rattled off the statistics: Over the past eight months, her company had helped three hundred corporations bring virtual health-care services to their employees; processed 56,000 COVID tests; and engaged with 135,000 patients, up from 35,000 last year. And yes, Sinha was able to rattle off those statistics without any notes, a practice all credible entrepreneurs should emulate. She continued, "We still need funding to invest in technology and hire talent, and we need to make some decisions about our e-health strategy and data model. We are meeting with investors now and assessing our priorities. While we still have a way to go, we've turned the corner and converted the crisis into an opportunity."

Although the future was still challenging, Sinha had turned a negative into a positive and shown resilience and agility in meeting the crisis head on. In fact, she had turned it into an opportunity—the perfect pivot. Just a couple of weeks after her presentation to my students, she secured $10 million in private investment, which she proudly posted on LinkedIn.

Perhaps you've heard this saying, which has been bandied about quite a bit during the pandemic: "Never let a serious crisis to go to waste; it's an opportunity to do things you thought you couldn't do before." Although Rahm Emanuel from the Obama administration is often credited with this counsel, the originator of the quote was Winston Churchill. He said "Never let a good crisis go to waste" in the mid-1940s as we were approaching the end of one of the greatest crises in modern times: World War II.

The pandemic presented everyone in every walk of life, in every industry, in every country with a challenge and therefore an opportunity—how to rethink the way we live, work, socialize, travel, and go to school, church, the gym, and so much more. Some businesses have adapted; others haven't. I would submit that Praava is one company that has successfully adapted—pivoted—to become stronger as a result of this crisis.

While we don't know what the future will bring as the world continues to emerge from the lockdowns, one thing is clear: we are a living experiment of the most massive global pivot we've faced in modern times. Post-COVID, nothing will be the same. It has produced a cascade of adaptations—a plethora of pivots, if you will—for organizations large and small.

For example, as consumer retail and restaurants pivoted to offering curbside-only services, they had to adjust again when businesses were allowed to open at reduced capacity with masking and social distancing. Many of us can recall the long lines outside grocery stores in the summer of 2020, when only fifty people were allowed in the store at any one time. There have been changes with places of work and schools, with parents and their children learning how to share WiFi and physical space as everyone was required to stay home.

"COVID has accelerated our acceptance of remote work environments by probably twenty years," said Spencer Rascoff, the former CEO of Zillow whom you met in the last chapter. "There's no one there to physically look over the employee's shoulder anymore. In some respects, a pivot is synonymous with managing change. That's certainly the case with COVID." At companies such as IBM, helping employees manage the change included things like issuing work-from-home guidelines that encouraged managers to make it acceptable or permissible for an employee's child or pet dog to be in their Zoom screen occasionally. "Heck, I built in a mandatory noon walk break to make sure employees were getting away from their desks, getting some physical activity," says one sales leader at IBM Watson Health.

Other companies that responded to the crisis positively by pivoting found new markets for their offerings and have made them a permanent part of their business. A good example is Fictiv, a Silicon Valley–based company that produces custom mechanical parts for use in the prototyping, product development, new product introduction, maintenance, and repair stages of a product's life cycle, with applications such as car parts for automakers, aerospace parts for manufacturers like Honeywell, robotic parts for companies like Intuitive Surgical, and the parts that go into fitness watches and smartphones. That's a lot of parts! Cofounder and CEO Dave Evans has been cited as a leading innovator in *Forbes Magazine*'s "30 under 30" list.

At a time when manufacturing has become global but remains rooted in outdated, time- and cost-intensive processes, Fictiv offers a modern approach: with its global manufacturing ecosystem comprised of 250 manufacturers across the globe, it can provide just-in-time sourcing of high-quality precision parts. It's a disruptive force in hardware manufacturing. As COVID's impact hit the manufacturing industry across China and then Europe, Evans envisioned a new role for Fictiv. "I could see how manufacturing supply chains were affected around the world," he said during a webinar where I was a guest commenting on the opportunities to improve the medical device supply chain during the pandemic. "Manufacturing of personal protective equipment and parts for medical devices came to a grinding halt in China. As the virus spread across Europe, manufacturing in Germany and Italy was impacted. And I could see that once the virus reached North America, we would have shortages in Mexico and the United States."

A reminder that it doesn't take a global pandemic for supply chain interruption was offered in the spring of 2021, when one of the world's largest container ships ran aground in the Suez Canal, bringing this most vital shipping channel to a floating halt.

In response to the COVID crisis, Fictiv put its globally connected digital ecosystem to work. The company sourced parts to develop and distribute face shields and then donated them to hospitals in the United States. It stayed one step ahead of the virus, sourcing critical parts for medical device companies while navigating the crisis and trying to find new suppliers. This ushered in new healthcare customers, a market segment that has become one of Fictiv's fastest growing.

Fictiv's pivot was successful. Not only did the company help with the crisis as good citizens but it has also expanded its capabilities into the medical area permanently, offering robotic and medical device parts for health care.

"This was a pivot that has had a long-term positive impact on our business because it gave us the opportunity to go after a new market segment," Evans said. "If it weren't for the crisis, I don't know if we would have explored health care as aggressively or we would have moved as fast as we did. Fortunately, the digitally powered ecosystem gave us an opportunity to serve our customers with the manufacturing agility they need when market conditions change. And these days change is a constant, hence the reason our business has grown four times in the past two and a half years."

Some say pivoting is bad. They say it means you don't know what you're doing, that you can pivot too much and use it as an excuse for a lack of strategy. Of course, any good approach can be used incorrectly or ineffectively, and pivoting is no exception. Silicon

Valley made the MVP famous, and critics claim some Silicon Valley entrepreneurs use pivoting as an approach to market research. The point is to do your homework. Launch with your best-laid plan, but don't be afraid to change course if the map is wrong.

WHY PIVOTING IS PIVOTAL FOR SUCCESS

A pivot is a change in strategy without a change in vision. But sometimes a pivot can be a change in strategy to *realign* with your vision.

Changing direction can be a good thing for a business, as the path to success is rarely a straight line. Let's look at a few historic and current-day examples.

In 1850, Cornelius Vanderbilt recognized that a new form of transportation was emerging that could move goods and products far faster and more efficiently than steamships. He pivoted to railroads.

At age thirteen, William Wrigley was a traveling soap salesperson for his father's company. As a salesperson in Chicago, he started offering baking powder and chewing gum with each box of soap. He switched his focus from baking powder to gum when he could see that the latter was more popular with customers. In 1893, his pivot produced a new popular brand: Wrigley's Spearmint chewing gum.

In the early 2000s, a podcasting company called Odeo recognized that it could not compete with a similar platform offered by Apple's iTunes. The company was rudderless when one of its employees, Jack Dorsey, had the idea of creating a platform that let people share their "status"—what they were doing at that moment. The company pivoted, and Twitter was born.

Yelp began as an automated email service in 2004 before it launched a crowdsource mobile app for consumer business reviews. YouTube was originally a dating site. Airbnb was launched as a rent-a-mattress company in San Francisco. Research shows that new ventures that reinvent their business even multiple times can reduce their chance of failing because they conserve resources, while continuing to learn more about customers, business partners, and new technologies.

History is filled with great pivots. Could your business be next? Maybe. But first, we have to remember *why* an organization might need to pivot.

WHAT ARE THE TOP REASONS FOR PIVOTING?

If you're paying attention to the market feedback and data you're getting for your product or service, you should see the signals that your strategy is not having the impact you expected. Here are some of the more common reasons you may want to reevaluate your product and your strategy and determine if changes are needed.

Reason 1. Customers aren't buying your product or service according to your forecast or expectations

Jabril Bensedrine, CEO of the Triana Group, describes working with a publicly traded Internet of Things (IoT) company. The company, formerly an electronics engineering firm whose revenue model was based on fee for service, decided to pivot to become a more scalable "IoT sensor" product company. However, by the time it pivoted, the real value in IoT had started to move away from hardware toward software and data: software as a service, and even data as a service, with new revenue models based on a pay-per-data model. The company initiated a second pivot to add software- and data-driven revenue sources, but that was challenging.

Bensedrine explained, "The company was used to providing technology that was deployed across numerous industries and applications. Its technology could power literally thousands of potential use cases. So we needed to explore how to narrow its scope to just a few applications. In the meantime, the company had raised substantial capital on the public market, thanks to ambitious revenue projections—ones that unfortunately didn't materialize. Investors were becoming impatient, and drastic decisions had to be made.

Resources were reallocated in a major move to make the company even more laser focused. That finally resulted in strategic partnerships with multibillion-dollar companies that needed to beef up their IoT portfolios. It is easy to say in hindsight, but a lesson was learned: when we pivot, we should do so in a way that doesn't just react to current market trends but anticipates the next wave," Bensedrine cautions.

Reason 2. The competitor has more brand awareness and the market segment is growing

If the market segment that you're serving is growing, your competitors are expanding market share, and you're not keeping up, it's time to reassess your market fit, understand customer need, and execute your plans. When I was working with an electronics manufacturer on increasing their market share in the health-care sector, our market assessment showed strong growth of the sector and the leading competitor, but our company's sales were flat. The pivot that turned things around involved two things: focusing on a different customer in the companies we were targeting and training the account team to align with the new customer focus. In this case, the account team had been calling on procurement and getting tangled in a morass of contracting processes. The customer who was using the company's product line didn't even know who they were. Instead, we trained the account team to have business conversations with leaders in R&D and engineering, the customer groups that owned the decision of which products and vendors they wanted to work with. This reboot had a dramatic effect, and though it took five months to fully execute, by the next business cycle the account team was beating the competition 40 percent of the time and subsequently expanding market share.

Reason 3. Your financial forecast is underperforming

It can be challenging to develop a realistic financial forecast, especially for a new product or service, but if sales and revenues are consistently falling short of expectations for more than a financial quarter, it's critical to assess why.

Reason 4. Your channel partners and/or strategic partners aren't engaged

Partners who can provide direct access to your customers and are willing to engage in a business relationship to help you get your product or service to customers are an efficient and key component of the go-to-market strategy for any brand. Amazon is a channel partner for millions of bricks-and-mortar and online brands. But if you fail to attract customers, a channel partner like Amazon will downgrade and even delist you. It's an important signal as to how relevant your product and your marketing are, and often this feedback can be used to plan a pivot. One of my student teams at Princeton developed a nutrient-infused beverage that they claimed could reduce hangover symptoms. They were an Amazon five-star seller for a few months, but when sales dropped precipitously because the start-up was struggling to fulfill orders on time, Amazon threatened to delist their product. After all, Amazon makes its money on a percentage of sales of the products it carries. After a painful delisting experience, the company bolstered its manufacturing capacity and launched a marketing campaign to get back on track.

Reason 5. External constraints are challenging your business

The global pandemic is a good example of what can happen when factors outside your control impede your ability to sell your original products and services. The airline industry came to an abrupt halt during the early days of the pandemic, but carriers such as United Airlines quickly adapted to becoming a different type of carrier— they transported supplies such as personal protective equipment and respirators to various destinations around the world. Even more importantly, they flew medical personnel and first responders to geographies that needed those resources. They were able to showcase their contribution in their messaging to customers during the pandemic, showing how they were contributing to the cause and keeping themselves top of mind with their customers until regular air travel could resume.

WHEN TO PIVOT: SEIZE THE OPPORTUNITY!

To get a great product or service to market and ensure that it grows, you need to respond to meaningful insights about your customers, regularly. That's why the decision to pivot in the Innovation Mindset comes *after* you've talked to one hundred customers. They will tell you whether you need to make a course change. Even if your start-up idea isn't resonating with customers, you don't have to throw everything away and start from scratch. In fact, pivoting is just the opposite! Keep a list or catalog of the things you've learned about customers along the way. Some of your best insights will come from understanding why your idea isn't delighting them. Don't be afraid to ask them

"What don't you like about this product?"

"What would be a better fit for your needs?"

"If we did X or added Y, would you be more likely to find it useful?"

Probing potential weaknesses in your original idea with the target market will make it easier to figure out how and where to pivot. Instead of failing, you'll just move in a new direction that gets you better aligned with your customer.

Here's a good example of what one might call a "realignment" pivot: I was a faculty adviser to a team, called Mountain Guitars, participating in the Princeton innovation accelerator. The company had designed a small, lightweight travel guitar for campers and hikers. Originally based in Salt Lake City and designing for campers in the wilds of Utah, the founders even launched a Kickstarter Program where they sold fifty of these small guitars. But once they started broadening their customer outreach, they learned that serious guitar players didn't like the idea of what they called a "kid-size" guitar. An interview with an avid backpacker who regularly took his guitar on trips produced an "aha" moment. He just happened to have a five-year-old child. He told the interviewers he wanted to buy a guitar, but not for himself—for his son! He didn't even recognize that the guitar was aimed at him. After exploring this further, they learned that the market for their guitar was much stronger among parents of school-age kids than it was for serious strummers. "Parents and kids liked the size and light weight of our guitar," said the company's founder, "but what was really critical was that, because it was made of carbon fiber, it was indestructible. Most kid guitars already on the market were really cheap and broke easily."

Once Mountain Guitar pivoted from being a lightweight version of the instrument for more serious players to a premium kid's model, it took off. "We created a catalog of feedback and started interviewing parents and music teachers," he said. "We then tested a new version of the product with school music programs. We ended up going through school music programs to sell the guitars, and it really worked out well. And we created a larger version of the adult guitar later, so ultimately were able to appeal to both markets."

UNDERSTAND YOUR CUSTOMERS: DON'T JUST LOOK AT THE STATISTICS

As we've stressed throughout this book, you need to get close to your customer. Steve Jobs inculcated this concept at Apple, and Spencer Rascoff did the same at Zillow. How close? You need to *become* your customer. That requires more than just looking at data. You need to watch customers in action, talk to them one-on-one and through surveys, see how they work and how your product or services fit into the way they work. This holds true at this stage of the process: Stay close to your customers as you pivot.

One of my clients was developing a new way to collect data from doctors' offices. Their first solution required too much data entry. The doctors and their office staff complained. The sales results, or lack thereof, were abysmal. But we didn't stop with that information—if we did, we might have thought we simply needed a more effective sales pitch. Instead, we met with a hundred physicians (yes, a hundred) and their data entry staff to examine their processes of entering patient data. The new solution allowed the doctors to copy and paste data from other records into our system. It was a pivot on the original product, but the strategy and the company goal remained the same—to collect patient data from the doctors' offices in a way that ensured accuracy and fit the doctors' work flows.

The takeaway? Pivot early and often! A change in direction is not a failure. Think of it as a necessary course correction that will help you make meaningful, successful changes as inexpensively as possible.

BUILD A CUSTOMER-FOCUSED CULTURE, NOT A PRODUCT-FOCUSED ONE

A pivot can seem obvious from the top, but to those responsible for executing the change in direction, it can be frustrating. To do so, you need to build a team culture focused on pleasing the customer. Your team should know that course changes based on customer feedback are to be expected—and should not be construed as failure.

DON'T STAY WITH THE STATUS QUO JUST BECAUSE YOU'RE DOWN THE PATH

Sometimes you can be afraid to pivot because you have so much invested in the product or service. You think that just one more week, one more quarter, will turn things around. When the status quo isn't leading to growth, it's time to take a deep breath and reevaluate. It's time to be bold and willing to make a major shift. It's time to pivot.

Albert Einstein is often credited with saying "The definition of insanity is doing the same thing over again and expecting a different result." In fact, Einstein never said that. The quote is attributed to a conversation at an Al-Anon (family members of alcoholics) meeting in October 1981.[1] A newspaper reporter in Knoxville, Tennessee, wrote an article quoting a discussion at an Al-Anon meeting and it really stuck, given how often it's attributed to Einstein. Too bad we don't know who really said it, but no matter the originator, the advice is sound.

I was helping a start-up with the launch of a "smart" deodorant bottle that dispensed the right amount of deodorant so you didn't end up with stains on your clothing. Initially, they had a very positive response on Kickstarter and had a queue of orders. They had put a lot into the design and premarketing, but after they fulfilled the Kickstarter orders, they found that demand was just not there. Customer research told them that most people who used deodorant were not willing to pay $35 for a smart dispenser, even if it did come with an inexpensive replacement cartridge of popular brands. The Kickstarter customers loved the novelty of the product, but the average consumer just didn't find the value proposition compelling enough to plunk down thirty-five bucks. We found a much more compelling application of their volume-measuring technology in the medical field. They pivoted to address the problem of topical dispensing of medications for skin conditions where applying too much could lead to adverse events. This was a much better use of the technology. While the technology didn't change, the market focus did, and just in time. They were able to establish a partnership with a consumer dermatology brand that offered the dispenser for free as an incentive for using their product over the competitor's.

HOW CAN YOU ENSURE STABILITY WHILE PIVOTING?

How do you execute a pivot and keep shareholders and other stakeholders engaged and confident while you change direction? First, you need clarity on the reason for your pivot and how you will execute it to drive forward momentum. If you can avoid putting things on hold or taking a big step back, that's ideal. But if the pivot does require a significant change that will delay or slow the business's trajectory, you need to clearly outline it and show how you will accelerate growth once you get on the new track. While executing a pivot for a diagnostics company, I showed investors how revenue-generating research partnerships could help keep the lights on while we completed the additional clinical studies needed to achieve regulatory approval and commercial partnerships with biopharma companies. Second, you need to ensure you are communicating clearly, consistently, and with regular frequency as you're planning and executing the pivot. Keeping your team and stakeholders apprised of critical milestones and their status is key to building trust and confidence in you as an innovation leader. And finally, stay true to the new plan. If you set a new course and then waffle on staying committed to it, you will confuse the organization and your investors. So, follow through with excellence.

FOCUS ON THE BIG PICTURE

Craft a broad narrative that leaves some room for you to navigate along the way. You may not want to show a precise road map but rather indicate your direction and show some of the options along the way that will be borne out with your research. Promise to reach a destination, but leave things open to change. For example, in the early days of Netflix, founder Reed Hastings, anticipating an eventual switch to streaming video, started with the stated purpose of offering the best home video viewing for everyone. He didn't lead with his product—DVDs by mail—but with the experience he wanted to create. As the business pivoted to digital distribution, the original sweeping ambition still made sense. Even the company name supported its future course. Hastings said he wanted to be ready for video on demand when technology permitted, and that is why he called the company Netflix. You can read more about

Hastings's reinvention of the home entertainment industry in his book, *No Rules Rules*, a New York Times Best Seller.[2]

STAY TRUE TO YOUR VISION

Research shows that when organizations are inconsistent in their messaging, customers view them as less legitimate and credible. To maintain credibility, founders need to make the connection between their strategic direction and their offering clear. For example, when the founders of Away, a luggage start-up, realized their first suitcase wouldn't be ready by Christmas, they created a coffee table book about travel. They distributed it with a coupon for an Away bag that could be redeemed after the holiday. But it seemed like a radical departure from their strategy and unnerved their investors. They were ultimately able to explain they were creating a travel experience brand, so the book fit with the broader strategy. They sold two thousand books (and redeemable coupons). And it's good they sold two thousand books, because COVID had a big impact on travel, which hurt the brand. They have since recovered. Staying true to being a brand that represents the travel experience was challenging, but their board credited them with a very creative and strategically sound pivot.[3]

MOVE QUICKLY: HOW THE MUSCULAR DYSTROPHY ASSOCIATION PIVOTED INTO A NEW ERA OF GIVING

Be decisive, and move in a new direction.

That's the essence of the pivot—and that's what a not for profit, best known for its gala fundraisers hosted by a 1950s comedian, did in 2020,

Once you decide to pivot, it's important to move quickly, marshal your resources, and focus on the new strategy. Dragging things out costs time and money and confuses stakeholders and the market. When pharmaceutical companies Pfizer and Moderna decided to pivot from their planned 2020 therapeutic pipeline and develop a COVID vaccine, they moved swiftly and decisively, announcing their plans and marshaling company resources in pursuit of bringing a vaccine to market before year's end. Both succeeded—in historic fashion.[4]

But not every successful pandemic pivot involved health or technology. Not-for-profits were hit hard by COVID-19. Half of their revenues disappeared almost overnight, and they had to furlough and reduce staff permanently. Many were heavily dependent on in-person events—the fund-raising dinners, charity walks, and golf tournaments that have been a staple for nonprofits for decades. During the pandemic all these events, not to mention important face-to-face meetings with large potential donors, had to stop.

One not for profit that responded with a creative pivot was the Muscular Dystrophy Association (MDA). Founded in 1950 as an advocacy organization for children with neuromuscular diseases, the organization was best known for its annual Labor Day telethon hosted by comedian Jerry Lewis. It raised a reported $2.45 billion from the telethon's inception in 1966 through 2009. After Lewis's last hosted event in 2010, the MDA experimented with other ways to raise funds, including in-person events. When COVID hit and in-person events were canceled, the organization needed a Big Idea. Then-MDA President and CEO Lynn O'Connor Vos and her team moved quickly over the summer to relaunch the iconic telethon, this time as a virtual fund-raising event featuring actor and comedian, Kevin Hart as host. Live gaming and sports content started seven weeks before the hour telethon to engage participants in the lead up to the big event. The telethon raised more than $10.5 million, an impressive sum for a first of its kind fund-raising event that exemplifies the spirit of the Pivot.

Vos said, "The telethon was instrumental in raising awareness and donations for muscular dystrophy that have been directly linked to life changing therapies. Our pivot created the opportunity to transform how we raise funds for not-for-profits. By tapping into Kevin Hart and his charity, we brought the power and magic of giving into a new era of giving."

HOW TO AVOID COMMON PIVOT PITFALLS

Common pitfalls of unsuccessful pivots include timing, execution, and communication. You need to account for excellent coordination of all three. Here are few examples of pivot errors.

Magic Leap was a pioneer in augmented, or virtual, reality (VR). It pitched its nascent product as a high-quality gaming headset for consumers and used the slogan "Free your Mind, Enter the Magic-verse." But when uptake of VR was slow, the company looked at other markets and bid on a government contract to sell VR headsets to the military. When it didn't win the contract, it was criticized for pivoting from a "delightful consumer tech" to "lethal military gear," according to a product review in a trade publication. Yikes. After that blunder, the company hired an ex-Microsoft executive as CEO and pursued broader applications of VR, including across education and health care.[5]

Another example of pivot pitfalls: Two finance companies formed an online community to mirror the financial transactions of skilled investors. The idea was to attract investors to sites, identify the most talented of them, and make money on their strategies. The companies started within six months of each other and had similar funding teams. Eventually both pivoted to become direct-to-consumer investing services with the potential to displace human financial advisers with automated software-based services. One became a leader in the automated investment advisory sector with more than $1 billion under management, while the other was forced to sell off its assets and shut down. After conducting an in-depth comparative analysis, a team from Harvard concluded that a key reason for their divergent trajectories was how the companies handled stakeholders. The successful company never wavered from its mission of democratizing finance, even as it shifted strategies. The CEO positioned the change in business plans as just another way to meet the same goal.

The unsuccessful company tried several changes in short succession and with each one rolled out a new goal: from "bring transparency to investing information" to "make investing social" to "trusted investment advisory." To make matters worse, the CEO didn't communicate with stakeholders adequately and ended up sowing seeds of doubt. He later admitted to "messaging whiplash" as the key reason for his inability to keep stakeholders on board. Lesson learned: After you pivot, your new positioning can be confusing to customers and partners if you haven't fully communicated why, when, and how you're pivoting.

Anki toys is another example of a pivot that didn't work. They promised to bring AI to kids' toys, but although they had many fans, it didn't provide enough value to kids. They didn't pivot quickly enough and so, in May 2019, the following message appeared on their website: "It is with a heavy heart to inform you that Anki has ceased product development and we are no longer manufacturing robots. To our partners and customers, thank you for all your support and joining us on this journey to bring robotics and AI out of research labs and into your homes."[6] It was no doubt a journey—one that, sadly, may have been cut short because the company couldn't chart a new course quickly enough.

'"SIX FAMOUS AND SUCCESSFUL PIVOTS

Even iconic companies like Uber, Airbnb, Starbucks, United Airlines and venerable events like the Muscular Dystrophy telethon have been upended by COVID. As we have seen, some pivoted well, others not so much. Recently, *CEO Magazine* published a list of some of the better-known and more successful pivots. Each is inspiring and instructive in its own way.[7]

1. Nintendo

The largest card-selling business in Japan. A taxi service. A short-stay hotel. A Ramen noodle manufacturer. A vacuum cleaner business. Has any company pivoted as many times as Nintendo? But in the 1980s, when the company decided to focus on the game and electronic toys industry, it finally made the perfect pivot. Donkey

Kong and Mario Brothers, Game Boy and Nintendo Switch followed, and in 2018 Nintendo earned nearly $10 billion in profit. That's a lot of noodles!

2. Play-Doh

Launched in 1930 as a wall cleaner, Kutol was designed to clean the black residue that coal heaters left on walls. However, as oil and gas heating became more popular, demand for the cleaner declined dramatically. Demonstrating a flexibility that would eventually become a leitmotif of its new product, the company heard of an arts and crafts teacher using Kutol not to clean but to create. Kutol transformed into Play-Doh, a multicolored modeling compound. Between 1955 and 2005, more than two billion cans of Play-Doh were sold, making the ionic brand one of the most successful pivots ever.

3. Starbucks

In 1971, Starbucks was launched as a business selling espresso makers and coffee beans. In 1983, after a visit to Italy, CEO Howard Schultz decided to actually brew the Starbucks coffee beans in a European-style coffeehouse. Thus, Starbucks took a cup of coffee and transformed it into a social experience where friends and colleagues gather around small tables, sipping overpriced coffee beverages while they swap business ideas, stories, and laughs. Starbucks has 31,256 stores globally and has become a common business hangout. "Meeting location: SBX" is found in many business calendar entries.

4. Instagram

Instagram started as Burbn, an app that allowed users to check their favorite sports, share photos, and arrange catch-ups. It was originally intended as a part-time project for cofounder Kevin Systrom to learn coding. When Systrom noticed that photo sharing was the most commonly used feature, he declared Burbn a false start and streamlined the app to create Instagram. Within hours of its launch, Instagram had more followers than Burbn had acquired in a year. Two years later, Facebook bought Instagram for $1 billion.

5. Airbnb

In 2007, friends Brian Chesky and Joe Gebbia rented out air mattresses in their San Francisco apartment to frugal travelers or those shut out of hotels during peak periods. They called their service Airbed and Breakfast. Initially, they realized their model was dependent on large conferences. They pivoted to the concept of helping travelers find cheap accommodations and an authentic local experience. Today Airbnb is estimated to be worth $38 billion and did an IPO in 2020.

6. YouTube

"Tune In, Hook Up" was the unofficial slogan of the video dating site YouTube that launched on Valentine's Day 2005. The concept never took off. The cofounders then learned that users were accessing the site not to meet people but to exchange funny videos, like one cofounder Jawed Karim had posted, titled "Elephants Have Really, Really, Really Long Trunks." It turned out to be a really, really, really good idea. Just one year later, Google bought YouTube for $1.65 billion. It's now the most popular video-sharing site, with an estimate value of up to $160 billion.

INNOVATOR IN FOCUS

Sylvana Q. Sinha, founder and CEO, Praava Health

When Sylvana Sinha was on vacation in her family's native home— Dhaka, Bangladesh—her mother became ill and had to have an emergency appendectomy. Despite being in the VIP suite of the hospital, they couldn't get the medical treatment she needed and had to travel to a neighboring country for her procedure. Sinha was struck by the experience and inspired to make a commitment to do what she could to address the health-care disparities in Bangladesh. In 2018, she founded Praava Health, a private for-profit health-care system that prides itself on being a patient-driven company—and one that is disrupting the standard of health care for Bangladesh's 170 million citizens. Praava is a "brick-and-click" health-care platform that integrates digital health and in-clinic experiences convenient to where everyone lives, works, and clicks. Tripling growth every year since launching in 2018, and currently serving 230,000 patients, Praava's tech-forward model is designed to be efficient, accessible, and scalable across emerging markets, where 85 percent of the world lives.

Lessons learned

The particular challenges and opportunities presented by the COVID epidemic enabled Sinha and her company to pivot toward growth. Within just a few months, Praava was able to effectively— and *remotely*—delegate and lead global teams to launch entirely new in-house tech products, including virtual primary care, a COVID symptom tracker, a telehealth platform, an e-pharmacy, and more. "Our pivot ultimately led to unprecedented growth in services," she says. "We had to learn how to launch new products quickly to provide patients with needed services, and we did."

The pandemic also highlighted for Praava the importance of government relations. "We had to quickly understand how we could be a broader and trusted support system to combat a global pandemic and national crisis," Sinha says, "and expand beyond our private-sector focus on preventive health."

Another area that was thrust into high gear was Praava's product line. "Overnight, our team had to suddenly reprioritize product offerings . . . and therefore entire development and training timelines . . . while still retaining utmost focus on our existing patients with non-COVID-19 immediate and/or in-person needs." During the pandemic, Praava emerged as one of the largest private providers in the country for COVID testing, processing about 3 percent of the tests in the country to date as of this publication.

While Sinha is proud of the way her company responded to the challenges posed by the pandemic, she also knows that work still needs to be done—not just for Praava, but for the Bangladeshi people. The eighth most populous country in the world, with a population three times as dense as India's, Bangladesh has enormous health-care needs: the average length of time doctors spend with patients is forty-eight seconds, there's only one internationally accredited lab, and more than 10 percent of drugs in the market are counterfeit. "How do we light the fire to attract outside funding at a time when many nations are focused on their own citizens?" she says. "I have to learn how to tell our story better."

You can't make this up

Sinha is proud of the role her family has played in what was once East Pakistan and is now the nation of Bangladesh—and she is conscious of continuing that legacy:

"When I think about my role and vision for Praava, I think about my paternal grandfather, who founded a pharmaceutical company in East Pakistan in 1954. It is now the oldest and one of the ten largest in the nation. The family legend is that he always said, 'We must stay committed to *quality*; we can never cheat the consumer.' Despite neither of us having medical backgrounds, we both sought to start *something* to transform the health-care landscape of Bangladesh and build trust in the system. Yet today, even after multiple decades, our nation still faces lack of access to *quality* health care. My grandfather helped start the foundation of this movement, and now I want to build it, accelerate it, see it through. So, I wonder, how can I put not just Praava on the map, but also Bangladesh itself?"

Insight for innovators

Know that people will underestimate you throughout your career. This is especially true if you are female or a person of color in the business world. Don't take the dismissive attitude personally. Just come prepared. If people underestimate you, you can only exceed their expectations.

Create your own space. If you're a square peg and can't fit into a round hole, you have to create dreams and opportunities for yourself that are most gratifying, impactful, and rewarding. Don't let someone else define what those dreams and opportunities should be.

Not having a background in an industry that you want to change should not stop you from trying to change it! Instead, learn about it, become immersed in it—and then figure out how to change it. "I took a deep dive into my own country to learn about the current health-care landscape," Sinha says. "I traveled around Bangladesh, speaking to patients, doctors, public health professionals, entrepreneurs, investors . . . anyone in the country, across Asia, and around the world who could teach me about what it means to have access to quality health care."

Keep going! Sometimes the hardest thing to do is wake up and fight for another day—but sometimes it's all you can do, and you must.

Learn more about Sinha at https://praavahealth.com and https://www.linkedin.com/sqsinha.

6

DEVELOPING YOUR BUSINESS
MODEL AND PLAN

I pulled my car off the main road and onto the gray gravel drive-way, listening to the concrete and pebbles crunching under my tires. My window was down, and I had enjoyed the cool early April breeze as I crossed the Pennsylvania border into New Jersey.

Signs of spring at long last after a long, dreary winter—the bud-ding cherry and pear trees, natural violets and buttercups dotting the highway islands, and tulips and daffodils in the manicured lawns along the highway storefronts. I took a deep breath as I greeted the contrast. The gravel road ended in a worn and broken black-paved parking lot.

The concrete, windowless building with the tall wire fence encasing it loomed ahead of me, aged and gray against a blue sky. A small sign stood in the entranceway. The words "Men's Correc-tional Facility" were carved in white letters in a brown wood sign as aged as the parking lot and building. "What were you expect-ing?" I asked myself as I looked at my smartwatch, which registered 9:15 A.M. "You knew you weren't' coming for a spa day at the Four Seasons."

Judging an Inmates-to-Entrepreneurs Business Plan Competi-tion had seemed like a good idea when I was approached about it a few months earlier. I was excited—what a meaningful way to sup-port potential entrepreneurs, address the problem of recidivism, and give back to the community. Now as a I waited to be buzzed into the building, holding only my car keys since I had left all my personal belongings locked in my trunk, I wondered if this was the best way to spend a Saturday morning, the first warm day of spring. I also began to wonder about the wisdom of voluntarily placing oneself in jail.

I brushed the thought away as the warden waved me through the security gate. Ted, my contact, was the first person I saw as I entered the cavernous room, clearly the gymnasium by the looks of the now-worn wooden floors and basketball hoops hooked against the green concrete walls. His brown hair was combed neatly to the side, and his perfect teeth were bright white against his sun-tanned face. He was wearing tan slacks and a white, open-collared shirt. Hardly the image of a prison official, he looked more like the Princeton graduate student that he was. In the corner I saw two police officers standing side by side, watching me closely, curiously. I didn't blame them. How many times had a professor from Princeton University visited their jail? I was pretty sure I was the first. Ted confirmed that.

"Hi, Professor Marchand. Thank you so much for coming out today. The guys are super excited that you'll be listening to their business plans, providing feedback, and helping us choose a winner among the business plan contestants. It's a big day for everyone in the program."

I shook Ted's hand warmly. His enthusiasm was infectious, and I found myself getting excited about the day's agenda. "Ted, I'm honored to be here and looking forward to meeting the men and hearing their plans," I replied, although to be honest, I had no idea what to expect. What kind of business plans would inmates have? Would their ventures even be legal?

Ted was a volunteer for a not-for-profit organization that offered entrepreneurship training programs to local prisons. He and a couple of his colleagues had led an eight-week business plan training program to interested inmates at the correctional facility located outside of Newark, New Jersey. Most of the inmates were African American males ages eighteen to thirty who were incarcerated for robbery, drug use and trafficking, and gang violence. Many were repeat offenders who struggled to get on their feet after being released because, with a criminal record, it was hard to find a job.

"Recidivism is a real problem," the warden told me when he joined us in the gym. "The program is designed to help these guys develop skills, plan their futures, and explore interests in starting their own small businesses."

Ted rejoined us, holding a stack of handwritten papers. "Here are the business plans," he said.

I was used to the slick printouts, PowerPoint decks, or PDFs that my students typically used to submit assignments. These plans were written on lined paper torn from spiral notebooks. Ted took some paper clips from his pants pockets and began organizing them. "They aren't allowed to have devices or paper clips or staplers," he said, looking apologetic. "So they have written these in their best handwriting—we asked them to print so you could read them more easily."

Ted told me I had two hours to read and comment on the plans. At 12:30 P.M. the men would meet as a group, and each would present his plan and hear my critique. We would then agree on the top three winners and share the good news with the group. We had to finish by 3:30 P.M. so the men could return to their cells.

Just the sound of that gave me the chills.

He left me alone at the one table and chair in the room. The two officers were still in the corner, talking. It was hardly the environment I was used to grading in. No backyard to gaze out at, no birds chirping, not even the warm cozy confines of my office at Princeton—just the bare walls of the prison gymnasium.

I started reading the plans and marking them up but stopped after the second one. A better approach was to read all the plans first to get a sense of what I had to work with and then comment according to the best paper. I used a paper by an inmate named James as a benchmark. It was the most complete and best written.

I'd never graded an assignment by an inmate before. Come to think of it, I could only think of one inmate I had ever met.

But while the circumstances and the students were a bit unorthodox, I wanted to give these men and their carefully thought-out plans the feedback they deserved. I tried to be very specific, positive, and clear in my comments, knowing I would have the in-person session to elaborate and make some points on what distinguished a good business plan from a mediocre one.

James's plan stood out as the best thought out. In his plan, he explained that he and his cousin Reggie had observed a problem at Newark Liberty Airport (familiar as EWR to business travelers in and out of the New York area). According to James, the airport had no barber shops for male travelers who might need a haircut and shave. James and Reggie, who operated the newsstand at the airport, wanted to lease a space to offer men's haircuts. They had conducted market research on the numbers of male travelers who passed through the airport in a given month, including the number of layovers, and confirmed that no barber shops were found within a ten-mile radius of the airport. Reggie had spoken to a couple of dozen men who had frequented the newsstand to ask about their interest in getting a haircut if a barber shop were nearby. About 65 percent said yes.

I was impressed that someone incarcerated could even conduct market research. Clearly, James's cousin and business partner Reggie had done it—and in doing so, demonstrated a sense of purpose, coordination, and good communications. All virtues for innovators.

"Good job quantifying market needs," I wrote in the margin. "That's the first step in a business plan—observing a problem that needs solving." The cousins had also done their homework on other aspects of the business plan. They knew that they needed to raise $10,000 to lease the space and set up the barber shop. James showed the costs in a table he had drawn freehand. The columns and rows were evenly laid out with headings: labor, lease, barber supplies, monthly utilities, fees, taxes. The next table had his income projections, based on average prices of the services he would offer and the number of men he thought he would service in a month. The two had $1,000 between them, so raising $9,000 was a concern, as there wasn't any clear return on investment (ROI)—a personal service business doesn't create a predictable recurring revenue.

James had a few ideas about funding sources: New Jersey had a state grant program for inmates who started new businesses and stayed out of jail for twelve months. He had an uncle who had agreed to give them $5,000 at 5 percent interest to get started. He even had a name for his proposed business—JR's of Newark (a blending of James's and Reggie's first initials, I correctly guessed). And a slogan: "Cool cuts for men on the go."

Not bad. I made a few more comments.

I had just finished my review and comments on the ten business plans when Ted returned. He clapped his hands together enthusiastically. "Are you ready for the students to join us now? They have a three-hour slot for your review. Then we can meet and agree on the top three winners."

Ted explained that each student would give a ten-minute presentation and I would have five minutes to comment. At 12:30 a parade of men in orange jumpuits, some with dreadlocks, others bald, all smiling and joking, filed in. Wearing my standard teaching attire, a business suit, I sat at the table and smiled. Each nodded my way and raised a hand in acknowledgment.

I'm not sure what I was expecting, but it wasn't this: They were a friendly group. And they looked happy to be here—time out of their cells at least, I thought. They sat in the ten folding chairs Ted had lined up on one side of the room. Ted, the other two students, and I sat at a table across from them.

Ted waved the first man forward and I pulled Gary's plan to the top of my stack. "I'm Gary," announced an African American man with brown dreadlocks down to his shoulders. He was about 6'4" and his hands were folded in a prayer pose at his waist. "My idea is what's known as a 'hardscaping' business. The people in my mom's neighborhood have small yards and it doesn't make sense to try and grow grass 'cause the ground is rocky. It's all patchy with weeds and stuff."

Right away, I'd learned something. I wasn't familiar with the term *hardscaping*, but when I googled it later, sure enough—it's a legitimate, and popular, service. And it made sense. "I'm good with my hands," said Gary, "and last spring I made my mom and aunt a rock garden. It's low maintenance and artistic." He paused and smiled proudly. "My mom decorates hers with small potted plants and it's the talk of the 'hood.'"

A few chuckles emanated from his fellow inmates.

Gary's plan was to start with five houses, charge for the rocks and supplies, and donate his labor to cultivate customer interest. "I plan to take photos of the rock gardens and promote it on Instagram and Facebook." Gary explained that he would charge $18 an hour for his labor plus a little markup on the rocks and supplies. If he could get five jobs a week, which he said was a conservative forecast, he could make $2,500–$3,000 a month to start.

I looked down at Gary's plan as he spoke. He had each section of the business plan outlined with a paragraph description. Very good.

The final page stated his cost of goods sold and revenues for the first year. He thought he could gross $25,000 in year one. And he planned to hire a part-time employee at the end of the first year.

"Gary, I like this idea, and the diagram of the rock garden you've sketched looks very attractive," I commented. He smiled, clearly pleased at my acknowledgment of his artwork. "This is a seasonal business, so you'll need to make enough revenue eight months of the year to cover the winter months. And what will you do after you've installed the rock gardens? Is this a one-time thing?"

"I've been thinking about that," said Gary, "and I need to add it the plan. I think I can charge a small monthly maintenance fee to trim the weeds, replace the rocks, you know."

"I think that's a good idea," I agreed. "In a service business you need to add other offerings to make additional revenues. For example, a lot of lawn maintenance companies switch over to snow plowing in the winter."

Gary, and the rest of the men sitting behind him, nodded thoughtfully. They were listening intently.

The last man came forward to present his plan. He was tall and thin with a bald head, cleanly shaved. His name was Tat and, you guessed it, his arms and the little I could see of his chest were covered in tattoos. His business idea was—again, no surprise—a tattoo parlor. Apparently, Tat was known far and wide for his body art. He was passionate about tattoos and had apparently visited an exhibit on the history of tattoos at a museum in Dunedin, Florida, as a boy—which is when he became enamored with the art.

"Tat," I said, "I can see that being a tattoo artist is something you're passionate about." "I'm my own best advertising," he replied, holding up his forearms with ornate designs of dragons and flying beasts.

"Well, that's important because starting a business is hard work, and you need to love what you do," I continued. "My concern is how much competition there is in this part of New Jersey. It seems to me there are tattoo parlors on every corner. So how will you differentiate your business?"

"I'm the best, and I know what my customers like," Tat said. "I do custom work, things that are special and personal. I made a tattoo of my friend's daughter's face from a photo. But I know what you mean, so I'm going to use word-of-mouth advertising and offer discounts for referrals."

"Good," I said. "Understanding your customer and having the right marketing and incentive plan to drive business are important. But your competition may try to do the same thing, so I want you to think more about that."

Tat nodded, "I will, ma'am," he said politely.

The presentations concluded, it was now time for me to offer these men some general lessons on business plans—a critical part of the Innovation Mindset.

"The teams did a good job overall," I began. "Everyone had a well-defined problem statement, research to support your solutions, and a financial forecast based on realistic assumptions."

They had avoided many of the most common business planning mistakes, I explained. So often, entrepreneurs include in their business plans overly aggressive financial forecasts based on weak assumptions and lack adequate customer and market research to confirm market need and fit.

"And the two that are my pet peeves," I said. The men looked at me intently; I think they were curious as to what might irritate Professor Marchand and were hopeful their plans had not done that.

"'We don't have any competitors,'" I said, mimicking the voice of overconfidence. "'No one is doing what we're offering, or we're better because of x, y and z.'"

I paused. "You have to be careful of that," I said. "It's like falling in love with your own baby, drinking your own Kool-Aid."

The guys laughed.

"Yes, that's Tat," one said playfully. "But it's true, you know, he *is* the best tat artist I've seen."

I smiled. "And the second is, not identifying the business risks. Let's say you can't raise money quickly enough—how do you bootstrap?"

I saw a few eyebrows raise at that—it sounded like a street term.

"Let's say in James's case, Newark Airport's legal department decides it's too much of a liability to allow services like barber shops and spas to be performed at the airport? He should have a plan B for location."

Next, I asked the group about business plans. "You've created one for the purposes of this competition," I said. "And I'm impressed with the work you've done. But let's step back a bit. What is a business plan, and what does it need to accomplish? Why do you even need one?"

Randy raised his hand. "You need a plan so you know how much money you need to get started and when you're going to break even," he answered evenly, as he looked down at his shoes

"That's right," I commended him. "Great answer. And for the most part, you all achieved that with your plans."

I noticed a few of the men exchanged satisfied glances and nods of approvals. Ted looked pleased too. He'd taught them well.

"A business plan also forces you to analyze the opportunity, assess the risks, understand the market, and determine what it's going to take to be successful. If you have a team, like James and his cousin Reggie, you gain important experience working together. You learn a lot about your business through the process of developing the plan because it forces you to outline assumptions and test them and debate and discuss and refine until you get it right."

The men nodded their heads in agreement. "That makes sense," said one, whose business plan was an app that could find the best prices on gasoline in the city. He had taken a coding class while incarcerated and was eager to put his new skill to work. "As we were going through the program, every week we had to complete one section of our plan and then describe why it made sense," he said. "And every week, after class we had to go back and make changes based on feedback from Ted and our instructors. At first that was kinda frustrating, but after a couple of times I realized it was a necessary part of the process. And it forced us to improve our ideas and our plans."

Ted smiled and gave a thumbs-up.

"That's right," I agreed, "and a business plan is different from a business model. Anyone know the difference?"

The men looked at each other shrugging, "I dunno." Then James raised his hand. "In the program we learned about the business model—there's something called a landscape or something like that?"

"The business model canvas?" I offered. "Yes, good. It's a tool created by two entrepreneurs named Alexander Osterwalder and Yves Pigneur that helps you figure out how you're going to make money."

James nodded, "Like it helps you figure out who your customer is and what channels you can use to get your service to market. For me, Newark Airport is a channel for taking my barber services to market. I could use other channels too, like offering services at my aunt's beauty salon, which I'm not going to do 'cause guys don't want to go to a little ol' lady's hair salon where they just gossip about the neighbors."

A ripple of laughter, and heads nodding. "My barber shop is going to have a flat screen and we're going to keep it on ESPN," James declared.

He was right. In a business *model*, you outline your customers, channel partners, and operating model to help you figure out how your business will make money. On the other hand, the business *plan* is a living document that you use to show how all the pieces of your business work—from reaching customers, to beating the competition, to who you're going to hire, to your plans for managing revenues and profits.

"At its simplest, a business plan is a written description of the future of a business," wrote business journalist John Palmer in the *Houston Chronicle*. "It's a document that not only gets a business concept on paper but also outlines the people and steps that will be involved to lead the business to success."

The business plan is where you do the things that the inmate-entrepreneurs had done: discuss the industry and the need for a particular product or service, the business structure, and how you will achieve success. "A business model, on the other hand," Palmer writes, "is a business's rationale and plan for making a profit. If the business plan is a road map that describes how much profit the business intends to make in a given period of time, the business model is the skeleton that explains how that money will be made." This should include everything from how a company is valued within an industry to how it will interact with suppliers, clients, and partners to generate profits.

And you need both to make a business work—a plan that lays out the business and how it works end to end, and a model for how that business is going to make money.

"I know it can sound a little overwhelming," I said. "And you can take shortcuts—but both the model and the plan help you figure out what you don't know. Developing both helps you challenge your assumptions, which can be wrong. You know what they say about that, right?

Artie, a short, thin man older than the others, who had said nothing outside of sharing his plan for an auto shop for vintage cars, spoke up. "It's what you think you got right that you didn't that will mess you up."

I raised my eyebrows and smiled appreciatively. "Close!" I said. "It ain't what you don't know that gets you into trouble, it's what you think you know that ain't so."

Like many business aphorisms, this one (popularized in the 2016 movie *The Big Short*) is widely attributed to someone famous—in this case, Mark Twain—and incorrectly so. We have no evidence that the great nineteenth-century writer ever said that. But I can tell you that, over the course of my career, I have seen a great deal of evidence attesting to its truth. Essentially, it's a reminder not to assume that what you think you know is correct. And it was a lesson that the inmates had obviously learned.

Ted and his fellow grad students, Rachel and Susan, beamed. Clearly, they had had more of an impact on this group then even they realized.

We convened at 3:15 to vote on the top three plans. Our criteria were based on addressing ten key components of the business plan: confirmation of a problem, a solution that could be easily implemented, customer and market research, financial forecast, marketing, delivery of products/services, sources of capital, risks, and competition. These are the same kinds of things you need to be thinking about with your new business or product, consistent with the Laws of Innovation.

We also considered preparation, thoroughness, and quality of work. The three men who won each stood and took a bow. I said a few words about what made their plans stand out. Everyone applauded. Even the warden and the security guards came over and joined in the celebration, smiling and fist-bumping the three winners. There was no cake or champagne or certificates of accomplishment, but there was a sense of satisfaction—I could feel it.

James, one of the winners, approached me. "Thank you," he said. "This means a lot to me. I really want to get this barber shop going with my cousin. I get out in six months, and it's given me a lot to look forward to. My girlfriend and I want to get married. She's put up with a lot, and I want to make her proud."

I was touched that James would share this with me. Regardless of what they had done in the past, he and many of his fellow inmates in this group were clearly looking ahead—and embracing an Innovation Mindset to chart a course to a better future. They are a reminder to us all that you don't have to be working at a high-tech firm, or working in corporate America, or even *working*, to have a good idea on a way to build a better mousetrap.

The Innovation Mindset can be adopted and embraced by anyone.

As the men filed back to their cells and I walked out with Ted, I was overcome with empathy for this group of men. They were earnest and eager to make a fresh start with their business ideas. I knew how hard it would be—transitioning back into society, staying away from the negative elements that had brought them here in the first place, and on top of that, raising money and putting these plans into action. They had the extra burden of trying to do all this with a criminal record. I felt ashamed that I had had second thoughts that morning about whether I wanted to be here. I was the one who had benefited from the experience.

"I'd be happy to talk to any of the guys if they want to follow up on their plans," I offered to Ted.

"That's so nice," he said, "but per the rules of the program, we can't share your contact information and you aren't allowed to have any contact with the men now or once they're released. It's just for your own safety." I nodded, although in the five hours I had been at the prison, I had certainly not felt that my safety was compromised in any way.

Several months later, I did follow up with Ted. He told me that he learned through the warden that James had been released and had started a barber shop with his cousin. It was in his uncle's basement—the one who had been willing to give him some starter funds. He hoped to get a shop of his own in a year or two. I gave a little cheer inside at this good news.

THE PLAN

As the men at the correctional facility's Inmates-to-Entrepreneurs Program learned that spring, the business plan is the culmination of a lengthy, arduous, creative process of articulating the problem and solution, marketplace fit, investment requirements, risks, and returns to inform your ability to take your goods and services to the marketplace and make money. This is true for both profit and not-for-profit entities. The main difference is how the profits are distributed. Both are sustained by revenues and profits.

The plan is also the start of your relationship with investors, future board members, strategic partners, and others who may be interested in your business's success. In a sense, it's your calling card, allowing them to evaluate you as well as the soundness of your innovation. The plan is what may get an investor excited enough to decide that they want to support you.

The other thing to know is that it's not immutable. Just as your idea and your business will evolve, so will the plan. It's a living document—so you ought to be revisiting your assumptions and findings with the marketplace in real time and updating your forecasts a couple of times a year. The exact numbers don't matter so much because you have imperfect information when you craft the plan, but the economics and market fit are critical.

Now, a nuance that is important to point out is that the business *plan*, as described earlier, is different from the business *model*, which lays out how this business is going to function, grow, and make money. Let's look at a famous example, the Nespresso coffee maker, a portable coffee machine developed and launched by the Nestlé company initially in Europe in 1986.[1] The idea was to enable anyone to create a perfect cup of espresso coffee—just like a skilled barista. It ended up redefining the way millions of people enjoy their espresso and shaped the global coffee culture.

Here's how it happened:

Nespresso launched with the first coffee machine (the C-100) and four signature portioned coffee blends. The coffee maker unit was priced at about $350, but that was obviously just a one-time sale. To accrue recurring revenue, the company would also sell the specially designed Nespresso capsules that could be purchased only from Nespresso or its distributors for about $20 for a box of ten.

If a consumer used a box a week, that was an additional $1,000 a year in coffee revenue. They made more from selling the capsules than they did from selling the expensive coffee unit. And after that the streets were paved with gold. This is known as the "razor and razor blade" business model, after Gillette's introduction of the first handheld razor with disposable blades. The profits came not from the sale of the razor, which could be used for years—but rather, from the blades. Same with Nespresso.

Now, contrast the business model with Nestle's business plan, which of course included a description of how they were going to make money but also detailed their target customer segments—in this case, middle- to upper-class professionals, singles or couples, who loved the convenience and luxury of espresso in their own homes. The business plan also examined the competition: Keurig was close on their heels with a lower-priced unit, so Nespresso needed to lock in customers and saturate the market quickly. And it included the size of the market, the cost of goods sold, relationships with retailers, operations such as how manufacturing and distribution would be handled, team structure, trademarks and intellectual property, accounting structures as they expanded into ultimately eighty-two countries, and investment in their growth plans and geographic expansion.

Business plan, business model—you need both.

As I told the men in the Inmates-to-Entrepreneurs Program that day in April, for every business success there are at least ten failures, often because of critical mistakes in business planning or a poorly thought-out model of how the business would make money. To help you avoid those pitfalls, let's look at the most common ones.

TOP BUSINESS PLAN MISTAKES

Mistake 1. Forgetting that cash is king

Many people think about profits (income after all costs) instead of cash as being their main focus. While you need profits to invest back into the business to fund future growth, you need cash to pay the bills and keep the business a going concern. So, the key metric you need to measure and manage is a cash flow statement—whether your cash is from investors, from a bank in the form of debt, or from your own savings account. This is why investors ask about monthly cash burn when evaluating a company they might invest in. Nearly nine out of ten businesses that shut their doors in the first year do so because they run out of cash.[2]

Mistake 2. Skipping problem/solution validation

An estimated 90 percent of innovations don't make it to market because they fail to solve a problem a customer wants to pay for.[3] Just ask Larry Berger, the head of R&D Innovation at Ecolab, a nearly hundred-year-old company in the water, hygiene, and infection-prevention business that has cultivated a successful model for problem/solution validation that needs to be emulated by more companies. Berger coordinates the R&D initiatives of a 1,200-member team supporting 24,000 field representatives managing cleaning, sanitizing, hygiene, and food safety needs at three million customer sites. Their customer-led response to the COVID-19 pandemic is a case in point. The company identified a performance gap for the quick and effective sanitization of surfaces under EPA use conditions, spanning a broad range of applications in restaurants, hotels, and healthcare environments. Ecolab knew that typical viral sanitization times of up to fifteen minutes to deliver claimed efficacy were too long for these customers. The company had been developing a unique combination cleaner and sanitizer that could be delivered as a concentrate and diluted on-site. Ecolab's R&D teams quickly recognized that the sanitizing performance of this product could be extended to address the customer needs created by the COVID-19 pandemic. The company successfully sought an EPA emergency use authorization based on extending the product's viral performance claims and delivered a combination cleaning and sanitizing solution that killed viruses in 15 seconds. Just weeks after the emergency use authorization, the product was launched across hospital and hotel markets, helping customers manage patient/guest interactions and turnover faster and more safely.

Mistake 3. Making incomplete plans

Every business has customers, products and services, operations, marketing and sales, a management team, and competitors. At an absolute minimum, your plan must cover all these areas. A complete plan should also include a discussion of the industry and trends affecting it, such as whether the market is growing or shrinking. Finally, your plan should include detailed financial projections— monthly cash flow and income statements as well as annual balance sheets—going out at least three years. When I see plans that skip any of these important fundamentals, I send the entrepreneur back to the drawing board to gather more research and engage in thoughtful deliberation with her team.

Mistake 4. Conducting inadequate research

Like incomplete plans, plans that reflect a static view of market and business opportunity and a lack of market awareness also won't cut it. Just as it's important to tie your assumptions to facts, it's equally important to make sure your voice of the customer and market research are robust. You need a minimum of one hundred customer interviews, as we discussed in chapter 4, and you need a thorough understanding of the marketplace, your competition, and pricing. Learn everything you can about your business and industry. You don't want to get bogged down by facts, but you should have numbers, charts, and statistics to back up your assumptions and projections. Well-prepared investors will check your numbers against industry data or third-party studies—if your numbers don't jibe with their numbers, they will question you and your credibility.

Mistake 5. Having unrealistic assumptions

By their nature, business plans are filled with assumptions, but the assumptions have to be based on facts and have evidence to support them. The best business plans highlight critical assumptions and provide justification for them. The worst business plans bury assumptions in the plan so no one can tell where the assumptions end and the facts begin, or they fail to conduct the proper research to back up their suppositions. Market size, acceptable pricing, customer purchasing behavior, time to commercialization—these all involve assumptions. Wherever possible, make sure you check your premises against benchmarks from the same industry, a similar industry, or some other acceptable standard. Tie your assumptions to relevant facts. A simple example of this is the real estate section of your plan. Many companies eventually need to lease real estate, whether it's office space, industrial space, or retail space. You should research the locations and costs of real estate in various areas and make careful estimates of how much space you'll need, when you'll need it, and what the costs are before presenting your plan to investors and lenders.

An example of a company burying this important component of their plan was a clinical research services business that hired me to help write their business plan. The CEO wanted to lease space in a very exclusive biotech office park in Manhattan to improve his brand awareness. The pitch to investors included only this real estate option, and the costs his CFO cited were a year old and didn't reflect the substantial rent increase that had just gone into effect. I had flagged this as a risk in the plan but they had waved it aside at the time. This turned out to be a nonstarter with one of the potential investors who knew the real estate market. He called out the CEO in public, accusing him of citing outdated costs; he also criticized him for not examining office space across the river in New Jersey—half the cost and a much better option for the company's employees, 80 percent of whom lived in Jersey City and Hoboken. Fortunately, they could address this issue quickly, secure space in Jersey City, and get back in front of investors.

Mistake 6. Neglecting to address risk

No risk? No way! Any sensible investor understands there is no such thing as a no-risk business. There are always risks. You must understand them before presenting your plan to investors or lenders. Since a business plan is a marketing tool for investors, we recommend addressing risks head-on, including a plan for how to mitigate the risks and contingency plans outlining what you'll do if the worst does occur. For example, software companies need to have disaster recovery plans in case their infrastructure and development teams encounter an economic event or even a natural disaster that closes offices. We have seen this time and time again, whether it was a tsunami in Thailand, an earthquake in Japan, hurricanes in Puerto Rico, or, of course, the COVID-19 pandemic that disrupted supply chains globally. Chances are, your business is not likely to be affected by a tsunami in Thailand, but there could be a power outage around the block, a new municipal ordnance, a swing in stock shares, or any number of other things, big or small, that are hard to predict. Regardless, you still need to be prepared for questions about risks.

These are dramatic examples of risks. Your examples may be more practical, such as whether you can hire a specialized type of talent, so be prepared for questions about risks and have sound risk mitigation and contingency plans prepared.

Mistake 7. Overlooking your competition

Any investor would be warranted in walking away from the pitch on this point alone. And yes, it's amazing how many potential business owners include a statement in their business plans that they are the first, the only, or the best at what they do. *Every* business has competitors, indirect and direct. Competition can come in the form of your customer not wanting to change. Competition can come from maintaining the status quo and doing nothing. It can come from substitutes and knockoffs. You may think your solution is uniquely valuable, but the customer may disagree. My advice: Plan for competition—*stiff* competition—from the beginning; you'll be more successful in the end. If you can't find any direct competitors today, try to imagine how the marketplace might look once you're established. Identify ways you will compete, and accentuate your competitive advantages—what we call your value proposition—in the business plan.

Example: An innovator from the San Francisco Bay area developed a new sinus surgical procedure that used a small balloon inserted into the nasal cavity as opposed to cracking the sinus cavity open, which was the standard approach at the time. But the otolaryngology community rejected the new method, even though it was less expensive and safer for the patients. The surgeons had been trained to perform nasal surgery in the old way, and the insurance system reimbursed them handsomely. They liked the status quo. Why should they change? The inventor of the sinus balloon surgery spent three years and a lot of capital on Food and Drug Administration (FDA) approval and market adoption among resistant surgical community. More market research earlier could have helped him anticipate this resistance and address it proactively.

Mistake 8. Failing to provide a road map to the future

A good business plan presents an overview of the business, now and in the short- and long-term future. However, it doesn't just describe what the business will look like at each stage. It describes how you will get from one stage to the next. In other words, the plan provides a road map for the business, one that is as specific as possible. It should contain concrete milestones—major targets that have real meaning for your business. For instance, reasonable milestones might be signing the one hundredth client, producing ten thousand units of product, adding a new line in the manufacturing plan, or raising capital from an investor. Outline all the major steps you need to complete to reach each milestone and how one milestone leads to the next.

Mistake 9. Getting bogged down in technical details

This is a common problem in technology-based start-ups. Keep the technical details to a minimum in the main plan and put the details in the appendix. Investors, whether for a start-up or a corporate entity, don't want to see engineering blueprints on how the technology works. They will send their technical experts for those discussions and trust that you know your subject matter or you wouldn't have gotten this far in the planning process. What they are more interested in is how you're going to commercialize the technology and make money so they get a return on their investment. So don't compromise "business" focus with too many technical details.

DEVELOPING YOUR BUSINESS PLAN

You can avoid the mistakes outlined above and make sure that your business plan stands out among the crowd, especially to potential investors. Here are several tips for developing a successful plan.

Tip 1. Follow a template

Here's a tried-and-true template for a good business plan: a two- to three-page executive summary followed by a ten- to twenty-page description of the market, customers, and financial forecasts, and an appendix with detailed assumptions, market research findings, financial tables, and technical specifications. It should be written in a conversational, easy-to-understand narrative that doesn't require a technical background.

Tip 2. Polish your plan so that it shines

As you can see, there are lots of potential pitfalls in a business plan. But they can be avoided! The value of the business plan is that it forces you to think the business through, test your assumptions, and learn all you can about the market. You may have great ideas, but have you carefully mapped out all the steps you need to make the business a reality? Have you considered how to build your management team, hire salespeople, set up operations, get your first customers, protect yourself from lawsuits, outmaneuver your competition, manage cash flow, and minimize expenses? Your business plan should reflect solid thinking about all these areas.

I once reviewed a business plan that was three pages of financial forecasts. When I asked where the thinking was behind the numbers, it forced the team to share their assumptions, many of which turned out to be unfounded. We developed a real plan, but it took three months. "I thought a high-level forecast was all we needed to attract funding in the very vibrant software market," the cofounder told me after the team had completed their sixth investor pitch with positive results. "But the diligence we put into the plan with your guidance showed us that there was so much we didn't know. We would have embarrassed ourselves in front of investors if we had set up meetings based only on our forecasts."

Tip 3. Do your homework

Investigate every aspect of your proposed business plan before you start writing and long before you start the business. If your plan is based on demographic projections, double-check and make sure you have interpreted the data correctly. If it's contingent on consumers being more or less likely to do this or that, make sure you can cite the source and give potential investors confidence in the behavioral predictions. If it's linked to some pricing trends, make sure the data are still trending in the same direction (remember the example I mentioned earlier about the CFO who got reamed out because he used outdated and incomplete information in his plan).

You'll also need to continue to research while you write the plan because inevitably things will change as you uncover critical information. Research questions could include:

- Is your product or service something people want, or is it just a cool idea?
- Is your market growing or shrinking?
- Do you need greater customer segmenting?
- Could new entrants, disruptive technology, or regulatory changes alter the market in a fundamental way?
- Why do you think people will buy your product or service?

As you develop the answers to all these questions, don't rely on one informant—corroborate with other sources. Remember: if you don't have customers yet, you'll need to convince investors that you have something people really want or need—and, more importantly, that they'll buy it at the price you expect. Make sure the value proposition and market need are watertight—they are fundamental to your ability to attract support and investment dollars.

Tip 4. Get feedback

Obtain as much feedback as you can from trusted advisers, friends, colleagues, potential investors, and lenders. You'll quickly find that almost everyone thinks they're an expert and could do a better job than you. This may be annoying, but it's part of the feedback process. You'll know when you're done when you've heard the same questions and criticisms again and again and have a good answer to almost everything anyone can throw at you.

When I established my ophthalmology diagnostic start-up, I spoke with experts in various sectors and functions, from ophthalmologists to experts in intellectual property, regulation, and clinical trials, as well as customers and potential investors and partners, over the course of a year, until I was satisfied that I had heard a representative sample of feedback, including one hundred customers to be exact!

Tip 5. Consider hiring a professional

I absolutely recommend identifying a professional you trust to guide you through the process and fill in knowledge gaps in marketing, finance, or other areas where you are spongy. There are many sources of established vendors and independent consultants who do this type of work. The *right* business plan consultants can provide additional unbiased feedback and prepare and package your plan in an attractive, easy-to-read format.

I emphasize the *right* consultant because you want someone who is knowledgeable about your industry and type of business and someone you can see yourself working with for several months. When I wrote the business plan for my first start-up, I hired a former pharmaceutical marketing expert turned independent consultant who not only knew all the right questions to ask but also helped me with researching the market and customers, testing assumptions, and crunching the numbers. Pamela worked with me as though she were my right hand. She cared about the business as much as I did, and it showed. Her level of engagement and role as a trusted adviser were invaluable. Twenty years later, we remain colleagues and friends, and she's among the first persons I turn to when I have a new business idea.

Tip 6. Use a business model canvas to paint your masterpiece

A business model canvas can be a great tool for collecting and processing your thoughts. Written by Alexander Osterwalder and Yves Pigneur, two business theorists, authors, and consultants, *Business Model Generation* is a practical guide for designing a business model. You can find the business model canvas outline and guidelines on applying it in appendix 2.

The business model canvas can even be useful if your innovation is your business model! When the founders of Diners Club introduced the first credit card in 1950, they created a new business model—making money on customer fees from paying for a customer's purchase. Xerox did the same when it introduced leasing photocopiers and the per-copy payment system in 1969. In fact, business model innovation traces all the way back to Johannes Gutenberg when he sought practical applications for the mechanical printing device he had created. The Roman Catholic Church was his first customer as he started his business printing Bibles, which spread Christianity across Europe. The core components of the canvas can help any innovator pressure-test the product, customers, partners, operating model, financial forecast, and time to get to market.

Tip 7. Continue to fine-tune and update your plan

The hard truth about business plans is that writing them is hard work. Many people spend a year or more writing their plans. I spend six months writing and fine-tuning the plans for all my businesses. And because the plan is dynamic and living, I update it every few months.

The men in the business program at the correctional facility had all too much time on their hands, but to their credit, they used it to think through their ideas and to research and develop solid business plans, under difficult circumstances. If they can do it, you can too. You can certainly devote the time to give your brilliant idea the best chance of success—and that's what the business plan and model, by securing funding, can provide.

The most difficult part is developing a coherent picture of the business that makes sense, appeals to others, and provides a reasonable road map for the future. Your products, services, business model, customers, marketing and sales plan, internal operations, management team, and financial projections must all be tied together seamlessly. But once you have it in place, you will feel a sense of satisfaction and have confidence in sharing your plans with investors, lenders, and other critical partners and stakeholders.

INNOVATOR IN FOCUS

Laurent Levy, CEO, Nanobiotix

Physicist, inventor, biotech entrepreneur, visionary—Laurent Levy is all that and more.

Nanobiotix, the company he founded in 2003, is a leader in developing medical nanotechnology. Nanoparticles, the specific technology advanced by the company, are tiny materials that are built atom by atom and can be used for various applications, from delivering medication more precisely to destroying tumor cells.

In 2019, Nanobiotix received approval to use its lead investigational product, NBTXR3—a first-in-class "radio enhancer" that is injected into solid tumors and paired with radiotherapy. The nanoparticles are designed to increase the dose of radiotherapy delivered within tumor cells without damaging surrounding healthy tissues, thus improving treatment for patients with this commonly used cancer-fighting regimen—without increasing harmful side effects. Under the brand name Hensify®, NBTXR3 is now commercially authorized in Europe for treating many types of soft-tissue sarcomas and is being developed globally across several other cancer indications.

Laurent has also authored more than thirty-five articles in international scientific publications. He holds several patents and regularly speaks on the topic of using nanoparticles to fight cancer and other diseases.

But his mission goes beyond developing technologies to treat and perhaps even cure diseases like cancer. Laurent and his team are on a mission to unlock humanity's limitless potential using revolutionary nanotechnologies and collaboration with other visionaries.

Laurent's true goal as an innovator, he says, is "to help inspire humanity to push beyond boundaries and discover a better way of life."

Lessons learned

Laurent knew early on that his ambitious ideas did not always translate easily to a PowerPoint or an investor prospectus. "Vision is what motivates you, but it's hard to sell a vision," he says. "If you say to an investor, 'I'm going to cure cancer,' they'll say to you 'yeah, right.'" That's where the business plan comes in. "When I told one of my former chairmen our vision, he said, 'Okay, well, maybe we should go step by step.' I thought I'd failed to communicate. 'Even my own chairman doesn't get it!' I said to myself. But now I understand that he was wise. We needed to take small bites before people could really digest this big elephant of an idea."

While he learned the importance of plans, Laurent also says that they should not be cast in concrete. "Creating innovation requires agility and flexibility," he says. "Yes, you need a plan, but you also need to recognize that the plan may need to change quickly."

Striking that balance—between what he calls "market pull and innovation push"—is the key to a successful new idea, product, or technology. "It's a constant back and forth between the demands of the market, and the dreams of the innovator," he says.

When they align? "It's a beautiful thing," he says.

You can't make this up

Laurent holds a doctorate in physical chemistry from the Pierre and Marie Curie University in Paris, as well as advanced degrees from other prestigious French institutes. But the work that resulted in Nanobiotix was conducted in, of all places, Buffalo, New York—a city best known to Americans for its beloved but hard-luck NFL franchise, not to mention prodigious amounts of snowfall in winter. It was at the State University of New York at Buffalo—specifically, the university's elite Institute for Lasers, Photonics and Biophotonics—that Laurent did the postdoctoral work that formed the foundation of his visionary company.

Tips for innovators

Go big or go home. "That's the way it was for me, and I'd encourage all those with a disruptive new idea to do the same. We only have one life. If this idea is your passion, then go for it!"

Take the road not chosen. "At Nanobiotix, we try not to do things that others have done. In my industry, there are many followers, many companies all going after the same target. I say, rather than following others, try to be the first in something new."

But don't hesitate to change direction. "There's always a path. Once you find it, follow it, but be mindful of better routes that may present themselves during the journey. That is the true nature of the innovative process. You must be an explorer."

Learn more about Levy at https://www.nanobiotix.com/management; https://fr.linkedin.com/laurent-levy.

7

HOW SERIAL ENTREPRENEURS INCREASE THEIR ODDS OF SUCCESS

The noon sun streamed through the wall-sized window of a conference room in Summit, New Jersey. I squinted from the podium as I surveyed the senior-level women and a handful of men in the audience.

The group of seventy-three was attending a leadership workshop sponsored by my company's women's affinity group, the Women's Information Network. I looked past them to take in the yellow, pink, and violet flowers dancing outside in the April breeze while inside, the women's pastel blouses, scarves, and jackets provided similar proof that—after a long, gray winter—spring was at long last here.

Each of the round tables to which the women had been assigned included one man. This arrangement was deliberate. Many women's leadership groups had learned over the years that the best way to advance the causes of corporate women was with the support of male peers. Increasingly, they cultivated advocates from the ranks of the most senior men in the organization. I guess the men felt honored or flattered, but whatever the case, they seemed sincere in their motivation—to help carry the torch and legitimize the need for female equity in the workplace. A workplace, I should add, that is challenged, even sometimes threatened, by the idea of women with new ideas, new ways of doing things—in other words, innovators.

The group was buzzing with chatting and laughter and I could feel the energy. We had just heard an inspiring motivational talk by athlete turned leadership speaker Robyn Benincasa, World Champion Adventure. Benincasa had been a competitor in several seasons of the Eco-Challenge, the multiday, ultra-endurance expedition race that itself was an innovation when it was first aired on the Discovery Channel. It was created by a then little-known TV producer named Mark Burnett, and the success of the Eco-Challenge sparked his creation of a more staged version of the event. This would be called *Survivor*, and with it, Burnett would help invent the reality show genre and change television history.

Benincasa's team won the 2000 Eco-Challenge in Borneo, a rugged island in Southeast Asia's Malay Archipelago known for its beaches, biodiverse rainforest, and abundance of wildlife, including orangutans and clouded leopards. She told the audience how her team won the twelve-day race, sailing over open oceans, biking the treacherous mountains, and slogging through torrential jungle rain while being assaulted by voracious leeches. They swam and canoed through a raging river and waded through caves filled with bat guano. At this particular event, a number of racers fell ill with a bacterial infection from the contaminated river waters and had to be hospitalized. Overcoming these intense physical challenges was a test of leadership, teamwork, and personal will, grit, and resilience. "Everything that could go wrong went wrong during this race, but I saw the most amazing leadership from our team captain. He kept all of us going," Benincasa said.

We were spellbound during her presentation. Our second speaker was a well-known New York psychologist who shared techniques on dealing with stress. She taught us the correct way to practice yoga breathing, taking us through several exercises to ensure we had perfected it. After Benincasa's harrowing and inspiring stories about endurance and bat guano, we needed it.

I was the third and final speaker and had been asked to share my personal experiences managing risk as a leader of innovation and entrepreneurship. "Those two women are hard acts to follow," I thought as I took a sip of water from the small bottle placed on the podium for me. They were professional leadership speakers who had clearly refined their talks to perfection—concise, well-crafted, motivational speeches designed to ensure that participants would be soaked in the immersive experience and convey their newfound wisdom to their office mates the next day. While I wouldn't be telling an epic tale of adventure or offering techniques based on treating thousands of stressed-out executives in the Big Apple, I did have a real-life case study that I was eager to share.

I adjusted the mic, smiled, and said, "Hi, I'm Lorraine Marchand, and before I share my story about business risk and leadership, I have a favor to ask." The eyes in the room were on me. "Answer this question: On a scale from 1 to 10, with 10 being the perfect 10, how effective are you at managing risk? Jot down your rating of yourself on the notepad at your seat. We'll come back to it a little later."

I saw a roomful of heads bend down, some with pens paused as they considered the question, and then heard the muffled sounds of seventy-three people scribbling down an answer—the men included.

"Imagine," I paused for effect. "You are a successful corporate executive in the life sciences industry and you've decided you want to run your own company, maybe even a start-up if the risk is manageable. An opportunity presents itself that is almost too good to be true, and you take the plunge. You cofound, as CEO, a molecular diagnostics start-up. Your business partner is a renowned physician who plans to continue running his practice but will devote time to serving as the company's scientific adviser. He puts in a healthy amount of seed capital to fund the entity. You have an impressive equity position, but he owns the majority of the company. Your plan is to get to a critical milestone required to secure venture capital (VC) funding within twelve months. This opportunity requires relocation, and you start the process of moving your family from Philadelphia to Baltimore."

I paused and let the details soak in. It was probably a scenario, or something like it, that many of those in attendance had thought about. "Okay, now," I continued, "let's say five months have passed and you've progressed on a number of fronts. Patents have been filed; clinical studies needed for regulatory approval are well under way; the laboratory is established and core staff hired; you have established an impressive advisory board and secured renowned regulatory and R&D experts to design and evaluate studies; several venture-capital companies have expressed interest in your technology, as have a few biotech companies."

"Everyone is waiting for feedback from the Patent Office preliminary human data. You and the cofounder are in sync, and things are progressing according to your expectations. You put your house on the market. Family weekends are spent looking at houses in the Baltimore suburbs and checking out schools for the kids."

Again, a pause, as I suspected that many of those in the audience—most of whom were mid-career women raising families—had probably experienced similar career-based family relocations.

"Then, on a humid summer morning in July, you walk into the office and are greeted with devastating news. Your cofounder was driving his motorcycle to work during rush hour on the Baltimore Beltway and has been in a multi-vehicle collision. He's in critical care in the trauma unit of a major hospital. He may not make it through the day. You try to keep the rest of your team motivated and hopeful, but they go through the workday mechanically; there is little conversation in the lunchroom. Thankfully, he survives the next forty-eight hours, the most critical time, the doctors say, but they know his spinal cord damage is significant. The next weeks and months are a roller coaster. He's still unconscious. The first order of business every day is an update on his prognosis. You try to keep the business running smoothly, but a few risks have arisen."

I then ticked off the realities of what actually happened in this situation, which—as the audience had begun to suspect—was something that had happened to me, earlier in my career.

"The attorneys have apprised you that there may be a patent challenge and they need a considerable budget to address it," I said, ticking off the challenges on my fingers. "The VCs have heard of your partner's accident and are asking about the viability of the company and your plans. The scientific advisers are pressing you for data, and several have threatened to rescind their role on the board based on the news that's now circulating publicly about your partner's prognosis." I paused and then offered the kicker: "Most importantly, the preliminary data have come back and are contradictory and ambiguous. Your statisticians are saying studies need to be redesigned and new data gathered because much of what has been collected is unusable."

I saw people shaking their heads as my crisis scenario grew more involved—a grim prognosis indeed. But there was one more problem:

"Finally, your partner's twenty-six-year-old son has been named his father's executor. You meet and he tells you you'll be reporting to him for the foreseeable future. The commitment that his father made to fund the company has to be revisited. He gives you sixty days to secure investor funding and drum up sales. 'Revenue is critical,' he emphasizes."

I let it all sink in. Every word—just as it had really happened to me.

"What do you do?" I asked. "Take a moment now and assess your readiness to handle this situation. What is your risk-management score now?

A few hands shot up. "My risk score went down," Sandy from procurement volunteered. "I honestly don't know if I am ready to handle something that unexpected and catastrophic. Even your other story about your dad's business shook me up; I was a kid during that recession and remember the gas lines."

An enthusiastic colleague named Susan who ran marketing stood up and grabbed the mic that was being circulated. "Listening to the story about the diagnostic start-up, I had answers to most of the risks. I feel pretty confident about my risk profile."

I then explained that many studies have been conducted on the attributes of entrepreneurs and innovators—the behavioral profile of an innovation leader comfortable with managing risk included. These attributes include resilience; tolerance of risk, ambiguity, and uncertainty; commitment and dedication to solving problems; an obsession with new opportunities; and vigilance, creativity, self-reliance, adaptability, and a motivation to excel.

I presented the group with a ten-minute exercise, a personal entrepreneurial risk assessment you can take yourself: https://www.bdc.ca/en/articles-tools/entrepreneur-toolkit/business-assessments/entrepreneurial-potential-self-assessment.

The assessment helped the women to determine if they had risk-management leadership behaviors. "Risk management is like a muscle," I said. "It has to be exercised to get stronger. You need to develop risk tolerance and good management skills and learn to think proactively about contingency and scenario planning, whether it's for a start-up or a new project at work."

One woman raised her hand, "I want to be better at managing risk. I'm in the middle of a tricky situation and don't know if I'm handling it well." She explained that her company had experienced a product failure and clients were bailing. She admitted that she recognized that signs of technical problems were present but had never planned for them. "Now we're managing a crisis," she said. "I'll know better next time."

I commented on how she could handle the situation—doing an objective assessment of the problem and what her customers were experiencing; being transparent with her team and customers about the steps she was taking to resolve the situation; and documenting her learning so she could share her experience with others to help them avoid making the same mistake she had made. I offered my six tips for managing risk under fire:

Tip 1. Focus on your strengths and talents.
Tip 2. Maintain a balanced perspective with the help of those you trust.
Tip 3. Emotionally detach from the situation and assess it as an observer.
Tip 4. Assess options and resources and set priorities.
Tip 5. Develop and execute a new plan with support from key stakeholders.
Tip 6. Forge ahead without looking back, but record the lessons learned.

I closed my talk by sharing the outcome of the story about the diagnostic start-up, the catastrophic injury to my original partner, and his young son's unexpected involvement.

"That story is true and the executive was me. It was important that I do the right thing, for my partner, for his family, and for the company."

At the time, I knew that given his health, my partner would never be able to return and support the company in the way it needed. Also, the landscape had changed during the time he was recovering. First, I had an honest discussion with him and his family about the state of the company. His appetite for running a commercial company had changed, but it was clear he didn't want to lose the focus on his research. I applied for grants and secured several million dollars in funding from the National Institutes of Health, the National Science Foundation, a private research foundation, and state and county biotech funds. We secured enough funding to put together a series of research studies that he could oversee, and I brought in a couple of R&D partners who were interested in the lab.

"He was able to run a small company that performed molecular diagnostic research studies," I said. "Which was really what he wanted."

As for me, I decided to move on. There wasn't enough value built up in the company to support a buyout, so I offered to stay on as an advisor while I explored new opportunities. Based on my start-up experience and expanded biotech network, I went on to found three start-ups, started my consulting practice, created a curriculum on innovation and entrepreneurship that I taught at Princeton and Columbia, and joined the boards of an angel investment group and a private equity fund. Eventually, I joined Cognizant Technology Solutions (the company I was addressing that day) to lead a new innovative venture that created revenue streams for the company and helped us increase market share in the pharma segment.

An Innovation Mindset embraces risk-taking. I don't mean taking crazy, uncalculated rolls of the dice. I mean carefully weighing risks, assessing their impact, building contingency plans, identifying ways to de-risk your plans, and demonstrating the resiliency to pivot when needed.

Even if that pivot may lead you away from your original innovative idea, another idea may be waiting just around the corner.

THE DIFFERENCE BETWEEN RISK AND UNCERTAINTY

Now that we've explored the risk-management DNA required of leaders of innovation, let's look at the definition and types of business risk. By their very nature, entrepreneurial and innovation ventures involve pursuing opportunity—doing something new—in an environment of scarce resources and many unknowns. This could mean developing a new technology or distribution channel or combining existing products or services into a solution. Newness brings with it uncertainty. Uncertainty is different from risk. Business uncertainty is when change introduces the potential for problems but the outcome or impact is unclear at the moment. You make decisions every day with an element of uncertainty. In fact, any innovation or start-up brings with it an element of uncertainty. But these uncertainties, changes, and challenges, and their potential impact on your business, can be assessed. For example, you face the risk that your innovation may not achieve its commercial results because of lack of customer interest and market fit—these are things you can anticipate and plan for. My partner's accident created a lot of uncertainty for our company, but I identified the key risks—for example, the investor community's response to the news—and worked through each one to reduce its negative impact on the business.

TYPES OF BUSINESS RISK

Risk 1. Uncontrollable

Uncontrollable risks are just that—unexpected things you can't really plan for, such as the oil crisis of 1973 that impacted my father's chemical manufacturing and distribution business, my cofounder's accident, and the black swan event of the COVID-19 pandemic, which created giant shocks to the global ecosystem, extending beyond health to include every facet of society, from business to education to finance and supply chain. These shocks are the greatest form of risk—external factors that cause risk. Some companies are swept under; others rise above and become stronger. Not all risks are of this seismic impact, but the ability to handle risk is the same—it requires proactive planning that helps to minimize, lower, or eliminate (de-risk) the negative impact of the situation or event. The added challenge is that in a situation like this you are diagnosing the problem, fixing what you can, and trying to anticipate what will happen next. That's a lot to manage at once!

Risk 2. Strategic

Strategic risks are desirable as they have the potential to help the business grow faster by taking the business in a new direction or offering the market new solutions. But high reward usually means high risk. Strategic risks include actions such as launching a new product to a new market segment or establishing a partnership that provides marketplace synergies. If these strategies are the right fit and executed well, they can help the business leapfrog the competition, but if not, they can slow the business down. Innovation typically involves doing something new with too few resources, people, and money. Timing and the right types of partnerships can close those gaps quickly and effectively. If the marriage is the right one, the terms make sense and both entities are committed to making the marriage work.

A good example of strategic risk is the partnership between Apple and IBM launched in 2014.[1] It was the second time the pair had attempted marriage. The first time was in the 1990s, and it failed because of disagreements over software development and licensing terms, creating a lot of collateral damage that had to be cleaned up. When the couple tried again in 2014, the focus was on bringing new business apps to market, leveraging IBM's big data and analytics capabilities to the iPhone and iPad. It required substantial commitment because mobile, cloud, and data analytics were and still are fast-moving competitive areas. This time the partnership worked out well. Both had learned from the mistakes of the past, and in 2021 the couple built on their success and launched IBM's COVID-19 vaccine medical record app on iOS. The two companies had come a long way since the famous "1984" Super Bowl commercial that had launched the Macintosh and—in its Orwellian depiction of a bold female runner striking a blow against a Big Brother–like figure on a giant screen—was widely seen as a symbolic and not-so-subtle attack against the dominance of IBM in the computer industry of that era.

Risk 3. Manageable

Manageable risks are the most common, and the good news is they are preventable, but they can also have the biggest impact on businesses success. Let's look at a few types of manageable risks.

MANAGEABLE RISK 1. TECHNICAL Technical risks involve anticipating what the options are if the new technology doesn't work as required. For example, when Astra Zeneca (AZ) initially launched its COVID-19 vaccine, the European Medicines Agency (EMA) quickly determined that there were cases of blood clots and neurological symptoms two weeks after vaccination, primarily in women under the age of sixty. The results presented technical risks to AZ, and countries suspended use of the vaccine until the EMA had conducted an investigation. The investigation determined that the risk of blood clots and low platelets was small and not significant enough to halt vaccine distribution. AZ explored what it could do to mitigate this side effect. Another example of technical risk is one that Google faces constantly—the need to scale and adapt its existing architecture to accommodate increased consumer traffic, technology advances, and even changing business requirements. The company has to proactively plan for and manage technical risks.

MANAGEABLE RISK 2. OPERATIONAL Operational risks are the result of failed or insufficient processes in day-to-day operations that impede the ability to get to market and earn revenues. In other words, they're the kind of snafus that creep into the daily grind of the business.

I was working with an early-stage software company that had failed to document its processes for developing a new product. This caused two problems. First, when the product failed to perform according to plan, the company didn't have adequate process documentation to assess what had broken down and why. Second, once they did get the problem fixed and started meeting with customers, the customers requested documentation of their product development processes. This second situation got their attention, and they hired me to help them with process design and documentation. During that work, the CEO, Todd, saw other issues and recognized the need for a full de-risking assessment. We then developed a risk matrix and set of strategies to anticipate and manage financial, operational, and market risks. The day he shared the plan with the board, Todd called me to say, "Thank you. I got this risk plan in place just in time. The board was worried that I didn't know what risks the business faced. They were getting ready to bring in a consultant. I'm so glad I earned their confidence and that we have tangible ways to de-risk the company going forward."

Contracts can present another form of operational risk: the business may be forced to live up to the fine print in a contract or fail to hold a vendor or customer accountable. Verbal contracts, while technically legal, are difficult to enforce, so always insist on a written contract, which will be more likely to stand up in court. It's important to have an attorney read nondisclosure agreements and the contract's fine print—they may insist that you sign their contracts, and a violation of terms could put you out of business.

A lack of resources—the right people to deliver your product—is another type of operational risk that can cause the business to fail to meet its objectives.

Examples of the impact of operational risks: Your website hosting company goes offline for several hours, interrupting e-commerce and resulting in sales loss; you have a product failure and lack the right resources to fix the problem; you are audited by a potential client as part of their new vendor diligence and your outdated standard operating procedure (SOP) documents cause you to lose the business when they signal a red flag about your credentials and attention to details.

MANAGEABLE RISK 3. **MARKET** Booz and Company reports that 66 percent of new products fail within two years of launch, and Doblin Group says 96 percent of all innovations fail to return their cost of capital.[2] This is a reminder that you need to examine dynamic market forces and big trends in the industry and conduct voice-of-the-customer research around behaviors, tastes, and things that would make work and life better.

This is not always as obvious as it sounds. If you're designing a product and ask customers what they need, they will likely regurgitate features based on existing competitive products. Remember the example we discussed in chapter 4 about Steve Jobs and how he first designed the iPhone and then tested it with customers, knowing that asking a customer if she wanted to take photos with her phone was a nonstarter? Another common problem in managing market risk is that companies segment customers according to their demographic and psychographic profiles, often missing insights into what job a customer hires a product to do. Do I need my phone to take great photos, search the web really fast, or store all my favorite videos? Which function is the most important to me? The innovator needs to know this.

This kind of research alone can go a long way toward de-risking your product's market fit. Let's look at a simple example of the drinking straw. The purpose of the straw is to make it easier for people to consumer liquids; straws have been around for centuries. The design hasn't changed much through the years because there was little need to change it. One innovator decided that a way to get children to drink juice and milk would be to create a fun straw bent in unusual shapes and packaged with milk and juice products.

The fun straws proved to be a huge success, and millions are sold every year. The innovator adapted to the changing demands of customers (parents wanting their kids to drink healthier beverages) and invented a new twist on an old product. He de-risked his product by confirming through market research that parents struggled to get their children to drink healthy beverages and testing the bent straw prototype at day-care programs in several states. Once he had a critical mass of data, he raised capital and got his fun straw to market.

MANAGEABLE RISK 4. **FINANCIAL** A steady stream of funding is obviously critical to the success of a new technology and a new company. You have to have the financial support to hit key milestones, get your product to market, and then sustain the business. Research shows that as many as 90 percent of all start-ups fail because they have inadequate capital just one year after launch.[3] When you develop a business plan, the most important component is the forecast, because it helps you determine how much capital you need for what activities over what period of time. Nothing will sink a company or a new technology faster than lack of capital.

Laurence Blumberg MD, a Columbia Business School alumnus and serial biotech entrepreneur who teaches a graduate course, Entrepreneurship in Life Sciences at Weill Cornell Medicine, is a regular guest lecturer in my course at Yeshiva University. He shares his experience raising money for early-stage companies in a way that really hits home for the students.

> When I did the investment plan for one start-up, I was afraid to take more money than I absolutely needed because I didn't want to dilute my and the co-founder's equity. First, we had some ideas about the therapeutic indication for the technology we wanted to develop, but our business plan reflected blue-sky thinking and had ambitious hiring plans—it lacked focus. Then the perfect storm hit—the market tanked and I couldn't raise funds later when I really needed the capital, despite good data in hand. I learned a hard lesson about the risks of being undercapitalized and unfocused.

When Blumberg launched his subsequent company, he de-risked his financial position by being more aggressive upfront about the amount of capital that he wanted to raise. Equally importantly, he crafted a detailed development and clinical plan for the drug he wanted to develop before he even tried to raise Series A funds.

"De-risking the company's financials and having a solid business plan turned out to be the two best things I could have done to optimize value creation," Blumberg comments. "I had a much longer runway this time around to get to a value inflection point with cushion and was more capital efficient by depending more on outside contractors rather than significant fixed internal costs. We got lucky that the capital markets remained robust, but we had planned for the worst."

Another way to de-risk your financials is to take advantage of free or less expensive forms of capital for as long as you can. For example, putting some of your own money into the company and asking friends and family members to invest or lend you the money provides a source of capital that is more attractive than taking money from a venture capitalist or debt from a bank. Nondilutive forms of capital, such as government and foundation grants, are also available. This money doesn't need to be paid back and can help you extend the period of time before you need VC money.

HOW VENTURE CAPITAL COMPANIES MANAGE FINANCIAL RISK

We'll examine the role of VCs and valuation methodologies in subsequent chapters, but a short note related to their role in risk is appropriate here. VCs manage risk by performing diligence on a company, using a methodology to place a value on the business, and then putting a member of their own team on the start-up's board so they can be involved in the operations of the enterprise they are funding. During diligence, their experts examine the technology, market fit, finances, and operational model, and they score each element of the business or new technology, applying a weighting algorithm and coming up with a risk assessment that they use to make a go/no-go decision on the technology from an investment perspective. When evaluating your company, a VC will look at financial risks through metrics called ratios: cash flow, EBITDA (earnings before interest, tax, depreciation, and amortization), ROI, and other measures.

Risk 4. Reputation

Before we leave the topic of types of risk, I want to mention a type of manageable risk that can occur at any time in a company's history. It speaks to the need to have a firm grasp of what you want your brand and your culture to stand for. If you do, you will be far better prepared to handle potential risks to your reputation should anything unforeseen happen.

Reputation risk involves anticipating how the company plans to handle an incident that could tarnish your reputation. Reputation can be affected by incompetence, dishonesty, disrespect, and a host of other causes. An example is Johnson & Johnson's (J&J's) handling of the infamous Tylenol recall of 1982. Seven people in the Chicago area died from taking cyanide-laced capsules of extra-strength Tylenol. Tylenol accounted for 17 percent of J&J's income and had 37 percent of pain-reliever market share. Marketers predicted that the company would never recover from the sabotage, but two months later Tylenol was back on the market with tamper-proof packaging and bolstered by an extensive media campaign. A year later its market share had climbed from 7 percent to 30 percent. It preserved its reputation by taking action and doing the right thing for consumers: it recalled 31 million bottles from store shelves and offered a replacement product in a safer tablet form, free of charge. The company was also open and honest in its communications to the public. Top J&J executives made themselves available to the media, refusing to hide behind a screen of "no comments."

Companies often fiddle around while Rome is burning—or retreat into a shell—during times of crisis. In this case the leadership took control of the situation, making the company a legend in consumer trust and a casebook study in reputation management.

HOW TO MANAGE RISK

The old adage "prepare for the worst and hope for the best" certainly holds true in the world of innovation. As we've said earlier, by its very nature, introducing a new product, business, or idea into the marketplace is chancy. This is where a risk assessment matrix comes in. This helps you defines the level of risk to your innovation by considering the probability or likelihood of an event against the severity of the consequences if the event were to occur.

The advantages of this risk matrix are that it helps the business to:

- Prioritize risks according to their level of severity to the business
- Neutralize the possible consequences by helping to focus on mitigation (reducing the seriousness of the impact) and contingency planning (always have a Plan B!)
- Analyze potential risks with minimal efforts
- Visually convey risks
- Identify the most critical areas to focus on de-risking

This is only a tool, not a complete solution. Developing a risk assessment involves considerable subjectivity and the assigning of arbitrary value to risks based on ambiguous information. Still, it gives you a place to start when it comes to risk assessment and mitigation strategy.

RISK MATRIX SAMPLE

Referring to the risk matrix (table 7.1 and figure 7.1), let's walk through an example. In the story about my diagnostic company, we faced three risks even before my partner's accident and before I completed this risk assessment.

Technical risk: Positive clinical data were required to secure our laboratory certification and to begin the Food and Drug Administration (FDA) approval process. So the risk was negative or inconclusive data. Negative or inconclusive data were possible, and the impact would be tolerable. Though unfortunate, this type of risk occurs all the time in new technologies and must be accounted for. The impact is on timeline and budget. It's critical to have backup

Category	Examples of questions to ask yourself	Manageable (Y/N)
Global	• Are there any global / regional trends that are likely to have an impact on your business (e.g., COVID-19 pandemic, global semiconductor chip shortage, financial markets, wars / regional unrest)? *While the source of the problem is uncontrollable, the impact on your business can be managed by capturing risks in the following sections and mitigating them.*	N
Strategic	• Is the core market need or problem statement guiding your organizational strategy still relevant?	Y
Technical	• What is your probability of technical success? • Are there other technological barriers that would likely affect your scalability / adaptability (e.g., iPhone vs. Android usage, privacy laws for apps)?	Y
Operational	• Do you have adequate expertise onboard to see the product through the next milestones? • Do you have adequate documentation of all processes and technical know-how? • Do you have contracts with all suppliers / buyers to ensure minimal disruption to process? • Do you have adequate protection for your intellectual property?	Y
Market	• Are your customer needs still in line with your products / services? • Are you suppliers well positioned to meet your changing needs? • Are there any new competitors who could disrupt your business?	Y
Financial	• How long will your cash reserves support your operating expenses at your current burn rate? • Do you have adequate funding for CAPEX (including new R&D investments)?	Y
Reputation	• What is your current reputation with customers, suppliers, and overall industry experts? • Is there any risk to your reputation with investors due to operational, performance-related, or market changes?	Y

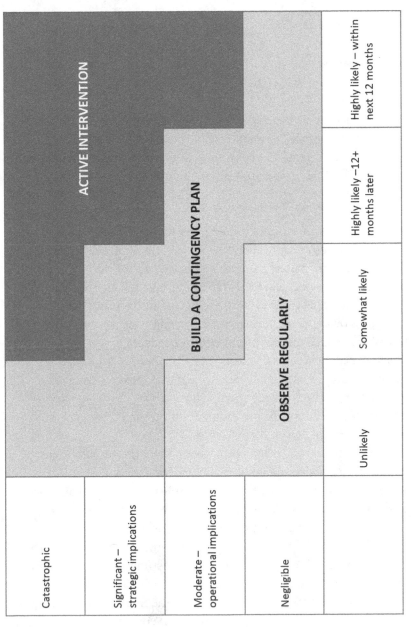

Figure 7.1 Risk prioritization and mitigation matrix

studies prepared or even running in parallel in case your data do not produce the expected results.

Financial risk: Investor capital of $3.5 million was required within nine months of the company's founding to cover the costs of hiring talent, setting up a laboratory, securing certifications, and setting up clinical studies. The risk was not raising capital in a nine-month horizon.

Not raising capital was possible, and the impact was unacceptable, as the timeline of getting to market would be seriously set back without the necessary capital. The contingency or de-risk strategy I implemented was applying for Small Business Innovation Research grants from NIH, grants from patient and research foundations for ophthalmology, and State Innovation Grants for new innovative companies. I applied for all three types of funding and was glad I did. When we failed to raise investor capital because of my partner's accident, those sources of funds ultimately sustained the company and allowed us to fund some of our research. Grants typically take a full year to secure, so you need to apply early, even when you're unsure you'll need the money. By slowing down hiring and managing expenses, we could slow cash burn until the grant funds were awarded.

Market risk: The ophthalmology market needed to adopt the concept of using a biomarker-based diagnostic test to determine who should receive drug treatment. The risk was that the market would be slow to adopt the technology and our ability to generate revenues after launch would be delayed.

Slow market adoption was probable, and the impact was unacceptable to intolerable, depending on how long it took doctors to use our test. We worked with key opinion leaders in ophthalmology and presented at conferences to share our research hypothesis, some early positive data, and the rationale for why our biomarker diagnostic test could be used to guide treatment decisions, but ultimately the combination of inconclusive study results, lack of funding to advance our research, and my partner's accident created the perfect storm. We could not move the market. We settled for research partnerships with pharmaceutical companies and additional research grants from NIH.

INNOVATOR IN FOCUS

Sarah Apgar, founder of FitFighter

INNOVATOR CLAIM TO FAME Now that Sarah Apgar has been awarded $250,000 on Shark Tank and earned national media exposure in the process, her worries about the risks of developing FitFighter, a strength and condition system, might seem unfounded. FitFighter is based on a patent-pending Steelhose—a twenty-four- to thirty-six-inch, semi-firm free weight made from real firehose and double-recycled steel shot. It can also be adapted to attach to other forms of gym equipment to create different workouts.

When Apgar started the business in January 2019, the uncertainty and the fears were real—just as they are for almost every innovator. She navigated the pitfalls by clearly imagining where she wanted to go. "I think you can hedge your risk upfront by creating a runway in front of you that has clear milestones and goals that you'll achieve," she says. "In my case, we raised capital, 20 percent of it my own money, to get our product development from the garage to the point we were ready to go to market."

For that financial support, Apgar went to friends and family, but carefully made each approach individual. "My friend Steve had been in the firehouse with me," said Sarah, a former volunteer for a firehouse in Halesite, on New York's Long Island. "He knew intimately what we were doing and was happy to invest. My uncle had always said he'd support me if I ever wanted to start a business, so I knew he had my back, too." Others needed a little more convincing before they would write a check. "In the case of another investor, it was more 'Let me lay this out in a more organized fashion and make a pitch.'"

Part of her presentation and promise to all of the approximately half-dozen people who invested time or money in developing Fit-Fighter's Steelhose was her two-year plan, with its sales/profitability benchmarks. "It was important for me to feel that I had hedged the risks a bit," she said. So if we didn't make it through this two-year period, I haven't ruined my life or the finances of my friends or family members."

As it turned out, she needn't have worried. What started as a tool to help firefighters stay in shape morphed into something even bigger. "I started having trainers and coaches outside of the fire service realm saying 'Gosh, this seems to be a really versatile tool. We could use this to help improve strength for a lot of people,'" she says. "I began to realize we had created something powerful."

Powerful, indeed. When Apgar appeared on Shark Tank in November 2020, she pitched FitFighter and the Steelhose and received an offer of $250,000 for a 25 percent stake in the company from guest investor Daniel Lubetzky, the creator of KIND bars. "We swam with the Sharks," Sarah posted on social media, shortly after the episode aired, "and are so incredibly honored to have a new FitFighter partner."

Lessons learned

Another way to manage risk, Sarah says, is to make sure your supply chain has multiple links. Currently, she says, most of her product is manufactured by one factory. "I realized that all my eggs are in one basket," she said. "What if that factory burns down? Or suddenly goes out business?" While she doesn't expect either of those scenarios to materialize and is happy with her production partner, these are the kinds of contingencies that those developing new products need to keep in mind. In Sarah's case, "We're lining up other manufacturers, and we could envision implementing a parallel manufacturing operation somewhere." Thinking through potential vulnerabilities in the supply chain, she says, can help a lot of innovators sleep better at night.

You can't make this up

A graduate of Princeton University, Sarah was a two-time All-American collegiate rugby player and member of Princeton's Army ROTC program. She served in Iraq, as platoon leader for an engineering battalion attached to the 101st Airborne Division in Mosul in 2003. Back in civilian life, she earned her master's degree from Dartmouth

College's Tuck School of Business. A volunteer firefighter and EMT, as well as a certified fitness professional, she is also a mom: she and her husband, Ben Smith, have two daughters, Emory and Arlyn. They live in Port Washington, on New York's Long Island.

Insight for innovators

"A good innovator needs to be stubbornly and doggedly curious, day after day. When it comes to your product, you need to be open-minded, and you need to ask questions and more questions—until there are no more, and then you need to think of one more. I've been called 'exhausting' and 'overly tenacious.' I think those are also qualities that makes you successful as an innovator.

"You need to have a village that supports you . . . a circle of people you love and trust. Being an innovator is not always a comfortable place to be. And you're going to have people that say your innovation sucks. I've had people comment on my social media about my product, 'That's useless!' or 'What? A firehose as a free weight? What a dumb idea.' Although I've developed a thicker skin, I'm still sensitive to people telling me my idea is stupid. It's like getting punched in the face. That's why you need to have this village of people who are unconditionally a call away, to prop you up."

Learn more about Apgar at https://www.sarahapgar.com.

8

COAXING CAPITAL

No Innovation Without Communication

I looked at the clock nervously. Rick had been speaking for fifteen minutes and was only on slide three of the capital-raising pitch deck for his health-care technology company. He was giving the presentation from his laptop on the conference room table because he couldn't get the projector to work. Fortunately, he had brought hard copies to distribute, always a good backup plan on pitch day. Unfortunately, his snail's pace as he went through the deck was starting to annoy this roomful of potential investors.

"Hey Rick, sorry to interrupt but I don't want to waste your time or ours," said Christopher, the president of the venture capital firm Rick was pitching. "I appreciate how passionate you are about the problem of people with diabetes not sticking with their therapies and diet to manage their health. Lots of people in health care have been working on that problem for years. I get it." He held up a copy of the presentation, the entirety of which he had flipped through while Rick was still on page three. "I've jumped ahead to the rest of the deck," Christopher continued, as Rick began to sweat. "Let's just cut to the chase. Help me understand how your solution is differentiated in a very crowded market, how you're going to scale your business model, and how you're going to make any serious money, enough to make it worth an investor's time."

Dressed in a starched white shirt and blue tie, Christopher was a successful serial entrepreneur and a professor of technology entrepreneurship at his alma mater, Princeton University. We were meeting in his office at Palmer Square in Princeton. Usually relaxed and affable, Christopher at this moment was smiling politely but his cheeks were pink and his brow was raised. You could tell he was losing patience.

I looked at Rick expectantly, wondering if I should jump in and help. I had set up the meeting as a favor to a colleague whose business judgment I respected. I had only recently met Rick and knew he was eager to get investor funding for his new business idea, which he had described as a direct-to-consumer health-care software product. Christopher's venture firm specialized in such technologies in the financial, entertainment, and health-care sectors. Like most VCs, the firm reviewed about 250 new ideas a year and invested in only two or three. That's about 1 percent. To overcome those kinds of odds, you'd better make sure you have a good idea and a good pitch with which to deliver it.

I had met with Rick and his team over the weekend to help them prepare for the meeting. Now, with a knot in the pit of my stomach, I realized that little of my input was reflected in today's Monday-morning presentation. To make matters worse, their slides were in a black-and-red color scheme, looking more like a Victoria's Secret Valentine's lingerie promotion than a health-care technology pitch deck. I realized I had made assumptions about Rick's credentials, business idea, and readiness to meet with investors.

Maybe, I thought now, those assumptions were wrong.

Should I come to Rick's rescue? I was about to cut in on why I thought this could be a worthwhile opportunity—particularly because I noticed that, again contrary to my advice, some of the most important selling points were buried in the appendix of the deck that Christopher now looked very close to tossing in the nearest wastebasket.

But Rick spoke up enthusiastically, "Well, Christopher, sure, I can answer that," he said, and went on to explain that Medicare had recently launched a new program offering patient education to high-risk people with diabetes. His idea would help deliver the kind of information that would improve compliance and treatment outcomes. "While we plan to start with a phone and web portal as a pilot, we'd like to eventually partner with a technology platform company and build a software solution with a patient-friendly user interface. . . ." Rick didn't get to finish his statement because Christopher's partner, who had been listening quietly, writing notes in the margins of his copy of the slide deck, shot up his hand. "I'm with Christopher; this is not a technology solution. You're offering a service—one that is undifferentiated and will be expensive to maintain. Let's look at your financials."

At the end of the table was the CFO of Rick's start-up, a retired executive from a multinational investment bank with headquarters in New York. His silver-white hair contrasted with his bronze golfer's tan. He was sporting a pink dress shirt with a white tie and white sports coat. He had a deep broadcaster's voice and was more poised than Rick, who was now fidgeting nervously.

The CFO's presentation was as crisp as his perfectly knotted tie. "Can he save the pitch?" I thought to myself. But Christopher had spotted a flaw in the methodology—one that I noticed, as well. "That's a pretty aggressive forecast, and you just told me the program is for the high-risk patients, so the 100 percent penetration really doesn't make sense," he commented. He winked at his partner and I recognized that "gotcha" moment. "The meeting is over," I thought to myself.

Rick jumped in. "We have five health-care systems who've signed contracts committing to bring on board 16,000 patients the first three months," he said, speaking in the rapid-fire cadence of the desperate. "And that will ramp up to 50,000 by the following quarter. Our business model is subscription based, so we'll get a guaranteed revenue per patient each month."

Christopher looked at the clock and stood up. Our forty-five-minute slot was up. "I think you're overly confident if you think you are going to achieve 100 percent patient penetration in those five health-care systems. I think you need to scrub your business model and your numbers. Why don't we talk again after you've refined your solution and business model?"

Rick tried valiantly to end on a positive note. "Christopher, we think we have something really unique here, and we believe it is a great business idea and one we'd like to work with you on. We can make some adjustments so it better fits your profile. We'd like to do that and get back in touch with you."

Christopher was already at the door. "Thanks for coming in today and good luck with your plans." He motioned me to his office. I told Rick to meet me at the Starbucks downstairs.

Christopher shut the door and invited me to sit down. "Let's talk about this for a minute," he said. "I don't think either of us should waste any more time with these guys. That was the worst pitch I've ever seen. There may be a business idea here, but I can't see it, and certainly not with this team." I was going to say something about them having an off day, but I thought better of it as Christopher continued. "What I saw were three retired corporate executives with a scheme to create a business around a Medicare subsidy to doctors. Lots of risk given that the program is new and the problem is old. And there is no technology play here, although what you've told me about the partnership with the software company sounds promising." He paused. "And Rick says they don't have any competition? That was naïve."

I had to agree with Christopher. These entrepreneurs I'd helped as a favor to a friend had failed to make a clear and compelling presentation of their business proposition. "Put it this way, Christopher," I said. "If they were in my class, they'd have gotten an F for this presentation. No doubt. And for that I apologize."

He smiled as he rose and walked me to the door. "You're too nice to give anyone an F," he said with a chuckle. "I probably wouldn't either. But if you decide to straighten these guys out, let me know and I'll be happy to talk to them again. I've learned not to pull any punches—it's best they get candid feedback early on."

When I joined the guys at Starbucks, they queried me before I even sat down.

"Well, what did he say?" Rick asked. "Do you think there's a possibility they will want to invest?"

Clearly, they hadn't read the room. "Guys, remember, this was your first pitch and clearly a practice exercise. Christopher did this as a favor to me. And quite frankly, this wasn't what he . . . or I . . . expected. What happened to the pitch we discussed last weekend? The technology platform and strategic partnerships? The revenues that were based on 5 percent market penetration in year one and ramped more slowly? I thought we were aligned on the strategy and business opportunity. What you presented today was very different from what we worked on last weekend. What happened?"

Rick explained that he had met earlier in the week with an old friend from his pharmaceutical sales days, who had his own views on what the presentation should emphasize. "I revamped it based on his input last night. I guess I had cold feet. I'm sorry. I should have run it past you."

While Rick made every mistake in the book that day, I learned a big lesson, too—the hard way, as is often the case early in one's career. I had trusted a team I really didn't know and a business plan I had not thoroughly vetted. And I had moved too quickly to put a naïve team of entrepreneurs in front of investors, even if it was designed as a practice pitch and a friendly, albeit candid, exchange. Entrepreneurs need to stay focused, I told them. While you need to stay responsive to customer feedback, you can't be swayed to change direction based on the last conversation you had with a friend or colleague without doing some affirmation with at least a few other stakeholders. What's more, entrepreneurs must be "on message" and communicate clearly, succinctly, and with compelling, fact-based information. Investors are evaluating you in this first meeting. They're assessing whether to invest in your idea *and* your team.

WHAT CAN WE LEARN FROM THESE MISTAKES?

Let's look at what went wrong, with the investment thesis and with the pitch.

First, Rick and team **didn't know their audience**. They should have opened with the direct-to-consumer technology solution they were planning to build. Christopher's firm's website clearly stated that they were interested only in direct-to-consumer software solutions. VC firms use their websites to post their investment thesis and list the companies they've invested in. This is basic research and the first step in your diligence on potential investors.

Second, they **failed to describe a vision for a business model that could scale**. The solution they presented was only an MVP designed for local deployment—in this case, to become a viable customer, each state had to participate in the diabetes education reimbursement credit program. It was also restricted by the number of Medicare diabetes patients. The program had a risk in that it could be abandoned easily by a state and health-care providers. The Big Idea that they failed to note was that a major national health-care insurance company had expressed interest in being a strategic investor of their platform, if the pilot succeeded. That investment would have provided the scale needed and made them less dependent on Medicare in the future. Rick got caught up in the problem and the immediate next steps and failed to present the bigger opportunity that would appeal to an investor.

Third, the **team lacked credibility**. Rick and team were not serial entrepreneurs or innovators with a track record in corporations or start-ups. Nothing is inherently wrong with that—everyone needs to start somewhere—but they needed to share some credentials about problems they had solved and new concepts they had taken to market. They also needed to show a solid understanding of the business area they were pursuing. They had launched new products in their careers, but this didn't come through as a credential that gave them credibility to launch this new start-up. As Christopher noted, they were retired pharmaceutical executives tackling an age-old problem with what appeared to be an age-old solution—not a winning combination.

Fourth, the **pitch lacked focus and the team was unprepared** for questions, appearing disorganized when the questions were asked in an interrogatory manner. Even the CFO—the most polished presenter of the group—was working with flawed data, which undercut the gravitas he momentarily brought to the table.

Fifth, Rick **didn't follow the 10–20–30 rule (10 slides, 20 minutes, 30-point font)**. He spent more than half his pitch time on the problem, leaving no time for a discussion of the solution. If he had apportioned his time better, he would have opened opportunities to get into the technology and health-care system interest in a partnership. Also, his slides were distracting with a red-and-black color scheme, and the font he used was small and hard to read.

No surprise that Christopher didn't end up investing. Rick didn't raise any venture capital, and after six months, the team went their separate ways. Rick ultimately launched his diabetes program as a not-for-profit funded by the five health-care systems in New Jersey who adopted his program. I learned an important lesson, too. Since then, I always make sure to schedule a rehearsal with clients in advance of their pitch—so I can make sure their message is clear, their priorities are right, and their slides don't look like advertisements for a lingerie store.

KEYS TO A POWERFUL PITCH

We've looked at what happens when a pitch goes wrong, and why. Let's now examine the elements of one that is successful. What are the keys to a powerful pitch, a compelling story, that communicates your business idea and leaves the audience wanting more? Here are three keys:

Key 1. **Start with a clear, well-organized vision.** Investors should be excited about your vision for the future and confident in your ability to execute. Showcase your unique insight or advantage. Answer the big question: Why? Why is this new product going to transform the market? Why is this going to generate revenue for the company and for me, the investor? The best pitches get to the heart of "why" this product, "why now" is the right time to invest in this technology, and "why this is the winning team."

Key 2. Show investors a return on their investment in a time horizon that fits their investment thesis. This time frame is usually three to five years for VCs. This means having a compelling business case, one that shows that the sector is growing and demonstrates how the business will grow and when it will generate revenue and be profitable.

Key 3. Tell your story in fifteen to twenty minutes. Show, with data from market and customer research, how your idea is better than available solutions. Provide proof that you can get market adoption, and outline a pricing strategy and revenue forecast based on realistic assumptions that you can back up. While being passionate about the problem is important, being prepared with a compelling business case, and answers to detailed questions at the tip of your fingers, trumps passion.

THE ALL-STAR PITCH DECK, SLIDE BY SLIDE

Now, let's get down to the specifics of the presentation. The optimal pitch deck is no more than ten slides. That ensures that you will communicate only the most critical information on each major section of the business plan and that you spend two minutes on each slide, for the perfect twenty-minute pitch.

Here are the ten points you need to cover in ten slides in twenty minutes. (The order and detail you need to present are outlined in a pitch template in appendix 5. This link is to pitches for popular brands like Airbnb and TikTok: https://www.venngage.com/blog/best-pitch-decks/.)

Point 1. **A big problem and a big market,** showing that your idea addresses an area of unmet need—and a large market opportunity. This is where you need to think big and think inclusively. This is not the place to stake out some lonely outpost of innovation. Remember that investors want to play where dollars are being spent already.

Point 2. **A solution** that clearly outlines how your technology solves this problem, is better than the competition, and is one that you have tested with ample customer research.

Point 3. **The technology,** how it works, and what's backing it up. Have you filed patents? Do you have research studies to verify its effectiveness?

Point 4. **Customer and market research** that qualifies and quantifies the need and willingness to pay for the product.

Point 5. **Competition**—an honest assessment of where you stand against competitors. It's helpful to create a chart outlining features and benefits the customer is looking for and then evaluating yourself and the competition against these features and benefits.

Point 6. **A strategy road map** that shows how you're going to get to market and over what period of time, with details in the backup about critical milestones and financial inflection points.

Point 7. **Sales plan**—a description of the partnerships, channel partners, and sales force and how they will ramp up over time.

Point 8. **Team roles and relevant experience,** including the relevant credentials and experience that ensure your business will succeed. In this section you should include advisers who complement the team's soft spots. Also point out any gaps in talent, as you may be raising capital to hire needed talent. For example, if no one on the team has financial experience, you could hire a consultant until you need a part-time or full-time CFO.

Point 9. **Financial forecast** for three years, including how you'll get to first revenues.

Point 10. **A summary** that succinctly closes the deal and presents why this is the right solution at the right time and place. Make sure you restate how the investors will make money and by when.

A VC investor, coaching students in my Columbia University course on Venture Creation, summarized what he wants to see during a pitch: "I'm looking for the pain point and how you'll solve it; how you'll make money; how you'll reach customers with low acquisition cost; how you'll manage your cash burn and stage your financing." His advice to first-timers: "Start small, and conduct conscious experiments; make fixed costs variable costs; manage the nature and timing of commitments; stage your financing over time to preserve your equity; and stay flexible and ready to pivot."

Let me contrast the story about Rick and his diabetes education company with an example of a new technology that successfully raised $12 million in its first fund-raising event with a VC—and an astounding $100 million in its second. (In the world of venture capital, these initial and second, larger meetings with VCs are called series A and B.)

A PITCH WORTH $112 MILLION: HOW C2I GENOMICS SEALED THE DEAL

C2i Genomics is a New York City–headquartered research-stage venture that provides an AI-based genomics software service to potentially detect changes in an individual cancer patient's tumor at the genetic level. More sensitive than other diagnostic tools, it measures minimal residual disease, or MRD. It could be useful for detecting shrinkage in the tumor before and after chemotherapy and surgery.

Why could C2i raise money so successfully? What advantages did the company have?

Advantage 1. **The ability to meet an unmet need in a large market.** Oncology genomics (the genetics underlying cancer) is a popular and trendy area, especially for AI software models that are easy to apply and can give life-or-death information. It's a growth area. In 2021, estimates were that the cancer genomics market would be worth $39.4 billion by 2027.[1] The company's technology met an unmet need, better, by providing early insights into a patient's tumor.

Advantage 2. **Experienced team with known advisers.** C2i has a well-credentialed executive team with experience in oncology, genomics, and software development. The CEO is new to the start-up world, but he has learned the ropes fast and is surrounded by other strong executives and an impressive board, all of whom have experience in health-care technology start-ups. I observed them perform in client and investor meetings. They could answer any question about the field, technology, applications, and pricing accurately and with confidence. Their deep knowledge and understanding of their domain and the business environment gave investors confidence. You need to demonstrate the same command of your material, your industry, and your Big Idea.

Advantage 3. **Strong value proposition.** C2i offered a unique technology in a growing market and a solid business model that benefited doctors, patients, and the health-care system. Importantly, the company's financial model showed how the business would scale globally over the next three to five years and produce a handsome return on investment (ROI).

Advantage 4. **Financial forecast based on sound assumptions.** C2i team members recognized that for the first two years they would be building and validating their technology. They knew the earliest they could achieve revenues would be at the end of year 2, once they could secure income-generating research partnerships. Sales would occur in year 3 once they had the necessary regulatory approvals and had converted research partners into paying clients. This was confirmed with other similar companies that had experienced similar ramp-up to revenue. Investors appreciated the rigor and accuracy of their forecast.

Advantage 5. **Followed the 10–20–30 pitch rule.** C2i's pitch followed this formula to the letter. Another advantage of this approach is that it leaves plenty of time for questions and answers. It was challenging to simplify the messages on the more technical slides because of the complex science underlying the technology, but the company used charts and graphs to communicate the results of its studies and compared results to those of competitors to emphasize the relevance of the findings. Investors responded positively to the data and the competitive assessment.

Advantage 6. **The team was prepared.** The C2i presenters knew that nothing less than the future of the company's innovation could be riding on these presentations. They rehearsed and practiced, tweaking and refining their presentation to the point that it sounded smooth and conversational, not stiff and technical. Team participants sounded like they were ready to engage in a productive dialogue, showing their desire for coaching, mentoring, and partnership. That's what potential investors love to hear.

SOURCES OF CAPITAL

The end goal of all this preparation and rehearsal is, of course, funding. Let's examine the various sources of financial fuel to nurture your new business or idea.

For founders—that would be you, the innovator bringing a new idea or business concept to market—the cardinal rule when raising capital is to hold onto your equity for as long as you can so you can increase the company's value over time and, as a result, your share of the ROI. Founders should also be aware of how long it can take to raise capital and prepare accordingly. C2i started planning their second round of funding as soon as the check from the first round was in the bank. It can easily take six months or longer to raise funds, and if you wait too long to get started, you could damage the company's viability, becoming desperate and possibly making a bad decision.

YOUR OWN SKIN IN THE GAME

It's best to start a company by investing some of your own money— not enough that requires a second mortgage on your home but enough to garner you instant equity and to show investors that you have skin in the game. There is no "right" number. I've seen entrepreneurs invest $1,000 of their own money to get started and others invest $1 million. It depends on the business, the stage, and your personal financials.

FRIENDS AND FAMILY

Next, you can ask friends and family members about their interest in investing alongside you. As you read in the last chapter, Sarah Apgar did this successfully when she launched what would become FitFighter. She started with a few trusted friends—including one who had worked alongside her in the firehouse and thoroughly understood the concept of this new fitness product—and an uncle who had always encouraged her entrepreneurial instincts and had said he would be willing to back her when the right idea came along.

This was the right idea—and Apgar found the right people from among her inner circle of friends and family to help her get it off the ground.

Friends and family usually invest modest amounts of starter capital to help you conduct market research, design and conduct your MVP, and secure key advisers and consultants to help with the next stages of business planning. You can convert their investment to stock or debt to be repaid once the company achieves a key financial milestone, such as generating revenues or securing other forms of investment.

A word of caution: even with these modest thresholds, I recommend approaching only those who are investment savvy and can afford to lose some money if your endeavor is not successful. It's tough enough (although common) to fail your first time out with an innovative product or new business—you don't need to lose a relationship with a close friend or loved one along with it.

CROWDFUNDING

In the age of the Internet, where just about any idea imaginable has been launched as an app, capital is accessible to anyone with a bank account and a computer. While crowdfunding (raising money from nonqualified investors in the general public) has been around for centuries, platform-based websites such as Kickstarter, Indiegogo, and Wefunder have gained considerable popularity since their arrival on the self-funding scene in the first decade of the 2000s. These crowdfunding platforms started out small, with funding seekers using the sites to raise money for concert tours, medical procedures, and creative projects like art exhibits. (You'll learn about one such artist in the Innovator in Focus section of this chapter.) However, these platforms have grown to become legitimate sourcing pools for major companies to raise capital.

In 2019, products such as PaMu Slide earphones raised $51.49 million; and in 2020, MATE X, a foldable eBike, raised $17.8 million. According to an August 2021 report published by statista.com, the crowdfunding market size globally is expected to reach $25.8 billion by 2027, with the largest markets in North America and Asia. Crowdfunding sites typically operate on several different models that can meet the needs of the project seeking funding. The most notable types of funding are reward based (you can earn points to spend on products), equity (stock), and digital (bitcoin). Funding can be bitcoin on the blockchain, debt with interest, and donation based (free money for a worthy cause). Kickstarter, Wefunder, and Indiegogo are appealing to investors because they can reduce the search and transaction costs of seeking investment opportunities through advisory firms. While they do not offer the large amounts of capital that VCs or angels can provide, crowdfunding platforms are a viable funding source for new and emerging companies with innovative ideas where several thousand dollars is all that's needed to get started. For more information, visit these crowdfunding websites: kickstarter.com, wefunder.com, and indiegogo.com.

ANGELS

The best source of seed or start-up capital is from the so-called angel community. The term *angel* can be traced back to 1978, when William Wetzel, a professor at the University of New Hampshire and founder of its Center for Venture Research, completed a study on how entrepreneurs raised seed capital in the United States.[2] He used the term *angel* to describe successful wealthy entrepreneurs and executives who wanted to invest in early-stage ideas. The term was also used on Broadway to describe wealthy individuals who backed new shows from producers and directors they admired.

Unlike friends and family and crowdfunding capital sources, an angel is considered a qualified investor. To be an angel investor you must fulfill the Securities and Exchange Commission (SEC) criteria, which include having a net worth of $1 million or more. These investors can be self-made millionaires who have made it on their own and have substantial business and financial expertise. Likely to be in their forties or fifties they are a well-educated group, with nearly all having achieved a four-year college degree. While angels are still dominated by men, that's changing, and there are now more female entrepreneurs and angel investment groups. Women investor groups such as 37 Angels, Golden Seeds, Springboard Enterprises, and others have been developed to help advance women entrepreneurs and investors. (We will look at the topic of women and innovation in more detail in chapter 10.)

And yes, as Apgar from FitFighter also demonstrated, the popular ABC program *Shark Tank* is a bona fide angel investing group, albeit a reality TV show and a form of entertainment. While *Shark Tank* makes pitching angels look one-sided and intimidating (the sharks hold the cards), one of the positive messages they communicate after they make a decision to invest is the strong relationship they form with the entrepreneur. Business is about people, and the best businesses are based on strong talent and effective partnerships. Similarly, a successful investor outcome is only as good as the partnership that underpins the business. Partnerships take time to cultivate because they must be built on mutual trust and values. An investment from an angel is personal because that person, unlike VCs and private equity and investment bankers, is investing his or her own money in a high-risk situation. Plan on spending about six months cultivating investor relationships. Anything less than that is reason for pause. You just can't learn everything you need to know about a potential investor relationship unless you really spend time together, discussing the business and meeting over lunch and dinner to learn more about each other.

ANGEL INVESTOR CRITERIA

According to *New Venture Creation*, the typical angel will invest $10,000–250,000 in a new venture, which is a very broad range.[3] They're looking for certain criteria:

- Ventures with capital requirements between $50,000 and $500,000
- Ventures with sales potential of between $2 million and $20 million in five to ten years
- Ventures with sales and profit growth of 10–20 percent per year

If your business or product doesn't fit into those parameters, that doesn't mean your innovative idea is dead on arrival. Each angel investor may have her or his own criteria. Remember, unlike friends and family and crowdfunding sources, these investors often add more than just capital. They offer domain expertise and a vast network. An angel investor's experience can be invaluable to a young company.

CHOOSING THE INVESTOR THAT'S RIGHT FOR YOUR INNOVATION

You should think of raising capital as a multistep process. In the first round, you'll want to choose investors based on their ability to open the door to future investors. Angels usually participate in an angel investment club or group to create a larger investing pool than they could provide on their own. They also share intelligence about those who are asking them for money. Finding these informal investors isn't always easy, but you can seek angels through the Angel Capital Association (https://www.angelcapitalassociation.org), the Angel Investment Network, (https://www.angelinvestmentnetwork. us), and PitchBook (https://pitchbook.com/), an investor database.

As you contact angels to schedule a meeting, be ready to provide an executive summary of your idea. Think of this as an even more abridged version of the nice, concise deck we discussed earlier. An executive summary (a sample can be found in appendix 4) is a one-page narrative or a couple of slides that describe in simple terms the market opportunity, your value proposition, how the business will make money, the team's credentials, and how the investor makes money. (Angels have an opportunity to exit and get their financial returns when the next set of investors, often VCs, take a significant share of the company.) We'll discuss exits in the next chapter, but suffice it to say that knowing your endgame is critical to you and investor. For example, do you want to partner and merge with a large strategic acquirer? Do you want to do an IPO and take the company public? Do you plan to exit in three to five years, or longer?

You can expect to raise capital in six months with both angels and VCs. Let's look at the next level of capital—venture.

VENTURE CAPITAL

The word *venture* suggests that this type of capital conveys a degree of risk. The VC industry supplies capital and other resources to entrepreneurs in business with high growth potential in hopes of achieving a high rate of return on invested funds. This process has many layers—but first, some background on the industry. Although the roots of VC go back to wealthy families in the 1920s and 1930s, most industry observers credit Ralph E. Flanders, then president of the Federal Reserve Bank of Boston (and later a U.S. senator from Vermont), with the first form of VC investing. In 1946 he founded the American Research and Development Corporation, which provided risk capital to new and rapidly growing companies in the Boston area. Indeed, some credit the firm with providing the initial money to some of the companies that would eventually make up Boston's famous Route 128 tech-belt, an early hotbed of digital innovation.[4]

The industry experienced a long-awaited growth spurt in the 1980s when academic institutions such as Harvard, Columbia, Yale, and Stanford decided to invest a portion of their endowments in high-risk, high-reward mechanisms. The VC industry decided that risk capital was a good way to spawn technologies out of academia and further develop them. A famous example is the Axel patents. Named after Nobel laureate and Columbia professor Richard Axel, these were originally issued in 1983 to protect the "co-transformation" technology developed in the 1970s by Axel, microbiologist

TABLE 8.1

VC investors: The basics

What you should know	What they are looking for
• VCs are organized as limited partners or limited liability corporations and represent a pooled investment vehicle for third parties, such as universities, corporations, and pension funds.	• Experienced teams that have start-up experience (serial entrepreneurs)
• They are a good choice when an investment is too risky for capital market or bank loans.	• Large markets with high growth rates where high customer pain is obvious
• VCs make their money on management fees (1–2 percent of fund) and carry (20–30 percent of what is left over after they have paid their investors).	• Great products with order-of-magnitude improvement and high barriers to entry
• They operate a portfolio of companies designed to maximize return to their investors.	• Like "hot" areas where others are investing
• They focus on exit by acquisition or IPO.	• Assess risk: upside and downside potential and trade-offs of market, technology, timing
• They invest where they have experience, network, and where others are investing.	• Anticipated growth rate (seek a multiple of three to seven times their investment)
• They like innovative, technically sound technology; strong market for $$ and great team.	• Age and stage of development (early-stage series A, later-stage series C)
• VCs are good at reducing risk (their risk, not yours!). A typical deal will give a VC 51 percent ownership. VC funding is considered the most expensive type of money.	• Amount of capital required (usually they raise a fund for a particular type of investment—e.g., digital health or green energy—and look for companies in that sector who need a certain amount of capital)
	• Founder's goals for growth, control, liquidity, and harvest. How much money does the founder want to walk away with at the time of exit, and when and how will exit be executed?
	• Fit with investors' goal and strategy
	• Capital markets at the point in time. Is it a good market, down market?
	• Carry fee—usually a management fee of 3 percent

Source: Professor Marchand lecture material on capital raising.

TABLE 8.2
VC investor selection criteria

Criteria	Good match	Bad match
Capital	• Can provide adequate capital to achieve all milestones tied with investment round	• Can provide partial capital, requiring you to engage another VC / other investors to meet your fund-raising objectives
Aligned interests and expertise	• Understands your industry, stage of business, and associated challenges and opportunities • Relevant experience (or access to experience) to increase likelihood of success, product adoption, or ability to penetrate new markets • True partner—invested in supporting your overall business (vs. narrowly interested in a component of business—e.g., intellectual property only)	• New to the industry, does not understand challenges / opportunities adequately, and ties success to purely financial metrics
Reputation	• Has served as a fair and ethical partner to other portfolio companies (do your due diligence on crowdsource sites—e.g., pitchbook.com)	• Reputation for treating portfolio companies unfairly
Track record	• Strong track record of successful deal making • Portfolio companies have benefited by partnership with VC	• Track record of predatory practices
Control	• Seeks to invest at a fair / acceptable valuation	• Seeks too much control over the company

Source: Professor Marchand lecture material on capital raising.

Saul Silverstein, and geneticist Michael Wigler. The patented process involves using genetically engineered cells to produce proteins used in many pharmaceutical drugs. It proved immensely profitable to Columbia over the seventeen years it was protected, generating $600 million in royalty revenues on drugs that produced more than $60 billion for the industry.[5] Columbia's success grabbed the attention of other esteemed universities that established technology transfer offices to help advance new technologies from the professor's lab to the market.

By 2000, VCs had taken off. According to *New Venture Creation*, there were seven hundred venture firms with $3.94 billion invested in 1,729 companies in the United States alone. Over time, individual VC funds have grown to greater than $500 million, with an average deal size of $20 million, $40 million, and even $80 million, especially during the dotcom frenzy.[6] Today, many VCs specialize in technology and digital, especially in health care, energy, and agriculture. VC investing is now a global enterprise, with funds in Germany and France and across China, Vietnam, India, and Latin America.

DO YOUR HOMEWORK AND USE THIS CHECKLIST

Raising capital takes six months for a reason. You need to use this time to investigate VCs. The following checklist will help you get started.

Step 1. **Research and create a short list of VCs you'd like to meet in person.** Pitchbook.com is the one of the best sources of information about VCs. Once you have names of a few, visit their blogs and check them out on Instagram and Twitter.

Step 2. **Get a personal introduction through your network.** Once you have singled out the firm, look at the resumes of the managing partners. Visit their LinkedIn profiles and identify those in your network who can make warm introductions.

Step 3. **Get to "no" quickly.** You don't want to waste your time and neither does the VC, so look for a match between the VC's investment criteria and your requirements. If the two don't align, move on, but make sure you stay on good terms.

QUESTIONS ENTREPRENEURS SHOULD ASK

VCs have enormous fiduciary responsibility to their limited partners and self-interest in making money for the firm and themselves. Remember, they see, on average, 250 new ideas a year and may invest in only two or three of those. That's 1 percent—and those are the odds that founders are typically facing.

Expect VCs to be thorough in their diligence, and use the experience to learn as much as you can about their opinions and view of your industry, technology, and team. You can ask the following:

- What do you think of our strategy and the competition? Anything we missed?
- Have we missed any competitors? Suggestions on how competitive we are?
- Any thoughts on our business plan to seize the opportunity?
- Team experience—do you have confidence in our team to execute based on what you saw today and have seen from us so far?

OTHER TYPES OF INVESTMENT TO CONSIDER

- **Academic medical center tech transfer.** If you have an affiliation with an academic research institution, such as Columbia University, you can work with its technology transfer office to determine if your technology is commercially viable and can attract investors. Tech transfer offices are staffed with patent attorneys and technical experts who work with a network of investors. They can be an ideal way to explore the commercial market, particularly if you are a first-timer.
- **Foundations.** Although highly competitive programs, foundations offer grants that don't have to be paid back. They can be a good source of capital for start-ups that need to conduct a research project to back their claims. In exchange for the grant, you may need to prepare a report discussing the outcome of the project you funded with the foundation's grant or publish a paper in a peer-reviewed journal of the foundation's choice. A few examples include the Bill

and Melinda Gates Foundation, the Michael J. Fox Foundation, the Juvenile Diabetes Foundation, and the Cystic Fibrosis Foundation.

- **Federal and state sponsorship.** Federal and state programs can offer innovation funds and tax incentive programs to supplement the development of a new technology or start-up of a new venture. Considered nondilutive because they are grants and do not have to be paid back, these are often seen as "free" forms of capital. They can help when you're getting started by funding key projects— for example, research to validate your technology. The downside is that these grants can take up to two years to secure because of the program cycle time, so they are not a good option if you need fast funding.

- **The Small Business Innovation Research (SBIR) and Small Business Technology Transfer (STTR) programs.** Federally sponsored, these programs are highly competitive and aim to encourage small businesses to engage in federal research and traditional R&D. SBIR and STTR create this engagement by facilitating a relationship between small/medium businesses and nonprofit research institutions. These programs require collaboration with a research institution throughout phase 1 (approximate grant of $170,000) and phase 2 (up to $1.2 million), with the goal of bridging the gap between basic science and commercialization of innovations. The SBIR website (https://www.sbir.gov/) lists the research institutions and agencies that work with SBIR and STTR. The amount of funds available is usually equivalent to 1 percent of each agency's budget. These are a few of the more popular agencies:

  - National Institutes of Health
  - Department of Defense
  - National Science Foundation

- **Biomedical Advanced Research and Development Authority (BARDA).** Nearly all corporations have internal VCs or make strategic investments in technology that fits their portfolio and even that doesn't. Corporations that earmark funds for early-stage ventures include Microsoft Corporation, Fidelity Investments, and Google Ventures.

A FINAL WORD: YOU NEVER KNOW WHERE FUNDING WILL COME FROM

On one end of the spectrum, you have the Gates Foundation, the NIH, or a successful VC firm. On the other, you have the more informal and grassroots forms of funding that have arisen in the past few years. Can successful innovations be launched through crowdfunding sites like GoFundMe? Certainly—although they are usually smaller initiatives, requiring less money, and are often focused on social causes. But they, along with social media, can be an effective if highly informal network of funds for a new business model—as our Innovator in Focus for this chapter has proven.

INNOVATOR IN FOCUS

"Nomad" Dan Navarro, Musician

Songwriter. Recording artist. Singer. Voice arts advocate.

To the list of credits that one can attribute to musician Dan Navarro—whose songs have enjoyed national radio airplay and been recorded by such rock and pop luminaries as Pat Benatar, the Temptations, the Bangles, Dionne Warwick, Dave Edmunds, and Austin country music outlaw Rusty Weir—we add entrepreneur and innovator.

Navarro demonstrated his business creativity during the COVID epidemic, when performers of all kinds were unable to ply their livelihood as theaters, concert venues, and even roadside joints were closed to live music—and to anything else, for that matter.

When the shutdowns went into effect, Navarro—who was typically touring three weeks a month before 2020—was suddenly stopped in his tracks. "I'm thinking 'What am I going to do?'" says the sixty-eight-year-old musician. He decided to stream a new song—"I Guess I'll See You Tomorrow," written expressly for the lockdown—that he played live to his 21,000 social media followers.

"I said, 'Hi, guys, looks like we're going to be stuck home for a while, so I'm just going to play for you."

The one-time, live Facebook show turned into six days a week. It was rechristened as "Songs from the Corona Zone," a sort of pandemic-era one-man social media show, in which Dan played and talked about his life in the music industry. The response of the audience convinced him that he needed to get back on the road. In early 2021, after getting vaccinated, he bought a 2020 Ram Pro Master with 6,000 miles on it and under his new sobriquet—NomadDan—began traversing the country, announcing his shows on social media hours, sometimes minutes, beforehand. (He also gave his RV a name—Vanessa.)

"I figured I could stream the entire way," he said. "It would be like 'Here I am in Ogallala, Nebraska, I'm going to play a few songs for you. Let's talk. I have a schedule of concerts, but we don't know what's going to be cancelled.'"

The hybrid approach and fluid, improvisational nature of the tour—so different from the structured, carefully orchestrated rock tours of the past—appealed to Dan, and apparently his audiences.

They began sending him money.

That was a surprise, as the NomadDan tour was not envisioned as a moneymaker. "I have a pretty good royalty stream," Dan said. And with no other band members, no roadies, and no hotels, he knew his expenses would be low. "So, I purposely did not monetize it," he noted.

But his fans had other ideas. As the NomadDan tour evolved—he would eventually do about fifty public performances in twenty-one states over six months—an adage he'd heard from friends in the not-for-profit worlds was confirmed. "They used to tell me, 'If you ask for money, you're going to get offered help. If you ask for help, you're going to get offered money.'"

Which is exactly what his fans have done. They send money—even though Dan has not solicited it. "One guy in Chicago sends me $200 a month, without fail," he said. It's not as if these fans see NomadDan as a charity—or that they just have money to burn. They're paying for a service they feel Dan has provided them during a very difficult time. Reading some of the comments he's gotten (along with checks or Zelle and Venmo deposits), he noted, "'You're saving me,' 'We wait all day for this,' and 'It's become a ritual for us.'"

"I wanted to break even," Dan said. "I'm doing that and able to pay a few bills. Which is all I need at this point in my life."

Lessons learned

After decades as a successful working artist, Dan feels he's grasped a truism about business that's relevant to all entrepreneurs, not only those who strum guitars for a living. "When you try to *think* where things are going, to predict a public, you probably miss," he says. "It's like trying to catch fish with your hands, you're always just one step behind. But when you *feel* it and use your inner sense of what is great, and what *you* want, and apply intelligence, sensitivity, and fearlessness to its execution and marketing, you wind up warping a paradigm."

You can't make this up

Dan's song that he wrote for Pat Benatar, "We Belong," was nominated for a Grammy. Dutch superstar Marco Borsato had a Top 10 hit with a Navarro-penned tune, and Japanese girl-group Wink hit #1 with his "One Night in Heaven."

His songs have also appeared in the films *Deadpool 2*, *Pitch Perfect 2*, and *Talladega Nights*; TV series *This Is Us*, *Stumptown*, *American Idol*, *The Voice*, *American Dad*, and *The Office*; and national commercials for Pepsi, Sheraton, Chase Bank, and the United Way.

Insight for innovators

"The only answer for an entrepreneur is 'yes.'"

"My uncle was in advertising, and I learned a lot about business and marketing from him. He once told me, 'If you don't get burned once in a while, you're not taking sufficient business risk.' That never left my head.

"There are three elements of success: talent, persistence, and luck. The most expendable—the one you need least—is talent. The most important is persistence, and that's how you create luck."

Learn more about Navarro at https://dannavarro.com.

9

EXECUTION AND EXIT

Managing Your Innovation, and If Necessary, Moving On

When my father founded his chemical manufacturing and distribution company in the 1960s, he wanted it to create wealth and a livelihood for his family in addition to offering a differentiated product to the market. "I want to translate my ideas into a business that I build and leave as a legacy," he told his wife and children. "It will be the inheritance I leave my family," he told my mother when he bought the intellectual property for a chemical formula that became the backbone of his business. Building a legacy business for his family was Dad's motivation for starting a regional company that would stand the test of time—a business with strong supplier and customer relationships. He looked for synergies and developed new products based on his customers' feedback and market demands. He called all the shots based on his creative ideas about growth and his financial and strategic goals. He wanted a company with a strong brand reputation and sustainable business model that he could pass on to his children. When he was ready to retire from the business and tackle new interests, he asked my husband, an experienced industrial electric supply sales executive, if he was interested in purchasing the business for cash that would be paid out over time.

We sat on the porch on a hot summer day in August, and my father presented Don with the term sheet and his expectations. In a neat twenty-page report, in a binder, Dad had carefully detailed the company's financials, suppliers, sales and marketing plans, operating reports, real estate, and equipment and customer lists. "And here are the terms of the acquisition, Don," he concluded, turning to the last page as he walked my husband through the proposal. "I'll stay involved for the first year while you transition. You can pay for the business in quarterly installments over a period we can agree to."

For the next several hours, they went over the details of the business, line by line. The decision wasn't easy, as my husband, Don, wasn't a chemist or an engineer; he had a successful sales career at the time. But this offered him the opportunity to try something new—running his own business. He knew my father would be around to help with the transition, and it afforded us some flexibility while raising a family of three young sons. Plus, he knew it was important to my dad that the business—a business that had been built on my dad's innovative ideas about chemical manufacturing and distribution—stay in the family.

My husband and I agreed to acquire the company that day in August. While the business has changed over the years, my husband continues to manage it today. Those solid relationships and the strategy my father put in place years ago have enabled the company to survive for the past fifty-five years.

Not all successful innovators have the same goal as my dad. Many aren't interested in legacy or in running the business in perpetuity. They're interested in selling or licensing. Or they may want to develop the business to a certain point and then cash out. Those are both common scenarios for many innovators.

Imagine it, build it, sell it, and move on to the next idea.

The innovator may design the product, and even the company, to fit the needs of an eventual strategic partner who will invest in or acquire the company.

All of these are laudable goals. What's yours? What's your ultimate objective with your Big Idea? Have you even thought that far ahead? I know that you've got a lot of work to do—the various steps and stages of the innovation process that we've laid out to this point. In this chapter, we offer you a few more suggestions on how to ensure success in the early going and increase the likelihood that your innovation will grow to the point that you have to determine what comes next—a successful legacy business, a successful salable business, or something else.

That's a good decision to have to make. I hope you will find yourself in that situation.

Now let's review a few more of the things that can help get you to that point. Let's look at what it takes to run an early-stage company successfully, regardless of what your endgame is.

IMPLEMENTATION SUCCESS
STARTS WITH THE RIGHT TEAM

Once you've vetted your innovation with stakeholders and customers and developed your launch plans, you're ready to take your product to market. It's time to execute the plan! You need people who can help you do just that. I've witnessed many innovators struggle to take their new solution to market because they lacked a team who could deliver. It's one thing to design conceptual plans; it's quite another to implement them.

Hiring the right talent starts with assessing your organization's needs, based on your business model and plans for growth. A typical start-up, even a new product launch in an established large organization, requires key roles, but we're not talking about a complex organizational hierarchy. For a start-up, it may be most efficient to staff your organization with two or three senior leaders with broad management and operational experience who can oversee several functions and perform multiple types of tasks. For example, the CEO may also serve as chairman of the board, lead strategy, represent the company to investors, clients, and other critical external stakeholders, and handle day-to-day operations. The chief financial officer (CFO) is an important link to investors but will also need to prepare financial forecasts, play a role in setting strategy, manage cash, and oversee operations, including administrative functions, contracts, salary planning, and even human resources. For this reason, it can make sense to hire a CFO who also plays the role of chief operations officer (COO). Often these roles are called CFO/COO. You'll also need a chief business officer or a director of business development to focus on partnerships and early stages of business development, marketing, and sales. As the company grows, sales and marketing may report directly to the CEO to ensure alignment with strategy and to signify the importance of the customer in the company's strategy. If you are launching a business that is dependent on R&D and continued product innovation, then you'll need a head of R&D to manage product development and a product manager to handle all aspects of the product, from product road-map planning to market assessments and customer engagement to pricing, sales, and marketing. This person is the mini-CEO of the product. If you decide to give these senior leaders fiduciary responsibilities in the company—holding them accountable for financial performance and having a vote on investment matters and a board seat—then you will title them officers (e.g., chief business officer) of the company. This role does come with the expectation of equity (the officer has ownership in the company commensurate with his or her responsibilities). While you probably want to start with three key roles—CEO, CFO/COO, and chief technology officer who also oversees R&D—you can fill in the gaps with contractors and part-time staff while the company grows.

And for solopreneurs, or those with innovative ideas for small, niche businesses, these roles might be filled, in part, by a wisely selected group of subcontractors, not-for-profits, or committed volunteers.

Serial biotech entrepreneur and Columbia Business School alumnus Laurence Blumberg, who we met in the chapter on capital raising, staffed one of his start-ups using a virtual model. He was the company's only employee as the CEO for the first two and a half years and outsourced every other position.

"I hired the best contractors in their respective fields for critical expertise in clinical development, regulatory, and legal," he explains. "It was a very efficient and cost-effective way for us to operate in the early years."

Often, start-up founders have questions about how to find good talent, whether contractors or full-time. This is an important question and one that the CEO spends a lot of time and energy on—identifying and recruiting the right talent. While it may sound obvious, I recommend starting with your own network and branching out from there. All the start-ups I cofounded or joined resulted from my own connections in industry. When the cofounder of our molecular diagnostics company was seeking a CEO, a colleague who had worked with me and knew my background referred him to me. When I assumed the lead at another start-up, it was for a company I had mentored at a start-up accelerator. It takes time to build trust, which is often the one thing a start-up is lacking. High-quality personal connections can help you bridge the gap and secure good talent that is reputable and comes recommended by people you know and trust.

You can also use networking sources such as LinkedIn to contact people or to ask for referrals. LinkedIn includes a feature for recruiters, and while it costs a little more, it can give you access to people who fit your specifications. Other sources of candidates can include business incubators and professional associations. For example, Columbia Business School, New York University, the University Sciences Center in Philadelphia, LaunchPad at Stanford University, and Techstars Austin Accelerators (to name a few) operate accelerator programs for start-ups. CEOs of the start-ups receive access to select mentors and coaches as part of their participation. These individuals are matched with companies based on functional expertise and industry knowledge. They can be a great way to secure talent for your advisory board, consultants for projects, and even part-time senior professionals in operations, fundraising, strategy, and marketing.

Finally, you can attract good talent using the services of recruiting agencies who specialize in searches for executives or management-level professionals. These firms work either on contingency or on a retainer. A retainer, an exclusive contract, is best suited to hiring hard-to-recruit senior-level talent. Other firms operate on contingency, meaning they accept the risk of identifying talent and you pay them only if you end up hiring the person they recommend. Some of these firms specialize in start-ups and have budgets that are consistent with the start-up's lean financials. Others will work in exchange for equity or debt in the company and adjust their rates and payment terms. To find these types of companies, you can check with VC and angel investor associations, which often list service providers such as talent-recruiting agencies, law firms, and accounting firms that specialize in providing services to early-stage innovators. Your needs may differ based on whether you are at seed stage or on your series C; these firms can grow with you.

THE BIG QUESTION:
HOW MUCH SHOULD I PAY MY NEW TEAM?

The next question to ask is, how do I compensate my team? How can I offer a competitive financial package to a high-quality senior leader who has worked in the corporate world or may have the financial expectations of a corporate executive? First off, individuals interested in a start-up should be aware that the job and compensation will be different. When I took my first job with a start-up as CEO, I took a salary cut, but in turn I received a handsome equity position. I knew the equity would be paid in the longer term and only if we were successful, but that was my incentive to perform and produce. So, the incentives and metrics in a start-up versus a corporation or even a growth company are very different. Make sure you and the person you are recruiting are aware of what they are stepping into. Some corporate executives find the start-up world alluring, but when they learn more about the lack of structure in the organization and the need to wear many hats, coupled with a different incentive model, many find they can't make the transition. Crowdsource websites, including glassdoor.com and ziprecruiter. com, provide compensation baselines for different industries, types, and stages of companies and geographies so you can get a sense of compensation packages.

I recommend that start-ups and early-stage companies seek compensation advice from a professional human resources (HR) consultancy (hr-guide.com). These firms specialize in market research on compensation; help with talent planning, including compensation models; and even help with governance models and compensation for the board. The investment you make for a few hours of their time to assess your situation and needs is well spent. These experts can help you avoid some common mistakes when you are hiring and planning compensation for your first new hires. The biggest mistake I see is offering too low a salary and too much equity. The problem here is that you don't want to disadvantage a new hire from a cash perspective. Equity is a long-term incentive. People have bills they need to pay now. Also, you may give away too much equity in your company at the expense of others you want to give equity to, including yourself. The HR professional can help you create a medium-term plan based on your growth and financial goals. They can help ensure you can woo good talent but at the same time aren't putting the company in jeopardy with the compensation models you're putting in place. They can also help in developing job descriptions, goals and objectives, and key performance indicators and in planning your training program and management system.

In addition to comprehensive talent planning and management, you'll also need a management system with helpful tools to run the company, depending on your size and growth goals. (Clearly, a very small company can handle the items below in-house or may not even need all these management components. But as a company scales, it's important to ensure that processes and technology can support the growing business.) A management system includes setting project management standards for how work will be done, how you'll manage resources and budgets, and how you'll run projects on time. You will also need a system for managing customers and stakeholder outreach.

Tools such as Salesforce are very popular for managing and tracking contacts, activities, and next steps, especially if several people in the company are interacting with customers, investors, and channel partners. While Salesforce can be a big investment for a start-up, less expensive and less robust systems are available for managing relationships. At a minimum, start with an Excel spreadsheet and a business development analyst who can manage and track for you weekly.

Your management system will also include creating processes for how you want tasks performed, managing and storing critical documentation, and even developing standard operating procedures and providing training to your employees. Training may include information security if you're handling client information in a database or interacting with sensitive data. There are also federal and state trainings on compliance with laws around discrimination. And then, of course, there is training in how to do the work at your company.

You'll want to identify the technology you'll use in the company—everything from email and messaging systems to HR tools for managing salary planning, payroll, insurance, and a website for customer interactions and engagement. You'll need someone to oversee IT. This is an area where you can use a consultant or agency for support.

A knowledge management system is an important means of creating a learning culture and encouraging continuous process improvement. Learning from your experiences is critical, as is capturing those learnings so you can share them with employees and inculcate them in the business. It's a great way to start things off on the right foot and ensure that you create the management system and culture you want.

START WITH STEPHEN COVEY IN MIND

How do successful companies chart a path toward growth and continuous value creation for owners and shareholders? Do you want to maintain your company as a going concern or form a strategic partnership or some other type of merger and acquisition (M&A)? In 1989, the self-help author Steven R. Covey's *Seven Habits of Highly Effective People* hit the bookstores with a firestorm. The number of workshops based on his book were dizzying. Even the National Institutes of Health (NIH), where I worked at the time, offered a two-day seminar to ensure that government employees were trained in the Covey method of performance management. The quintessential chapter, "Start with the End in Mind," opened with an exercise that encouraged you to imagine your funeral and what friends, family, and coworkers were saying about you. That drew a lot of attention and was an effective way to get people to think about their future goals.

This metaphor, start with the end in mind, is appropriate when planning your start-up. It's important to ask yourself, first, what is my goal? What does my exit or harvest look like? You're not going to be working forever, and your company may not outlive you. You need to know what you want to do with your company, your innovation, when you are no longer managing it. Earlier in the book we met Leslie Aisner Novak from HowdaDesignz, the inventor of a specially designed chair for adults with back problems and children with autism. Leslie took the long view on her now-successful business from the get-go. "I realized the most important question I needed to ask myself when founding Howda was what my exit strategy was," she said. "Did I want to run the business as a lifestyle company, sell it off, or merge at some point? Once I answered that question, everything fell into place."

Leslie makes an important point: Know your endgame. Having a vision of the kind of company you're developing, and over what time horizon, is critical to your strategy and affects all your decision-making.

At ZipStitch, a technology that could replace traditional sutures in certain types of surgery, the founders designed their technology to be acquired by a large medical device manufacturing company that served the vast surgery suture market. They studied the acquirers, designed the clinical studies needed for regulatory approval, and developed the customer relationships needed in a way that fit the pool of the acquiring company's business model. They then met with several members of the acquiring team early in the development process to cultivate their interest and input in the technology.

When the time was right, they had positioned themselves for a successful merger.

WHAT IS YOUR EXIT STRATEGY?

Exit strategies are imperative to becoming a successful innovator, as they offer big payoffs for years of hard work. My dad had his exit strategy in mind for years—and the fact that his business is still profitable and still being run by a member of his family shows that his end goal strategy was a sound one.

While the reward of being a great innovator can be derived from your ideas' becoming reality, financial success can be a significant incentive to creating and tweaking both new and existing ideas. The security offered by large income streams can also help innovators take bigger risks with their ideas and investments. This type of behavior helps break the mold of status quo thinking and encourages innovative products and services. Elon Musk would not have been able to expand into new areas of business, such as space travel and electric cars, if he had not cashed out of his first commercially successful venture, PayPal, to the tune of $180 million as reported by the billionaire.

HARVEST GOALS

While an exit is a transfer-of-business event in the company's history, a harvest is an opportunity for the founder to extract value from the company. There are some factors to keep in mind when evaluating a successful exit strategy and effectively navigating harvest options that separate serial entrepreneurs from one-time failures. Successful entrepreneurs create jobs and wealth, not just a means of living.

A harvest goal can be used by someone seeking to enter a new venture to assess what type of end results they want to realize when the venture is finished. The harvest goal could be to sell off the company to a strategic partner by the third year of a venture or it could be to go public in the same time window. Either way, a harvest goal provides focus for the venture. In the mid-1980s, a time when the computer software industry was performing poorly, entrepreneurship author Steve Holmberg surveyed one hundred companies and found that 80 percent of them were focused on short-term strategy. This isn't surprising. When a company struggles to survive and then starts its ascent, the furthest thing from the founder's mind may be planning an exit—but that's exactly what he or she should be doing. Often, it isn't until a financial crisis hits that founders think about selling. By then, they are scrambling to develop an exit plan and are at risk of considerably undervaluing their company. Harvest goals are just one step in creating a successful strategy and are necessary for ensuring a company is sustainable.

TIMING

Timing can be the difference between making $200,000 or $200,000,000 from a transaction. When Mark Zuckerberg was offered $1 billion for Facebook in 2006, he turned down the investors at Yahoo. Many financial analysts at the time called it a completely misguided and miscalculated sense of optimism that Zuckerberg would spend the rest of his life regretting. Today, Facebook is worth more than $300 billion. In the early 2000s, Blockbuster Video was presented with the opportunity of acquiring a DVD delivery service called Netflix. Blockbuster declined and eventually filed for bankruptcy in 2010. Obviously, hindsight is 20/20, but these two are prime examples of how the right timing can determine how much value you derive from your venture.

Many founders choose to exit out of fear brought on by a tough economic downturn or struggles within the company. Acting out of fear is not considered a practical strategy when planning an exit scenario. Instead, having harvest goals well in advance can help you assess when the timing is right to cash out of a venture. This is easier said than done. It requires patience, outside consultations, and realistic expectations to find a viable timing window for your harvest goals.

Here are three guidelines for harvest goals:

1. **Be patient.** Harvest goals are usually three to five years or seven to ten years.
2. **Have a realistic valuation of your company's worth.** Manage expectations and don't be greedy.
3. **Get advice from well-credentialed professionals.** Corroborate your plans with at least three different advisers.

THE MOST COMMON TYPES OF EXITS

A good public speaker or Broadway actor knows when to get off the stage. Innovators should be similarly sensitive to the timing of their exit.

Several types of exits are available, such as a management buyout, a merger or acquisition, or an IPO. All of these have different levels of attraction for an owner depending on the type of venture and risk tolerance. For example, an acquisition with cash up front has lower risk than a stock transaction because the stock price of the purchasing company is not something anyone can control.

CAPITAL COW

For some reason, investors love bovine analogies. So let's talk about the "cows" and how they fit into our topic of exit strategy.

A capital cow is not an exit, but it is an option for an owner who is not necessarily exit based but requires large amounts of cash and capital to invest in new activities. The previously mentioned innovator Elon Musk has used money from his diverse range of projects to fund his new ventures, such as SpaceX. Money invested in SpaceX produces capital gains that can be reinvested in other projects, which produce a diverse range of revenue streams. A capital cow also offers the opportunity to inject liquidity into companies that might be having cash flow problems. Capital cows are rare but can pay huge dividends for those who can take advantage of them.

M&A AND STRATEGIC ALLIANCE

Merging with another, larger firm is another way for a founder to exit and realize a financial gain. In a reference book I use in my course, *New Venture Creation: Entrepreneurship for the 21st Century*, authors Stephen Spinelli, Jr., and Robert J. Adams, Jr., provide a typical start-up M&A example. Two founders with experience developing training programs for the personal computing industry merged with another company. These entrepreneurs had computer backgrounds but lacked marketing skills and general management experience. This was obvious in their first year's revenues and the company's inability to attract venture capital. They merged with a firm that had $15 million in sales annually with an excellent reputation for management training and an established customer base. The buyer obtained an 80 percent share of the smaller firm and consolidated the company's revenues into its financial statement. The two founders of the small company got 20 percent ownership in their company. They also obtained employment contracts with the new owner.

Many M&As start out as a strategic alliance, where founders can attract badly needed capital from a large company interested in their technology and where there are strategic and financial synergies. Such arrangements can eventually lead to complete buyouts of the founders.

PUBLIC OFFERING

An IPO might be the dream for many an entrepreneur, but taking a company public is a rare event. The challenge with the IPO market is its cyclical, bust-and-boom nature: bust in 2000, when the red-hot dot.com bubble burst; boom in 2020, a year that has been called one of the best ever for IPOs, despite the pandemic. Companies such as DoorDash, Snowflake, and Airbnb had big IPOs in 2020, with DoorDash and Airbnb each raising more than $3 billion, according to Barron's. And so it goes.

Though tricky to pull off successfully, going public offers several advantages. First, it helps the company fund rapid growth. Public markets provide access to immediate or short-term capital while also meeting the company's longer-term funding needs. Companies may use the proceeds of an IPO to expand the business in the existing market or to move into a related market. The founders and initial investors might be seeking liquidity (to cash out), but this is limited by the SEC, which monitors the timing and amount of stock that the officers, directors, and insiders can dispose of in the public market. As a result, it can take several years after an IPO before the founders see a liquid gain. An IPO is also positive for generating brand awareness and improving the company's market attractiveness.

Disadvantages include the short-term focus on profits and performance, running the business with a quarter-to-quarter mentality. Also, because of the disclosure requirements, public companies lose the ability to hold some information in confidence, not to mention having to spend money on public disclosures, audits, and tax filings. With public shareholders, the management of the company must be careful about the flow of information because of the risk of insider trading.[1]

MANAGEMENT BUYOUT

Owners who want to exit a venture also have the option of selling their shares to an existing owner. This is a good option if you want to keep the company in the same hands. Investment banks usually broker these types of transactions. The management buyout can be risky if the purchasers don't have the money they need to buy the seller's shares outright. In this case, the parties have to create an agreement stipulating when the balance will be paid over time. This term can be tied to the company's performance to help manage the buyer's risk.

SALE

No doubt, selling the company is the best option for all parties and mitigates the risks of changes in stock prices, which, as noted previously, can leave the seller at a disadvantage. This is the route my father used to exit his company but keep it in the family. He sold his company to my husband, who in turn paid him cash over a short period of time.

FINALLY, A WORD ABOUT VALUATIONS

In preparing for both investment and your exit strategy, expect to be asked what you think the value of your company is. And expect that those asking are going to prepare their own valuation exercise as part of their diligence. Valuations are part science, part benchmarking with peers in your industry, and part assessment of exit potential. They are also part art, meaning a valuation can be influenced by trends, fads, intuition, and emotions—the psychology of investing. Expect a combined approach when assessing your valuation. I recommend that you hire a consultant who has the expertise to perform your valuation. The consultant will be an expert in key criteria that influence valuation, including the following:

- Valuation is based in part on stage (i.e., growth, shipping product, line extension).
- The strength of the economy affects the going rate for a particular stage.
- The industry affects the perception of what the company is worth; currently, health care, energy, and agriculture are "hot" areas.
- Final value is based on how much the VCs want the company and the availability of competitors.

- Higher valuations come in "hot" areas for savvy companies with multiple term sheets.

My dad was clear on his goals and objectives in translating his innovative ideas into a business that would last a couple of generations. You need to do the same. As Novak demonstrated in her implementation plans for Howda Designz, you need to be clear from the outset, and you need to be able to answer some key questions:

- Why are you creating a company, what does success looks like, and when and how do you want to exit?
- Who is depending on your business to succeed, and who will benefit the most?
- Conversely, if things don't proceed according to your plans, who will be affected by that outcome?

The answers to these questions will guide your decisions about the design of your business, your fund-raising strategies, the talent you hire, and even how you plan your own personal exit from the company. It may sound counterintuitive, but the key lesson here is to remember that even while immersed in the start-up of a new idea, the savvy innovator is already thinking about how to leave it.

10

UNIQUE CHALLENGES WOMEN INNOVATORS FACE AND WHY

The unfortunate reality is that only 5 percent of patents are held by women. Only 25 percent of top innovation firms are led by women. Women account for 20 percent of Fortune 500 chief innovation officers. Women are underrepresented in science, technology, math, and engineering (STEM), and the gender wage gap among STEM professionals is 16 percent. Half as many women as men are likely to start their own business, and 95 percent of women who do start their own business fail within a year because they can't secure funding and other necessary support.[1]

Why is innovation so challenging for women? Or should we be asking a different question: Why aren't more women encouraged to be innovators? And are their contributions fully recognized?

In this chapter we explore the stories behind famous and not-so-famous women innovators and examine why females find it difficult to patent their ideas, raise funding for their innovations, and launch and maintain successful businesses. It's more complicated than you might think. I share findings based on research with women innovators in both small companies and corporations as well as with attorneys, investors, policy makers, and other stakeholders who see the valuable role women innovators can play in society. There's much we can do to close the gap on disparities and encourage more women in innovation and entrepreneurship.

And, of course, I offer my own perspective as a female who has devoted her career to invention and innovation. As a woman in what has been a predominantly male preserve, I've learned a few things along the way that you might find illuminating and instructive, regardless of your gender.

THE LEAGUE OF EXTRAORDINARY
GENTLEMEN—AND WOMEN

With my adrenaline flowing in anticipation of the day ahead, I quickened my pace as I approached the Broad Street entrance of the Union League of Philadelphia—an imposing edifice with its French Renaissance brick and brown façade and dramatic, twin circular staircase. Two colorful flags, one bearing the Union League crest and the other the crest of the City of Philadelphia, floated over the portico in the cool April morning breeze. My heels clicked the old stone steps, and I paused on the landing to take in the view. My moment of reflection was cut short when a bellman in a gray vest with matching cap opened the large wooden door with a flourish of his arm, waving me in. He then touched his cap as he tipped his head and said, "Morning, Ma'am." A courteous gesture that I appreciated—but I wondered if my ideas would be dismissed as quickly, if politely, as I had been ushered in.

The Union League of Philadelphia, ranked the number one city club in the United States for many years, is considered a historic treasure of Philadelphia. Founded in 1862 as a men's patriotic society to support the Union and the policies of President Abraham Lincoln, it laid the philosophical foundation for other Union Leagues across the nation torn by civil war. Since its founding, it had evolved into a social club for male and, yes, female professionals representing the region's leaders in business, education, technology, health care, government, religion, art, and culture.

Today, I was a guest at the club participating in the Angel Venture Fair, an annual capital-raising event for CEOs of start-ups in the greater Philadelphia region. I walked down the plush floral-carpeted hallway past the two restaurants, the cocktail lounge, and meeting rooms of the block-long building to the grand ballroom where the Angel Venture Fair was being held.

As I checked in at the registration table and enthusiastically picked up my name badge and participant packet, a woman whose name tag said "Joan" greeted me in a businesslike manner. "Your company's exhibit is set up," she said. "You can find the location on the map in your packet." She went on to crisply inform me that I was scheduled for six investor pitches—or, as they called it, "speed-dating sessions"—with ten investors each.

"You'll have ten minutes to present and ten minutes for Q&A," she concluded. "There will be a digital clock in the room, and the timekeeper will hold up a card when you have one minute left to wrap up."

My time was already up. "Any questions?" she asked, staring at the line that had formed behind me. Taking her cue, I said, "I'm all set. Thank you."

I walked into the ballroom with its white decorative ceiling and dim chandelier lighting, imagining the important meetings and celebratory galas that must have taken place there. I studied the exhibit area, which was already filled with investors and entrepreneurs engaged in light banter and product demos. Checking the map, I saw I was in the first aisle, a great location. As I displayed the company signage and set up the demo, a couple of investors stopped by to say they had a lot of interest in ophthalmology diagnostics and looked forward to my pitch. An investor named Lou from Ben Franklin Technology Partners stopped by. His foundation, formed with money from the tobacco settlements in Pennsylvania in 1998, invested in new technologies in the City of Brotherly Love. "You might be a good fit for our program. Give me a call next week," he said.

I went into the green room where presenters could make final adjustments to their presentations and have one-on-one discussions with investors. I was grateful I was the only one in the room. I needed a few quiet minutes to mentally prepare for my first speed-dating session at 10 a.m.

As I sat in the green room, scanning the list of twenty-five CEO participants, I saw that I was one of only two women presenting at the Angel Venture Fair. I felt honored but at the same time perplexed about the lack of female participation. Something was not right. I made a commitment then to do my part to improve the metrics.

I reflected on how I had ended up at this significant event, a milestone in our company's brief, one-year tenure. I had been meeting with investors on the East Coast for three months, and while I had had some promising discussions, none had resulted in a term sheet. I knew it was partially related to timing—it was 2010 and the country was still climbing out of the 2008 real estate–induced recession. The investor community had been hit hard. NASDAQ (the stock exchange for technology, the riskiest of investments) had plummeted, and the VC private equity and banking community had also suffered significant losses. While psychologically the financial and business communities were eager to invest and get back to growth, some trepidation lingered. Coupled with that, I was a relative newcomer to the world of raising capital. The investor community was well established along the East Coast and particularly in Philadelphia. The investors and the serial entrepreneurs knew each other well, had worked together for years, and were almost in a "rinse and repeat" model, having perfected a formula for success over the years.

On top of that, while I was well credentialed and established in my field of biotech, having served in senior roles in life science organizations, I was a first-timer to the start-up world—one very different from running a department in a large corporation. I had helped lead innovative projects at the National Institutes of Health, Omnicom, Bristol Myers Squibb, and Covance (now Labcorp), but this was my first experience taking a technology from the research bench to the commercial market. It was thrilling and at times overwhelming, figuring out things for the first time, creating a new network of other start-up professionals, and learning the ropes while running the company. And finally, I was a woman in a man's world, as even just a quick glance around the conference room confirmed. The only other women I saw were the hotel staff.

My start-up was lean in every sense of the word—I had a team of five scientists, seed capital from my cofounder, and a laboratory in an office building in Towson, Maryland. I knew we had a compelling value proposition—to improve clinical outcomes for people with eye disease—coupled with an impressive patent portfolio, research studies, and science-based technology.

Knowing I needed to "join" the start-up community to improve my chances of successfully transitioning into this new world of entrepreneurs and investors, I had joined a few well-appointed organizations: BIO (Biotechnology Innovation Organization) chapters in New York, New Jersey, and Pennsylvania; the New Jersey Technology Council; the University City Science Center start-up program; and the Alliance of Women Entrepreneurs (AWE). AWE was one of my favorites. Women make up only 28 percent of the workforce in science, technology, engineering, and math (STEM), and increasing that number was critical for cultivating more women innovators. Established by three female Philadelphia entrepreneurs with backgrounds in science, AWE had a mission to increase the number of women in STEM, help women develop and launch start-ups, and advance women-led economic development in the region. I was active in the STEM mentorship program and the committee that sponsored capital-raising seminars for women. Not only had I personally learned a lot about fund-raising, but also the networking was invaluable. One AWE member, a partner at a Philadelphia VC, had met with me, mostly as a favor, but since the first fifteen investor meetings had been exclusively with men, I was grateful. I felt like I could be myself with her.

"We prefer digital technologies that can get to market in three years," she told me. "Your eye diagnostic test could take three to five years." But she gave me some helpful pointers and referred me to another investor group she thought was a better fit. The investor meetings with men usually went one of two ways. I noticed, anecdotally, that men over sixty responded with avuncular encouragement, acknowledging our technology's potential and my strong clinical and business background. Several offered to schedule meetings with others in their networks and introduced me to attorneys and accountants whom they thought could help shore up my business and legal story. The younger investors were all business. They took a few notes, asked probing questions, then offered feedback and usually told me to come back after we had more clinical data to support our product claims. I could tell I wouldn't be breaking into the men's investor circles easily. "Yes, but that's OK," a friend told me. "You are a master at making your way around boulders, and you'll find the path forward. I've watched you do that your entire career."

I appreciated the encouragement. And the investors had a legitimate question when they asked about needing more data to back up our technology's claims. "How do I get more data without funding?" I thought to myself. This was a Catch-22, a vicious circle. The feedback spurred me to apply for federal, state, and foundation research grants, which I knew would take a year or more to secure but could provide nondilutive (essentially, free) funding, because the money didn't have to be paid back. At least I could show investors I was pursuing all forms of funding to advance the development of our technology.

I was thrilled in February when I got the phone call from the chairman of the Angel Venture Fair selection committee saying I had made the cut. My cofounder was sure it was because our technology was ahead of its time and investors would be clamoring to invest. While I thought we had a good story to tell, I also knew that my colleagues from AWE had put in a good word for me with the selection committee. Gloria, who had retired from a senior-level science position at DuPont and was a member of Golden Seeds, an investment fund that favored women CEOs, had positioned me to the committee as a successful life-sciences executive and innovator who had a compelling business case and interesting technology. In one of our mentoring lunches, Gloria shared with me her own challenging climb up the DuPont corporate ladder. She credited a couple of mentors with helping her navigate successfully. Now retired and a member of the investment community, she wanted to do her part to help women succeed in the innovation and entrepreneurship ecosystem. I've strived to help advance women entrepreneurs throughout my career, too, and Gloria was an early inspiration for my dedication to women and their careers as innovators.

I focused my attention back to the present and saw that the clock in the green room said 9:50 a.m., just a few minutes shy of show-time, so I made my way to the Lincoln Room for my first speed-dating capital-raising pitch. Ten white men in dark suits, ranging in age from about thirty-five to seventy, sat around a large rectangular mahogany conference table, reclining in leather chairs. I knew that many had made it big during the dotcom boom and had been fortu-nate to cash out before that market went bust. They were looking for someplace to invest their extra cash.

My presentation, which I had memorized, was smooth, and I had timed it out to the second. The woman in the corner with the digital sign signaled the one-minute mark just as I was finishing my summary statement. "Our company is offering a novel solution to the problem of age-related eye disease," I said in the final seconds allotted to me. "We have a solid team, strategic partner commit-ments, and a fast path to revenue. We need $1.5 million to get to our first milestone, completion of our clinical study. I hope you'll consider joining us as we build a company that is changing the way eye disease is treated, offering hope to many who would otherwise go blind." The audience clapped, and a few hands went up.

Bernie, a well-respected, active angel investor asked, "Tell me more about the design of your study and the statistical plan."

Paul from a local VC wanted to know if we had spoken to the FDA about our technology, and an older Middle Eastern gentleman I didn't recognize, whose name badge just said "Tal," asked about the patients from whom we were collecting samples. "Nothing I couldn't handle," I thought as I breathed a sigh of relief and left the room.

The other pitches were similar, although one investor from a national VC really prodded me on the validity of our science. He asked questions about our patent language and seemed to already know a lot about our patent filings. I wondered if he was funding a competitive product. I found out later that indeed he was, and that he had been dismissive of me and my pitch during the investor debrief. These types of forums are designed for the entrepreneur to share nonconfidential information. I was glad I hadn't gone into too much detail about our intellectual property strategy and clinical development plans during the Q&A. My job was to provide just enough information to be credible and to get a meeting, for which a nondisclosure agreement would be signed by the interested investor and me.

Three of my six speed-dating sessions included one woman investor. Looking at the roster, I noted that five out of the sixty-five investors were women, mirroring the proportion of women investors who were angels and VCs—about 5 percent. And yes, there is a correlation, albeit anecdotal, between the number of women investors (5 percent) and the number of women entrepreneurs who receive angel and VC investment (3 percent).

That day I met a dozen new investors, deepened relationships with a few I already knew, and met some amazing entrepreneurs, many of whom became colleagues and friends—among them, Dan and Eric from ZipStitch, a new technology that reduced surgical complications and recovery time, and Cid, who had invented a "smart" child's car seat that told parents if the seat was properly installed and secured. He had lost a grandchild to an improperly secured child restrainer and had designed this one himself. I had one serious angel investor who put together a syndicate (a team of other interested angels) to perform diligence (as you'll recall from the previous chapter, this is a top-to-bottom assessment of the technology and the company). They decided to wait to invest until we had clinical data. And a local VC gave me a term sheet—a draft of the deal—but they wanted too much equity and we decided to pass. My company secured research grants and strategic partnerships and ultimately did not need VC funding, given the pivot we made after my cofounder's accident.

As for me, I met some of the most creative, innovative, and agile results-oriented professionals during that period. I became even more involved in the innovation and entrepreneurial culture and ecosystem. I cofounded several other companies and raised funds for my companies and those of my colleagues from angels and VCs.

I also redoubled my focus on women in innovation, looking for ways to share my experiences and newfound expertise with other women. At one of my workshops, I secured a DC-based reporter, author, consultant, and professor who specialized in women and entrepreneurship as a guest speaker. Sharon Hadary wrote a seminal piece in the *Wall Street Journal* in 2010 based on research she had conducted on why it was so tough for women to break into and be successful in entrepreneurship.[2]

In that article, Hadary noted that while the number of women-owned businesses had been growing for the past three decades, with women launching new enterprises at twice the rate of men, women-owned businesses were small compared with those owned by men. She reported that the average revenues of women-owned businesses were only 27 percent of the average revenues of men-owned businesses.

"And yet a quarter million women in the United States own and lead businesses with annual revenue topping 1 million, proof that women have the capacity, vision, and perseverance needed to be successful entrepreneurs," she concluded in that article. "So, what's holding them back?" Her research revealed a twofold problem: (1) women have self-limiting views of themselves, their businesses, and the opportunities available to them; and (2) women face stereotypical perceptions and expectations among business and government leaders.

As a start-up professional, I can tell you that it's hard enough to be an innovator and entrepreneur of a start-up in the best of circumstances, much less to be a female in this arena. As we've seen throughout this book, it can take time to develop and launch a commercially viable idea, raise capital, and become a financially self-sustaining business. It also takes a toll on an entrepreneur's personal financial situation. I don't think that being a woman affected my ability to be successful. Women are every bit as intelligent, confident, inquisitive, and resilient as men. However, I, like many of my women peers, had financial and family obligations as the mother of a young family that influenced my medium-term plans. Serial entrepreneurs get good at start-ups after they've done three or four—and that can require ten, fifteen, twenty years of continual effort. It's why serial entrepreneurs are so attractive to investors and to the community. After five years as an innovator in the start-up world, I had launched several companies and raised capital. But I hadn't hit it big enough to generate the kind of revenue and exit to be financially independent. And I couldn't afford to incur personal risk for an uncertain period. I ultimately returned to the corporate world for security.

Of course, as we've discussed in this book, innovation happens in many ways and under many circumstances. I decided to focus my innovative spirit and start-up aspiration on corporate innovation, or what I call intrapreneurial endeavors, helping large organizations embrace innovation and advance new technologies to market with a start-up approach I had learned and applied. At the same time, I stayed involved in the start-up world as a professor, adviser, coach, and angel investor myself. So, I have the best of two worlds. I help corporations innovate, and I stay involved in the start-up community as a resource to innovators. And I do this proudly, as a professional, an innovator, an educator, and even as a parent when I've had the opportunity to guide the entrepreneurial interests of my children and their friends.

Fast-forward to 2021: How are things different for women in STEM and the start-up world? According to a 2020 *Harvard Business Review* article, over the past decade U.S. venture capital has grown fourfold and the number of businesses started by women grew to 40 percent. Yet the percentage of venture capital dollars raised by women-founded companies has barely budged since 2012. In the United States, about 3 percent of venture capital goes to all female-founded companies.[3] Only 15 percent goes to companies that have even one woman on the founding team, according to entrepreneurial resources Pitchbook in 2018 and a 2019 report by the European Investment Bank's InnovFin Advisory.

We're not much better off than when Hadary wrote her analysis in 2010.

The statistics aren't any better in Europe. The European Commission issued a report in July 2020 stating that more than 90 percent of capital raised by technology companies backed by European ventures in 2018 went to companies with male founders. Only 5 percent of capital went to mixed-gender management teams, and a mere 2 percent went to all-female teams.

What's ironic is that the data on the importance of gender diversity in ensuring corporate success are positive. Women-led companies tend to require less capital while delivering higher returns. A study by the Boston Consulting Group showed that women outperformed their male counterparts' start-ups despite raising less money. For every dollar raised, female-run start-ups generated 78 cents in revenue, whereas male counterparts generated 31 cents. A survey of six hundred founders by First Year Capital found that those who were part of a team with a female founder performed 63 percent better than their all-male counterparts.

What's more, the issues facing women are the same ones Hadary wrote about in 2010. A report by Eurostat in 2018 found that women in Europe and the United States are half as likely to be self-employed, perceive themselves as having less entrepreneurial experience than men, have less diversity in their networks, have inadequate fundraising connections, face societal perceptions that affect their confidence to launch a start-up, and experience tax and family systems that do not encourage a dual-earner model. The disparity is particularly high in the technology sector, where fewer than 15 percent of founders are women, a reminder of the challenges of not having enough women in STEM.

Women-led start-ups tend to be smaller and are often less capital intensive and growth oriented and more geared to services such as health care and social work. One study found that women who do succeed in raising capital tend to be leading companies with a social mission. A disproportionate number of ventures that emphasize social impact seem to be founded by women, according to a 2018 *Harvard Business Review* article.[4] The researchers comment on the huge role of stereotypes in how entrepreneurs are evaluated. An iconic image surrounds successful entrepreneurs—they are expected to be aggressive and ambitious. This poses a challenge for women entrepreneurs, as research shows that females who project an aggressive and nonfeminine persona may be viewed as more competent but may also suffer for violating societal expectations of warmth and care. Women face a double bind. What is expected of them as entrepreneurs is at odds with what is expected of them as women. Social-impact framing seems to break the double bind by avoiding discrimination while also meeting gender expectations.

HOW CAN WOMEN INNOVATORS LEVERAGE THE CURRENT ENVIRONMENT?

Based on what I've seen and experienced, as well as what the data show us, I offer these suggestions to other female innovators on how to get noticed in what is, sadly, still very much a man's world.

Work with what you've got. Take advantage of the perception of women being good leaders of social-impact start-ups and talk about sustainability and social impact in your messaging if relevant. Social enterprises are on the rise, and women can take advantage of this.

Tap into the growing number of women-focused angel networks. Women now make up 26 percent of angel investors, according to the University of Berkeley. Golden Seeds, Plum Alley, Astia, and 37 Angels are providing seed capital to high-potential female founders. Morgan Stanley and Goldman Sachs have started accelerators for women and multicultural entrepreneurs. Andreesen Horowitz and SoftBank have announced funds to provide capital to underserved founders and entrepreneurs, including women and people of color.

Take advantage of the growing number of innovation accelerator programs to create a network that can jumpstart your business. Innovation and entrepreneurship are popular career paths promoted by most colleges and universities and a focus of federal, state, and local economic development programs. In both academia and government, there is a coordinated and strong focus on promoting entrepreneurship as a career path and as a means of creating new jobs, opportunity, and wealth for communities. Women in Innovation (WIN) is an international organization with four thousand members in New York, San Francisco, and London that hosts events and training programs. Women can take advantage of a number of programs like WIN and others in their regions by taking classes, participating in accelerator labs, and attending networking events to bolster their network of investors, bankers, financial professionals, and legal and other professionals who can help them get their ideas off the ground. These forums are also an ideal opportunity to meet other innovators and entrepreneurs, men and women alike, to share experiences, trade stories, and swap recommendations on consultants and other helpful resources.

Leverage the community-based focus on women in STEM to get involved in local efforts to advance women in innovation. The best way to recruit more women into technical fields that feed the pool of future innovators and entrepreneurs is to encourage more young women to pursue careers in science and engineering. STEM programs are easy to identify at the high school and college levels, and women have an opportunity to influence, coach, and mentor young women to consider technical careers. Consider being a guest speaker at an event or even being a mentor to a female student. By getting more involved in the STEM community, women can have a positive impact on other women and advance the innovation ecosystem in general. There is an equal focus on increasing diversity in STEM, and women can be important advocates here as well.

WHAT CAN LEADERS DO TO ENCOURAGE MORE WOMEN ENTREPRENEURS AND INNOVATORS?

Let's not stop at the local level. We need a call to action. Women and men need to create a unified voice demanding change in the entrepreneurial ecosystem. We need the attention and involvement of the entire ecosystem—financial, academic, government, and business. Here are some changes that will make a difference now and in the future.

Hold VCs accountable by requiring long-established VC fund managers to report the number of companies with diverse leadership they are investing in and the capital committed to these companies, during diligence and at annual performance reviews. While 65 percent of limited partners in VC say they care about diversity, only 25 percent ask about it in diligence. What gets measured gets done! According to the University of Berkeley, 6 percent of VCs today have female partners. Monitor the number of women in senior positions at VC funds. Investors have taken on big societal issues before. As of mid-2020, nearly 450 institutional investors representing more than $41 trillion in assets joined Climate Action 100+.[5] They set targets for board representation and emission reduction and put market pressure on companies to make climate-friendly choices. The result is greater transparency about a company's carbon footprint and better data about capital flow to companies based on climate-relevant activities. They created an urgency and a momentum for climate action that did not exist at that scale

Change the mindset and encourage women to think big by providing more training on setting goals, especially around finance—how to raise capital and build relationships. This training should be sponsored by universities, technology transfer offices, and large corporations with innovation offices. Companies such as IBM that have a commitment to advancing women innovators have sponsored programs to encourage STEM in high school and to upskill women entrepreneurs.

Create an environment and make the necessary culture change to encourage more women to study STEM subjects and enter STEM careers. Meaningful innovation happens when smart, passionate people are trained in technical fields so they have the knowledge and skills to create products and services that can improve the way we live, work, and play. Women hold a smaller number of computer science positions today than they did in the 1980s, according to an Ernst and Young report in March 2019. The U.S. Center for Talent Innovation explains that women are twice as likely as men to quit the technology industry. We need to reverse this trend. We need to get women into STEM as a first step; then we need to support them in those careers by helping them balance work-life, achieve career advancement, and receive equal incentives, including compensation.

Follow the lead of Babson. One academic institution that is doing a laudable job of encouraging women innovators is Babson College. Located in Babson Park, Massachusetts, the college is a leader in undergraduate education in entrepreneurship and home to the College Center for Women's Entrepreneurial Leadership. It's an academic leader in advancing female entrepreneurs' leadership and supporting women innovators and founders.

Babson's Women Innovating Now, or WIN, Lab, established in 2013, is a venture accelerator for women entrepreneurs. It provides a community-based, rigorous experiential process that catalyzes innovation thinking and enables successful business scaling. The five-month curriculum is supported by one-to-one coaching, access to experts, interactions with company executives, a peer-based community, and a program that holds students accountable for their progress.

The challenges women face as innovators and entrepreneurs clearly cannot be addressed overnight, but there is reason for continued hope, and we must stay focused and vigilant in driving change. Today, a young woman in the United States, Europe, and parts of Asia has more opportunity than ever before to have a successful career as an innovator because awareness of the need for diversity is greater—the data prove that women leaders are good for business. The Third Mastercard Index of Women Entrepreneurs, which evaluates countries based on women's advancement outcomes, including participation in the workforce, financial access, and entrepreneurial support, ranked the United States first, followed by New Zealand, Canada, and Israel. We need to continue to press for change. Consider the suffrage movement. It took eighty years for women to gain the right to vote. Susan B. Anthony, a courageous innovator for social and political change, died fourteen years before the Nineteenth Amendment was passed. She reminds us that meaningful and measurable change can take a couple of generations until it becomes the new way of operating. Importantly, as we've discussed in this book, adversity and necessity bring out the best in the innovator. Innovators have a passion for novel ideas and positive change and possess drive and resiliency to push through until they're successful.

Hundreds of women innovators throughout history are noteworthy (the ones we know about), including more than a dozen I personally admire. These women saw a problem, developed a viable solution, and then persevered until they were successful. I'd like to share with you my Women Innovators Hall of Fame.

PROFESSOR MARCHAND'S WOMEN INNOVATORS
HALL OF FAME

My criteria for nominating a woman to the Hall of Fame include her ability to identify a problem worth solving and examine multiple solutions and the patentability of her idea. These women also adhered to many of the Laws of Innovation mentioned in this book—including the spirit of pivoting and personal resilience. I have looked also for diversity among women innovators and provide a few additional resources at the end of this section for your perusing pleasure. I've included details about the inventor's life and a quotation when available. You can refer to Susan Fourtané's article cited in the notes for more information about woman innovators of historical significance.[6]

JOSEPHINE COCHRANE (1839-1913), ASHTABULA, OHIO Invented the automatic dishwasher

> "I couldn't get men to do the things I wanted in my way until they had tried and failed on their own. They insisted on having their own way with my invention until they convinced themselves my way was the best, no matter how I had arrived at it."
>
> —JOSEPHINE COCHRANE

Cochrane designed the dishwasher by measuring the dishes and making wire compartments to fit each dish type. The individual compartments were placed inside a wheel that lay flat within a copper boiler. A motor turned the wheel while hot soapy water squirted from the bottom and rained down on the dishes. She showed the dishwasher at the 1893 Chicago World's Fair and won the highest prize for best mechanical construction, durability, and adaptation to its line of work. She founded Garis-Cochrane Company to manufacture her dishwashers, a precursor to KitchenAid. She was inducted posthumously into the National Inventors Hall of Fame in 2006.

MARIE CURIE (1867–1934), WARSAW, POLAND Discovered radioactivity

"The use of X-rays during the war saved the lives of many wounded men; it also saves many from long suffering and lasting infirmity."
—MARIE CURIE

Curie coined the word *radioactivity*, and her work on uranium rays created the field of atomic physics. Based on her discovery of radioactivity, and her discovery with her husband Pierre Curie of the radioactive elements polonium and radium, Curie was the first woman to win a Nobel Prize and the first person to be awarded it twice. Educational and research institutes, including the Curie Institute and Pierre and Marie Curie University, were named after her.

She died from aplastic anemia, a disorder she developed because she carried test tubes of radium in her lab coat and worked with radioactive materials. Her book *Radioactivity* was published posthumously in 1935. Her remains were interred with Pierre's in the Pantheon in Paris; she was the first of only five women laid to rest there. (https://www.nobelprize.org/prizes/physics/1903/marie-curie/biographical/)

HEDY LAMARR (1914–2000), VIENNA, AUSTRIA Invented a secret communication system that presaged Bluetooth, GPS, and WiFi

"Any girl can be glamorous; all you have to do is stand still and look stupid."

—HEDY LAMARR

A movie actress and self-taught inventor, Lamarr and colleague George Antheil developed a radio guidance system that used spread-spectrum and frequency-hopping technology to jam radio signals. They created it for use on Allied torpedo ships in World War II, but the U.S. Navy didn't adopt the technology until 1960. Lamarr was inducted posthumously into the National Inventor Hall of Fame in 2014. Several books have been written about her life and her invention, including *The Only Woman in the Room*, by Marie Benedict. (https://www.biography.com/people/hedy-lamarr-9542252)

JOY MANGANO (B. 1956), EAST MEADOW, NEW YORK Invented the Miracle Mop

"All you need is one person to say yes to an idea."

—JOY MANGANO

In 1990, Mangano invented the Miracle Mop, a self-wringing plastic mop that generated $10 million a year. Subsequently, she invented other products, including velvet-covered Huggable Hangars, house odor neutralizer Forever Fragrant, and the SpinBall Luggage Wheel. Her product line has generated more than $3 billion in revenues. Her autobiography, *Inventing Joy: Dare to Build a Brave and Creative Life*, was published in 2017. (https://nypost.com/2017/10/02/how-to-turn-your-invention-into-a-billion-dollar-success/)

MADAME C. J. WALKER (1867–1919), BORN SARAH BREEDLOVE IN A LOUISIANA SLAVE PLANTATION Invented hair-care products for Black women and is recorded as America's first female self-made millionaire

"I am not merely satisfied in making money for myself, I am endeavoring to provide employment for hundreds of women of my race.

I want to say to every Negro woman, don't sit down and wait for opportunities to come. Get up and make them."

—MADAME C. J. WALKER

Walker developed the hair treatments herself and recruited twenty-five thousand Black women to be door-to-door beauty consultants across North and Central America and the Caribbean. Her story was the basis for a Netflix series, inspired by the book *On Her Own Ground*, written by her great-great granddaughter A'Lelia Bundles. (https://tech .co/21-successful-black-entrepreneurs-throughout-history-2015-02)

MARY ANDERSON (1886–1953), GREENE COUNTY, ALABAMA Invented the windshield wiper blade

Anderson, a real estate developer and rancher, was riding a trolley car during a wintertime visit to New York City in 1902. She observed the motorman driving with the front windows open because of the difficulty keeping the windshield clear of falling sleet. Once home, she hired a designer and constructed a hand-operated device and then had a company produce a working prototype of her invention. In 1905, Anderson tried to sell the rights to her invention to a Canadian-based firm, but her application was rejected for the following reason: "We do not consider it to be of commercial value as would warrant our undertaking its sale." In 1920, after the patent expired and automobile manufacturing grew, windshield wipers using Anderson's design became standard equipment. Cadillac was the first car manufacturer to adopt them in 1922. (https://www .famousinventors.org/mary-anderson)

GERTRUDE BELLE ELION (1918–1999), NEW YORK Developed novel drugs for herpes, organ transplants, and leukemia

Elion developed forty-five patents in medicine. In 1944, she was hired by Burroughs-Wellcome, where she began a forty-year partnership with Dr. George H. Hitchings to create medicines by studying the composition of diseased cells. They used the differences in biochemistry of normal cells and disease-causing agents to design drugs that would block viral infections. Elion was awarded the Nobel Prize in Medicine together with George Hitchings and Sir James Black. In 1991 she became the first woman inducted into the National Inventors Hall of Fame. (https://www.biography.com /people/gertrude-b-elion-9285981)

BETTE NESMITH GRAHAM (1924–1980), DALLAS, TEXAS Invented Liquid Paper

> "Graham ran her company with a focus on spirituality, egalitarianism and pragmatism. She believed in de-centralized decision making and emphasized product quality over profits. She believed that women could bring a more nurturing and humanistic quality to the male world of business."
>
> —EDWARD T. JAMES, *NOTABLE AMERICAN WOMEN*

Graham was an executive secretary at Texas Bank and Trust when the first electric typewriters were introduced. She dealt with the problem of not being able to easily erase errors by developing a typewriting correction fluid with tempera water-based paints. She put it in a bottle and took it to work secretly for five years. Her son's chemistry teacher helped her develop the product, which she called "paint out." Graham got a patent, renamed her invention Liquid Paper, got a trademark, and started her own company. She sold her company to Gillette Corporation for $47.5 million in 1979. (Meanwhile, her son, Mike Nesmith, became famous as a member of the 1960s band and television show *The Monkees*. (https://lemelson .mit.edu/resources/bette-graham)

ADA LOVELACE (1815–1852), LONDON, ENGLAND Invented the first computer program

> "The brain of mine is something more than merely mortal, as time will show."
>
> —ADA LOVELACE

The daughter of poet Lord George Byron, Lovelace worked alongside Charles Babbage as he developed the first general-purpose computer, called the Analytical Engine. In 1842 she wrote the instructions for the first computer program that ran on the Analytical Engine. (https://www.britannica.com/biography/Ada-Lovelace)

PATRICIA BATH (B. 1942), HARLEM, NEW YORK Invented laser cataract surgery

"The ability to restore sight is the ultimate reward."

—PATRICIA BATH

Bath completed a fellowship in ophthalmology at Columbia University. In 1981, she began working on her invention, the Laserphaco Probe, which enabled accurate laser surgery to be performed on cataracts, previously a manual procedure. In 1986 she filed a patent for her discovery, becoming the first African American woman physician to receive a medical patent. She has spent her career working on behalf of the blind in her clinical practice, academic work, and engagement with advocacy organizations as president and cofounder of the American Institution for the Prevention of Blindness, which advocates that "eyesight is a basic human right." (https://brogans.wordpress.com/dr-patricia-era-bath-/eye-surgery -of-the-time-and-the-laserphaco-probe/)

RUNNERS-UP

KATHARINE BURR BLODGETT (1898–1979), SCHENECTADY, NEW YORK Invented invisible or nonreflective glass

Blodgett's invention was significant because it enabled the work of physicists, chemists, and metallurgists who needed transparent glass, and it was used in consumer products such as camera lenses, pictures frames, and optical devices. She was the first woman to be hired as a scientist by General Electric. She was issued eight patents during her lifetime and was the sole inventor on two of them. (https://en.wikipedia.org/wiki/Katharine _Burr_Blodgett)

OLGA D. GONZALEZ-SANABRIA (NO BIRTHDATE AVAILABLE), PUERTO RICO Coinvented long cycle-life nickel-hydrogen batteries (holds a patent)

The batteries are significant in enabling the International Space Station power system. Gonzalez-Sanabria is the highest-ranking Hispanic at NASA Glenn Research Center and a member of the Ohio Women's Hall of Fame. She also received the Women of Color in Technology Career Achievement Award in 2000. (https://en.wikipedia .org/wiki/Olga_D._Gonzpercent C3percentA1lez-Sanabria)

MARIA TELKES (1900-1995), BUDAPEST, HUNGARY Invented the thermo-electric power generator

Telkes used thermoelectric power to design the first solar heating system for the Dover Sun House in Dover, Massachusetts. In 1953 she built the first thermoelectric refrigerator using the principles of semiconductor thermoelectricity. She was granted seven U.S. patents and was inducted into the National Inventors Hall of Fame posthumously in 2012. (https://patents.justia.com/inventor /maria-telkes)

BARBARA MCCLINTOCK (1902-1992), HARTFORD, CONNECTICUT Discovered genetic transposition

McClintock's breakthrough discovery was that genes could move along the chromosome and cause mutations and other characteristic changes. She won the Nobel Prize for Physiology or Medicine for her study of corn chromosomes. (https://www.britannica.com /biography/Barbara-McClintock)

GRACE HOPPER (1906-1992), NEW YORK Invented the computer language compiler

"You don't manage people; you manage things. You lead people."

—ADMIRAL GRACE HOPPER

Hopper was a computer pioneer and naval officer. She earned a master's degree and a PhD in mathematics from Yale. She is best known for her contributions to computer programming, software development, and the design and implementation of programming languages. (https://president.yale.edu/biography-grace-murray-hopper)

ROSALIND FRANKLIN (1920-1958), LONDON, ENGLAND Used X-ray crystallography to understand the molecular structures of DNA and RNA

HONORABLE MENTION

MELITTA BENTZ (1873-1950), DRESDEN, GERMANY Invented the coffee filter

CARESSE CROSBY (1891-1970) Invented the modern bra, which she patented

JACLYN FU (B. 1990), CALIFORNIA Founded Pepper, a company that makes bras for small-chested women

RUTH HANDLER (1916-2002), DENVER, COLORADO Invented the Barbie doll

RUTH GRAVES WAKEFIELD (1903-1977), EASTON, MASSACHUSETTS Invented chocolate chip cookies

ELIZABETH J. MAGIE (1866-1948), MACOMB, ILLINOIS Invented the Landlord's Game, the original Monopoly board game by Parker Brothers. Magie's invention was not known until after her death.

MARY SHERMAN MORGAN (1921-2004) Invented the rocket fuel Hydyne, which powered the Jupiter-C rocket that boosted the first U.S. satellite, *Explorer*

SELECT RESOURCES ON WOMEN OF COLOR INNOVATORS

99 Black Women-Owned Brands and Entrepreneurs to Support Now and Always, https://www.createcultivate.com/blog/black-female-entrepreneurs-you-should-know?format=amp

How Asia's Female Entrepreneurs Are Reshaping Tech for Good, https://www.reutersevents.com/sustainability/how-asias-female-entrepreneurs-are-reshaping-tech-good

9 Latin American Women Innovators Shaking Up the Tech World, https://remezcla.com/lists/culture/9-latin-american-women-innovators-shaking-tech-world

Searchable Directory of Agricultural Technology Women Innovators, https://agfundernews.com/a-new-searchable-directory-focuses-on-women-innovators-in-agrifoodtech.html

Women of Color in Tech, https://www.amazon.com/Women-Color-Tech-Generation-Technology/dp/1119633486

ORGANIZATIONS RECOGNIZING HISTORICAL AND CURRENT WOMEN INNOVATORS

We all have an opportunity to influence the number of women inducted into the National Women's Hall of Fame (www.womenofthehall.org) in Seneca Falls, New York. Get on the board, investigate the nomination process, and nominate women you know and work with. Share information about this organization with the women innovators you know.

Founded in 1969 to advance the rights of women, the National Women's Hall of Fame is also home to a plethora of women innovators in social and political crusades such as women's rights. It includes women such as Mary Church Terrell, a Civil War–era woman whose career in the civil rights movement went into the 1950s. She was one of the first Black women to earn a college degree at Oberlin College and to teach at the first Black public high school in Washington, DC. These organizations are home to some of the great women leaders of our times. We should do all we can to support and participate in these organizations and the activities and fund-raising for which they advocate.

The National Innovators Hall of Fame includes some women innovators. To learn more about this organization, visit https://www.invent.org.

APPENDIX 1

TYPES OF CUSTOMER RESEARCH

- **Focus groups**

A group of eight to twelve customers meet in a room, or a virtual room, where they share their beliefs, perceptions, and opinions about your product or service. The group participants are free to talk openly with one another. This data collection method is used to gain insights into customer prioritization of needs or to test concepts and get feedback. Focus groups are used to inform surveys and interviews, going from broad to specific, but they can also come at the end of the process to test messages and concepts. This method works well when testing a new idea about a problem to be solved. For example, when the not-for-profit group National Alliance on Mental Illness (NAMI) wanted to explore the topic of depression, they asked us to conduct focus groups with people with depression, their family members, and their friends to better understand stigma and the lengths to which people would go to hide a love one's depression from family, friends, and coworkers. We delved into the shame they felt and their fear of being discovered and discriminated against. We then developed messages to help destigmatize mental illness and launched a new campaign to dispel myths and stigmas around the disorder.

- **Individual interviews**

This traditional technique is commonly used to understand a particular customer point of view regarding products, services, issues, attributes, and performance measures. You can do this for a particular customer or for a group of customers with some common attribute. You can conduct interviews in person, by phone, or through email. This is the method I used when I interviewed the retinal surgeons about the new diagnostic. It is one of the more expensive research methods, but it's also the most useful and trusted because it's based on interacting with the customer.

• **Online surveys**

Another way to capture the voice of the customer is through online surveys. These help you understand customer issues. Keep in mind the need for a survey that is short and to the point, with open-ended questions. Using a platform like SurveyMonkey or VWO, you can easily set up a survey with yes-or-no questions, multiple options, drop-down menus, and fill-in-the-blank questions. Ecolab, the global leader in water, food safety, and infection prevention solutions and services, conducted a survey of consumers about how comfortable they felt going to restaurants and hotels based on the establishment's use of hospital-grade disinfectants and third-party audits. The research showed that hotel guests feel extremely safe or very safe knowing a hotel is cleaned with hospital-grade disinfectants. The company was able to share this information with hotels and restaurants using their products and give them the Ecolab Science Certificate to display in their windows. A clever use of a survey to generate data to share with your customer!

• **Social media**

Research via social media provides potent feedback because it allows two-way communication with your customers. On any of the most commonly used social platforms, such as Twitter, Facebook, or LinkedIn, you can tap into relevant ongoing conversations and connect with customers by actively participating or quietly listening. The core strength of social media lies in allowing you to have a more direct, real-time conversation with the people using your products and services.

• **Live chat**

According to a 2021 study by forrester.com, 42 percent of online shoppers feel the best feature of an e-commerce website is the live chat. This is a great way to capture feedback, not just complaints, interacting with customers and learning more about what's on their minds. It's also an opportunity to schedule a follow-up survey with customers, even a call for deeper feedback. You can use HubSpot Messages to get live chat up and running on a website.

- **Website traffic**

Websites are a good place to capture voice-of-the-customer data. Besides chat and on-site surveys, another way to collect these data is by analyzing your customers' behavior on the website. You can do this quickly by leverage tools like heat maps, scrolls, and visitor recordings. You can also invest in a single platform like Crazy Egg so you don't need multiple tools.

- **Net promoter score (NPS)**

NPS is a management tool used to measure the loyalty of a company's customers. The customer loyalty metric was developed by Fred Reichheld, Bain & Company, and Satmetrix Systems. NPS gives you quick and reliable feedback from customers. The way the system works is easy. Customers use a simple 1–10 scale to answer questions such as "How likely are you to recommend our company to a friend for colleague?"

- **Emails**

This is a flexible way to gather feedback and can be either formal or informal based on needs. You can send highly personalized emails to customers or create a template for feedback that can be used to target a wide variety of customers. You can also request feedback in the form of an email or through an online survey link.

- **Feedback forms**

It is now standard to include a feedback form on your website, but you can also choose to administer a feedback form after an event or demo, either live or via email.

- **Online customer reviews**

Crowdsourcing of customer reviews has become very popular. People love reading the commentary on Angie's List, Nextdoor, Wayfair—anywhere users are gathering and want to share their feedback on a product or service.

APPENDIX 2

BUSINESS MODEL CANVAS

The Business Model Canvas allows an observer to describe any business model based on nine fundamental building blocks. It is used to evaluate a company as it goes through its life cycle. Following these nine building blocks will help you build a compelling Business Model Canvas.

1. Customer segments

Clearly describe the group of users, people, or organizations you are creating value for. There are two ways of doing this:

- Traditional description (demographics, psychographics, behavior)
- New way of segmenting customers: focusing on jobs customers are trying to get done to see how they will use services—e.g., for a wealth management firm, a customer segment may be described as people who want to "have an impact / retire at 45 / send kids to college"

Identify your direct customers (intermediaries to adoption) and indirect customers (end users).

Is your product / service serving a double-sided market (e.g., advertisers and consumers)?

2. Value proposition

Describe your value proposition to each customer segment: specific bundles of products and services that create value for each customer segment, addressing a fundamental problem and attracting customers to you.

Identify value drivers:

- Functional (e.g., performance, getting job done better, customization, accessibility, functional design, price / cost reduction)
- Social (e.g., brand status, communication)
- Emotional (e.g., reduced anxiety, design creation)

3. Channels

Note touchpoints through which the firm both interacts with and delivers value to the customers:

- Direct channels (e.g., own stores, websites, senior executives, sales force)
- Indirect customers (e.g., third-party stores, third-party sales force, wholesalers, media)

4. Customer relationships

Outline the type of relationship that a firm is establishing with its customers:

- Type of relationships (direct, indirect, combined)
- Bond established with customers (transactional, long-term, both)
- Intimacy of relationship (automated, personal, both)
- Relationship life cycle (acquisition strategies, retention strategies, cross-selling strategies)

5. Revenue streams

Make clear how and through which pricing mechanisms a company is capturing value:

- How do you make money from each customer segment?
- How do you capture value ($) in return for delivered value?
- What are the outcomes of your choices regarding value proposition, customer segments, channels, and relationships?

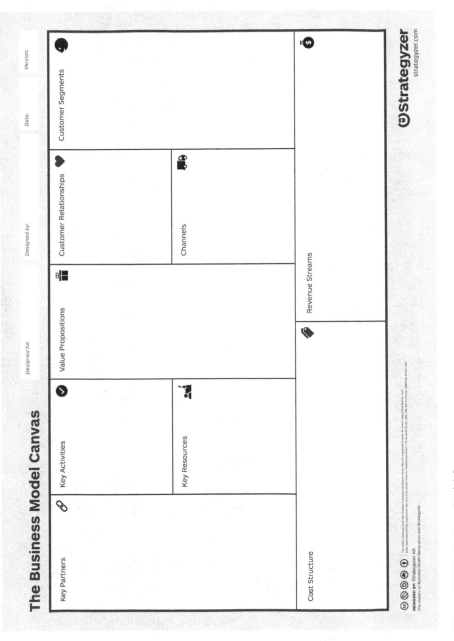

Figure A2.1 The Business Model Canvas

Courtesy of Strategyzer AG under CC BY-SA 3.0.

- Make sure revenue streams are larger than cost structure.
- Consider all types of revenue streams (asset sale, rental fee, usage fee, licensing fee, advertising fee, subscription fee, brokerage fee, etc.).
- Describe pricing structure (static vs. dynamic) and mechanisms (yield mechanisms depending on inventory and time of purchase—e.g., airline seats; real-time market supply/demand-dependent cost—e.g., stock market, auction; avoid orphan revenue stream).

6. Key resources

List assets indispensable to the firm, including:

- Tangible resources (computers, employees, capital)
- Intangible resources (intellectual property, brand, traffic, trust, etc.)

7. Key activities

Note processes useful for interacting with key partners.

8. Key partnerships

List other firms that can help your firm leverage current business model. Consider all partners, including:

- Strategic alliances between noncompetitors
- Strategic alliances between competitors
- Joint ventures
- Buyer-supplier relationships

9. Cost structure

Describe all costs incurred from operating your business model, including:

- Fixes costs (e.g., salaries, rents, production facilities, etc.)
- Variable costs (e.g., COGS)

Consider cost-driven business models, economies of scale / economies of scope, and value-driven business models

APPENDIX 3

EXAMPLE OF ACTUAL BUSINESS PLAN: OCULAR PROTEOMICS, LLC

℗Ocular Proteomics, LLC

Market Opportunity
Ocular Proteomics, LLC. Is poised for near term success with its unique platform of technologies that provides access to the large and growing degenerative eye disease diagnostic and therapeutic market that is estimated to be several billion per year. Initial focus is being placed on developing the company's vitreous-based diagnostic test for wet-age-related macular degeneration.

Investment Highlights
A validated and proprietary vitreous-proteome discovery technology.
• Developing accurate and cost effective diagnostic tests that could be used to measure therapeutic efficacy.
• Diagnostic eye disease market focus.
• Near term revenue opportunity with Age-related macular degeneration treatment responsiveness test.
• Multiple Product opportunities: PCADM-1, PCADM-2, HGPIN, CAM-1 & DNA ZYM-1.
• Experienced management & scientific team.
• Broad based IP protection.

Executive Management
Lorraine H. Marchand, MBA,
        President and CEO
George Scarlatis, M.D., Ph.D.,
        Clinical Advisor
Svetlana Novikova, Ph.D.,
        Manager, Bioinformatics
For more information, contact:
Lorraine H. Marchand, MBA,
        President and CEO
Ocular Proteomics, LLC.
Phone 443-921-1351
Fax 443-921-1369
Email lmarchand@ocularproteomics.com
http://www.nationalretina.org/innovativetechnology/centerforocularproteomics.asp

Corporate Overview

Ocular Proteomics, LLC is an early stage biotechnology company formed to capitalize on the growing need for more efficient and effective technology to rapidly identify and develop:
• Novel diagnostic markers for the early detection and staging of age-related macular degeneration and other eye diseases.
• Novel proteomic slide kit for identification of targets for drug discovery.
• Novel device for the collection of sample vitreous fluid for diagnostic purposes.

Core Technologies include:
• Proteomics platform for novel marker discovery.
• Proprietary methods for identification of proteins.
• Proprietary immunoassays for tissue/fluid markers.
• Linking diagnostic markers to therapeutics.
• Broad patent application covering discovery process, diagnostics, and therapeutics applications.

Age-Related Macular Degeneration Programs
MacroArray Technology will initially focus its efforts on developing age-related macular degeneration diagnostic products. The primary objective is to obtain FDA approval to commercialize vitreous proteome sampling and analysis as a clinical diagnostic test customized medical treatment of age-related macular degeneration.

VEGFR Y1175, VEGFR Y1175, and PDGFRβ Y716
A vitreous-based diagnostic test battery for predicting which patients with wet age-related macular degeneration will respond to current intravitreal anti-VEGFr treatments. This test is designed to be the first diagnostic of its kind introduced into the personalized medicine for eye-disease market. The availability of a simple yet reliable vitreous-based test would facilitate the selection of appropriate therapeutic regiments thus reduce overall medical costs and improve visual outcomes for patients with wet age-related macular degeneration. Periodic testing of patients to more accurately assess response to ongoing treatment can also be performed.

℗Ocular Proteomics, LLC

Scientific Advisors

***********, **M.D.**, Ophthalmologist
******** Hospital, city
*******************, **M.D., Ph.D.**,
******* University College of Medicine
*********, **MD**
Chairman of Ophthalmology
*************** University

Research Centers/Collaborators
National Retina Institute
Bert M. Glaser, M.D.
Founder and Executive Director
George Mason University
**************, Ph.D.
Research Scientistists
University of **************
*************, M.D.
Director of *************,
(Location)
**************,, M.D.
Director of *************, and
Chairman of Ophthalmology

Investors
• NIH-NEI (Grants thru 2010)
• National Retina Institute
· LORE
• Ben Franklin Technology Partners
• BioAdvance
• Innovation Philadelphia

Intellectual Property
Ocular Proteomics has patented intellectual property. The patent provides exclusive rights to the proteomics discovery technology and discoveries made for diagnostic and therapeutic applications.

Pipeline Products
Our early development stage products include MMP-9, a vitreous proteome-based marker for subretinal fluid in age-related macular degeneration; Human Vitreous Proteomic Slide kit, a vitreous-based set of slides for drug discover target marker identification; and The Vitreous Aspirator, a device for safe and easy in-office acquisition of vitreous samples for diagnostic purposes. Markers for other retinal and ophthalmic diseases are also being explored.

MMP-9
Matrix Metalloproteinase-9, a.k.a gelatinase B, specifically targets type IV collagen, the predominant structure of the vitreous. Our initial studies have shown that levels of this protein in the vitreous directly correlate with the amount of subretinal fluid seen in patients with wet age-related macular degeneration. It is hoped that by monitoring intravitreal levels of MMP-9 we can **predict** recurrent accumulation of subretinal fluid and initiate retreatment to **prevent** subretinal accumulation rather than the current method of reacting to subretinal accumulation after it has already occurred and damaged the retina.

Human Vitreous Proteomic Slide kit
Drawing upon our extensive library of almost 2000 samples taken from over 500 patients, we plan to construct a slide kit of pooled vitreous proteins from patients grouped by eye disease and other demographics. These slides will be sold to large pharmaceutical companies for testing of potential targets in their drug-discover stages of drug development. These kits will be used to test for the binding of certain key targets of their new drugs within the vitreous proteome of a pool of patients with their target disease. If this protein is present, they will then have initial validation that the proposed drug may have some effect in altering the course of said disease.

The Vitreous Aspirator
This specialized tool is intended to replace the current bimanual technique of aspirating vitreous samples with a needle and syringe. The tool is currently being designed to allow one-handed collection of the sample, allowing the other hand to be used to stabilize the globe and apply external pressure to the sampling wound immediately after withdrawal of the aspirator; minimize oblique-angled penetrations and thus reduce the risk of retinal detachment; and prevent the occurrence of "dry taps", the situation where an attempt to collect a sample provides an insufficient volume of vitreous for testing purposes.

APPENDIX 4

SAMPLE APPLICATION
FOR ANGEL INVESTOR FUNDING

COMPANY NAME
Address | Website | Contact No.
INVESTOR PITCH PREPARED FOR 'XX'

BUSINESS SUMMARY
Deliver a clear, concise, and compelling elevator pitch while referencing industry themes to anchor reader's interest in business plan. Approximately 75 words

Customer Problem
Describe problem from the perspective of end user who will ultimately benefit from the product / services and will pay for them, if different. Approximately 45 words

Product / Services
Describe the product while explaining how it addresses the above problem. Include references to other partners needed to develop and deliver the product/services. Approximately 75 words

Target Market
Describe customer segments, size and growth trends including spending capacity. Approximately 75 words

Sales / Marketing Strategy
Describe pricing strategy, sales channels, market enablers and partners. Approximately 75 words

Competitors and Unique Value Proposition
Describe key competitors for each product / service along with your differentiation. Approximately 75 words

Team and Expertise
Add key management team's photo, name, title and experience

Advisors
Key external advisors including consultants, attorneys, accountants

Investors
Add names of investors, and (if applicable) funds raised in previous rounds

Referred By

Achievements to date
Include number of customers, employees, development stage of product, etc.

Upcoming milestones
Any upcoming development milestones, launch activities, etc.

Financials
Include revenue projections, costs, net income over next 3-5 years in table format
Investment Asks—how funds will be used—on which activities and how much—and business impact.

EXAMPLE OF ACTUAL PITCH DECK: OCULAR PROTEOMICS

Illustrative sample of investor pitch deck for a new technology

Ocular Proteomics

An Ophthalmic Diagnostics Company

Lorraine Marchand
President and CEO

1

The Current Problem

- Age-related Macular Degeneration (wet AMD) in U.S.
  - Leading cause of blindness over 50; growing problem among aging populations in Western countries
  - 1.75 million patients growing to 3 million by 2020
    - 200,000 new cases annually

- Current diagnostics measure morphological/structural changes; lag time between treatment and response

- Gold standard @ 25k per year not effective in all patients; dozen new drugs in development

Solution – Ocular Proteomics

Biomarker diagnostic predicts patient response to drugs
Biomarkers help drug companies accelerate cycle time

Proprietary Panel of 45 protein biomarkers (IP protection)
- Diagnostic capability--predict patient response to drug treatment
- Technology platform novel, reproducible

Robust database
- NIH supported study
- 600 pts., 24 mos. data, 2,500 samples

Broad IP
- **Covering 3 patentable technologies**
  - Discovery Process--system and method for identifying biomarkers
  - Diagnostics and Therapeutic applications--ocular fluid markers
  - Device design--sampling ocular fluid

ACCOMPLISHMENTS SUMMARY

2009 - Q1 2010

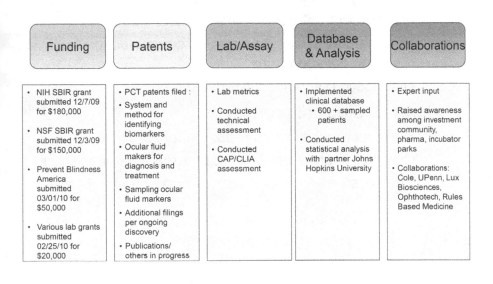

Funding	Patents	Lab/Assay	Database & Analysis	Collaborations
• NIH SBIR grant submitted 12/7/09 for $180,000 • NSF SBIR grant submitted 12/3/09 for $150,000 • Prevent Blindness America submitted 03/01/10 for $50,000 • Various lab grants submitted 02/25/10 for $20,000	• PCT patents filed : • System and method for identifying biomarkers • Ocular fluid makers for diagnosis and treatment • Sampling ocular fluid markers • Additional filings per ongoing discovery • Publications/ others in progress	• Lab metrics • Conducted technical assessment • Conducted CAP/CLIA assessment	• Implemented clinical database • 600 + sampled patients • Conducted statistical analysis with partner Johns Hopkins University	• Expert input • Raised awareness among investment community, pharma, incubator parks • Collaborations: Cole, UPenn, Lux Biosciences, Ophthotech, Rules Based Medicine

Strategic Tracks & Timelines

	2010	2011	2012	2013
Track 1 Biomarker Diagnostic	Identify & validate biomarker for wet AMD: 3 months	Design & execute prospective study for proof of concept: 12–18 mths . Requires $2 million in 2010 and additional $2 mil per year in 2011 and 2012 License biomarkers once validation/data complete.	Identify & validate biomarkers for additional indications including DME; License select validated markers FDA approval wet AMD. Launch and revenues of $1.5million	Launch next indication, DME
Track 2 Biomarker Lab Service	Conduct lab feasibility/ Product concept: 3 mths	Government certification (upgrade lab): 12–18 months. Will require $1.3 million in 2010 Develop lab offerings (samples, assay, PK/PD, infrastructure, technical talent: 12–18 months. Revenues to begin in 2010 (150k) and grow to over $1.7 million by 2011		Continue to progress lab offerings and services revenues

Ocular Proteomics
An Ophthalmic Diagnostics Company

Customers and Sales

- Customers
  - Retinal physicians/surgeons: determine who will respond to treatments (personalized medicine)
  - Pharma companies: companion diagnostic for drugs; research collaborations
  - Diagnostic companies: license biomarkers
- Sales Strategy (3 prongs)
  - Contract medical sales reps: retinal surgeons
  - Contract pharma sales reps: pharma and diagnostics
  - Business development: license agreements, royalties

cular
roteomics
An Ophthalmic Diagnostics Company

Competition

- EyeGene, Korea: Proteomics for diagnosis and treatment of diabetic macular edema drugs

- Diagnostic labs investing in ocular diseases

- Ophthalmic Contract Research Organization

- Academics with ocular sample banks
  - Cole Eye Institute

cular
roteomics
An Ophthalmic Diagnostics Company

Financial Projections

	2010	2011	2012	2013
Licenses	-	$ 500,000	$1,000,000	$2,500,000
Services	$150,000	$1,170,000	$1,950,000	$2,950,000
Diagnostic	-	-	$1,500,000	$7,300,000
Total Sales	$150,000	$1, 670, 000	$4,450,000	$12,750,000
Expenses	$1,550,000	$2,150,000	$3,150,000	$3,925,000
EBITDA	($1,400,000)	($ 480,000)	$ 1,300,000	$8,825,000

8

Partners and Collaborators

*Partners and collaborators are an important signal to investors that you are engaging with key stakeholders to advance your product to market and securing their permission to include their names and logos is typically what you do on this slide

COLLABORATOR 'X'   PARTNER 'A'

COLLABORATOR 'Y'

Executive Team

- **Names goes here**
  Founder/CSO (retinal surgeon/entrepreneur)
- **Lorraine Marchand, MBA**
  President/CEO (clinical operations BMS/Covance)

- **Advisors:**
  - Name goes here, MD/PHD, biomarkers/clinical development (BMS, Amicus)

  - Name goes here, MD/PHD/JD, regulatory/clinical development (MIT and Boston College)

  - Name goes here, PharmD, commercialization (BMS, J&J)

10

Summary

Seeking $1.5 M: clinical studies for diagnostic and laboratory services expansion

- Wet AMD drug response 1st indication; diabetes 2nd

- Strong IP in novel area; minimal competition
  - 4 yrs. research; largest human vitreous sample bank
  - Technology platform ideal for biomarker discovery
  - Proprietary panel of protein biomarkers
  - Three revenue streams/high margin potential

11

Why Now?

Demand for better eye health growing rapidly
Personalized therapy benefits patients and doctors
Strong revenue potential with several exit scenarios

For information, please contact:
Lorraine Marchand

Ocular
Proteomics
An Ophthalmic Diagnostics Company

APPENDIX 6

GUIDELINES FOR COMPLETING THE INVESTOR PITCH

The following slides will guide you in developing a clear, compelling, and concise investor pitch.

Sample Investor Pitch Deck

Investor Presentation
Company Name
Prepared for 'xx'

Company logo

Presenter's name and contact details

Presentation Guidelines

Maximum 8–10 mins presentation
- Deliver a clear, concise, and compelling message
- Answer questions: What is your "Ask" of the audience?
- Why should an investor fund your idea or company?

10-20-30 Pitch format (10 slides, 20 min, 30 pt font)

Problem	Strategy Roadmap
Solution	Sales
Technology	Team
Market/Customer Research	Financials
Competition	Summary

Problem Being Solved

What is the Pain Point or Problem You are Solving?

Who is involved?

The Evidence to Support Your Observation

Solution

Define the Solution and How it Addresses the Problem

Explain How the Solution will be Provided; Describe Features & Benefits; Commercialization Opportunity

Technology that Underpins the Solution

- One page describing the technology and its role in the solution
- Explained to a lay audience
- Intellectual property (patent, trademark, copyright) supporting diagrams or charts
- Identify dependencies and risks

Don't confuse with the venture

Don't over-index on technology

Market Size

- **Quantify the Size**

What is Addressable Market? Identify the Initial Target Niche Explain Expansion Opportunities

- **Offer Visuals**

- **Cite Research & Evidence**

Customers

- Explain Your Understanding of Your Customer Description of End User Pain

- Current Profile Market Segments

- Factors that Influence the Customer Strategies Associated with Penetrating Market Segments

- Changing Profile of Your Customer with Expansion

Competition

Direct
- Same Targeted Customers Solving Same Pain

- Similar Product Features & Benefits

Indirect
- Pain point Solved by Product/Service that is Tangential

Future

Where will Competitors Emerge in the Future

Achievements to Date/ Key Milestones

Key factors that impact venture growth

What have you accomplished? Where are you going revenue year to year projections (5 years)?

Expansion of management team key hires such as sales team addition of number of customers

Grid, time line, or chart works well here

Be realistic – acknowledge internal and external risks and dependencies required to achieve upcoming milestones

Sales Strategy

Direct: Expansion of Sales Staff Sales Cycle

Target Purchaser

Channel: Partners Scale & Size

Division of Territories

Strategic Partners (if any)

Management team

Communicating that IT is not ALL ABOUT YOU Understanding Scalability & Infrastructure Building

Current Role
Titles & Bios
Relevancy to Current Venture Entrepreneurial Experience

Future
Expansion Needs Timing

Outside Supporting Resources

Advisory Board
• Area of Expertise Name & Title Relevance to Venture

Law Firm
• Reputable Background in Venture Funding

Accounting Firm
• Rarely Sole Practitioner Background in Industry

Financial Projections

1 to 5 years

1st Year: Monthly

2nd & 3d Years: Quarterly 4th & 5th Years: Annual

Key Assumptions: Ratios, Margins, Factors Impacting Growth

Key Milestones: Break even

Sales Acceleration Change in Cost Structure

Funding Summary

Personal Funds
- Family & Friends Current Round

Future Rounds
- Conditions Foreseen

Use of Funds
- Prior Funds Used Most Optimally Key Future Use with Greatest Impact Milestones that will be Passed

Exit strategy

Acquisition

IPO

Summary

For Investor, Why is Now the Right Time, Right Venture?

Dramatic Impact on Venture of New Funding Evidence to Support Level of Confidence based on Prior Results

Fulfilling Investor's Needs: Passion, Profile, ROI, Return on Principle

Contact information

Logo

Name

Email Address

Phone Number

Address Web Site

APPENDIX 7

RESOURCE GUIDE
FOR WOMEN INNOVATORS

CATEGORY 1: FUNDING

If you are a woman seeking funds for your new idea or start-up, below is a broad list of reputable funding sources. Please refer to the organizations' websites for more information.

37 Angels

http://www.37angels.com/

Contact: admin@37angels.com

37 Angels is a network of more than ninety women who invest in a variety of start-ups, led by both female and male entrepreneurs, but with a strong focus on women entrepreneurs. Technology comprises 80 percent of their portfolio, and 65 percent of their investments are based in New York City. They typically invest $50,000–$200,000 in each start-up, and companies are selected through a bimonthly pitch contest. Since they are seed investors, they prefer to invest in start-ups valued at between $3 million and $8 million, and they require at least six months of customer data. Please refer to their list of resources for women entrepreneurs: http://www.37angels.com/female.

Amber Grant

https://ambergrantsforwomen.com/get-an-amber-grant/

Founded by Women's Net, Amber Grant's portfolio is composed of businesses of all types that are at least 50 percent owned by women. They select twelve new companies/grantees annually, on a monthly basis, and make an award of $10,000 to each business. Each year they select one grant recipient to receive an additional $25,000 at the end of the year.

BBG (Built by Girls) Ventures

https://www.bbgventures.com

BBG invests in consumer Internet start-ups with at least one female founder.

Chloe Capital

https://chloecapital.com

Chloe Capital invests in start-ups and early-stage companies. Their signature programs include a private investor dinner, a fund-raising workshop, and a Shark Tank–style pitch event. These programs are held in various cities across the United States, including Los Angeles and Boston, and they also have a virtual program. One hundred percent of their portfolio is women-led business, and 30 percent of their portfolio represents women of color.

Golden Seeds

https://goldenseeds.com/venture-capital/

This venture fund invests in early and revenue growth stage companies that have at least one woman in the executive C-suite. Their portfolio focuses primarily on B2B technology and services and health-care companies.

Hypatia Capital

https://hypatiacapital.com

This is a privately funded private equity fund focused on sponsoring female CEOs. Their investment fund mandate is to sponsor female CEOs in growth equity and buyout transactions. Through their fund, Hypatia Invests, they provide a platform for investing in women leaders. They offer education and funding to women.

Intel: Capital Diversity Fund

diversity.fund@intelcapital.com

The fund's investments cover a broad spectrum of innovative industries, starting with a five-year goal to invest a total of $125 million in technology companies led by women and underrepresented populations, including Black, Latinx, and Native American. They invest in companies of all sizes, and funded companies gain access to Intel Capital's industry-leading business development programs, global network, technology expertise, and brand capital.

Pivotal Ventures

https://www.pivotalventures.org

Founded by Melinda French Gates, PV uses investment capital to fund early-stage, untested, or provocative approaches that create a path to impact. Their work is specifically focused on expanding women's power and influence. They held an Equality Can't Wait Challenge in 2020, in which four women-led businesses received $10 million grants each to create a more equal America for women of all backgrounds.

Valor Ventures

https://www.valor.vc

Based in Atlanta, Valor funds female founders and people of color whose technology businesses are located in the Southeast region of the United States.

Women Founders Network

https://www.womenfoundersnetwork.com

Women's Founders Network hosts an annual Fast Pitch competition for women-founded businesses, which offers $25,000 or more in cash prizes. Competition finalists also receive investor connections, financial mentorship, and access to a pitch coach. Early-stage woman-founded businesses with high growth potential are encouraged to apply to their annual competition.

Contact: info@womenfoundersnetwork.com

Women in Tech

https://onlinefestival.women-in-technology.com

Initiated by Standard Charter Bank, Women in Tech is a global initiative with more than nine locations, including New York, Kenya, Pakistan, Nigeria, and Bahrain. Their objective is to empower female-led businesses by providing networking, mentorship, and funding opportunities as part of an enabling accelerator program. Their most recent chapter is in the UAE. They are a good fit for early-stage start-ups with at least one female cofounder of a business one to three years old developing an innovative and scalable tech-enabled product. Funding is up to $100,000.

CATEGORY 2: ACCELERATORS AND INCUBATORS

If you are a woman entrepreneur looking to expand your business and innovation knowledge and to accelerate the growth of your business, accelerator and incubator programs provide training, coaching, mentoring, access to capital, and fund-raising advice.

Astia

https://www.astia.org

Astia invests in high-growth start-ups and women-led companies. It offers funding, acceleration programs, networking, access to capital, and training/support for women entrepreneurs.

Female Innovators Lab

https://home.barclays/who-we-are/innovation/female-innovators
-lab-/
This New York City–based studio by Barclays and Anthemis is
dedicated to cultivating entrepreneurial talent in women. Its mission is to identify female founders at the idea stage of their journey and match them with the resources and mentorship required
to develop a company and bring it to its first round of fund-raising.

Global Invest Her

https://globalinvesther.com
Empowering and helping women entrepreneurs raise funds
for their innovations, the organization focuses on demystify-
ing funding by offering access to investors, mentorship, coaching, education, and related support programs and activities. The
goal is to increase the number of women getting funded and to
help them get funded faster—one million women entrepreneurs
funded by 2030.

Pipeline

https://www.pipelineentrepreneurs.com
Pipeline is an accelerator program for underserved entrepreneurs based in the Midwest region of the United States.

MergeLane

https://www.mergelane.com
MergeLane is a venture fund that invests in high-growth
start-ups with at least one female leader. It offers a network of
investors and mentors to encourage conscious leadership to demonstrate that diverse leadership teams drive superior returns. It
seeks to be an on-ramp for early-stage technology products and
services.

Women Innovating Now

https://www.thewinlab.org

A twelve-week growth lab, this Babson College–based accelerator provides women entrepreneurs in early start-ups from all industries with an inspiring community and a rigorous, experiential process that catalyzes innovative thinking and enables them to successfully scale their businesses.

Contact: Program director Kara Miller at kmiller5@babson.edu

CATEGORY 3: NETWORKING

No matter your stage of entrepreneurial maturity, every innovator knows that entrepreneurship is a team sport. Building the right network is a critical component of lifelong success. If you are a woman entrepreneur seeking to join a network of innovative and dedicated women in business across various industries, below is a broad list of organizations. Please visit their websites for a more detailed description.

EveryWoman

https://everywoman.com

With a presence in more than one hundred countries and a successful active network of more than thirty thousand members, this organization champions the advancement of women in business to close the gender pay gap. Networking opportunities include events, awards, and leadership programs.

Global Women's Innovation Network (GlobalWIN)

https://www/globalwin.org

GlobalWIN is committed to women's leadership in innovation. It focuses on gathering insights from the experiences of women across business, academia, and government who work in innovation-driven fields to develop mentorship, career guidance, and a network of powerful women helping women advance professionally.

She Innovates Global Programme

https://www.unwomen.org

A program headed by UN Women, this initiative led by the United Nations aims to support women in innovation by providing access to development tools, programs, and resources, connecting women innovators worldwide, and providing support for the development of innovations that meet the needs of women and girls.

We Are the City

Contact: info@wearethecity.com

This organization supports women with career planning, offers educational conferences, and grants recognition awards. The Rising Stars Awards aim to highlight future stars across multiple categories showcasing female talent. Tech Women 100 Awards recognize rising talent within the technology sector.

Women Who Startup

https://www.womenwhostartup.com

This is a U.S.-based learning platform for a global community of female entrepreneurs and innovators. It provides a network, a platform, multiple sources of collaboration, and rapid learning to female entrepreneurs and innovators who are committed to building successful companies. A yearly virtual seminar, the Women Who Startup Rally, features successful women founders.

Women in Innovation

https://womenininnovation.com

A nonprofit organization with more than four thousand members in New York, San Francisco, and London, this is a professional association for women championing innovation in their work—at companies and organizations large and small.

COLUMBIA UNIVERSITY RESOURCES (BOTH FEMALE AND MALE STUDENTS AND ALUMS)

116 Street Ventures

https://www.avgfunds.com/116streetventures/
A community of Columbia alums who pool money into a VC fund to invest in venture-backed companies. They create a diverse portfolio for their investors, coinvesting with leading VC funds across industry, stage, and geography. The goal is to raise a new fund each year that benefits entrepreneurs, the school's ecosystem, and their investors.

Columbia Angel Network

https://columbiaangelnetwork.com/
A nonprofit group of Columbia alums interested in investing in Columbia-affiliated early-stage ventures. Available to all university alums and current students.
Contact: info@columbiaangelnetwork.com

Columbia Innovation Grants

https://entrepreneurship.columbia.edu/resources/innovation -grants/
Innovation grants of $5,000 to $15,000 are awarded by Columbia Entrepreneurship to incentivize and support the creation of novel products and unique business models. Grants are open to current students with the stipulation that one founder be an undergraduate of Columbia College or General Studies.

Eugene M. Lang Fund for Entrepreneurial Initiatives

https://www8.gsb.columbia.edu/entrepreneurship/resources/
lang-fund
This fund provides early-stage investing opportunities to qualifying graduate student business initiatives. Funds are provided in the form of a $25,000 to $50,000 convertible note. The program is designed for Columbia Business School students.
Contact: langcenter@gsb.columbia.edu

Eugene M. Lang Entrepreneurship Center

Contact: langcenter@gsb.columbia.edu
This Columbia Business School Center offers courses focused on launching a company, investing in ventures, and joining a start-up or other innovation role. Courses available to CBS students include Foundations of Innovation and Entrepreneurial Strategy.

NON-U.S. RESOURCES (REPRESENTATIVE SAMPLE)

India

THE WOMEN ENTREPRENEURSHIP PLATFORM https://wep.gov.in/
The government of India through NITI Aayog sponsors an initiative that brings together women entrepreneurs and sponsors. It provides services such as free credit ratings, mentorship, funding support to women entrepreneurs, apprenticeships, and corporate partnerships. It is designed for women entrepreneurs who are at the ideation stage of their business, have just launched a start-up, or are an established early-stage start-up. It also offers incubation and acceleration support to women-founded/cofounded start-ups.

Canada

CANADIAN WOMEN'S FOUNDATION https://canadianwomen.org

The foundation operates a grant program for nonprofit Canadian organizations that have a valid charitable number from the Canada Revenue Agency. In their effort to support gender equality, they fund projects primarily focused on those who identify as women, girls, or trans, Two Spirit, and nonbinary people.

Contact: info@canadianwomen.org

United Kingdom

ANGEL ACADEME https://www.angelacademe.com

A UK-based angel network, their investors are entrepreneurs, senior professionals, and people enjoying portfolio careers. They invest in ambitious and highly scalable technologies and businesses with at least one woman with 20 percent ownership on the founding team. They host regular pitch events with a thorough four-stage selection process, investor workshops, and networking events. They fund UK-based technology start-ups that offer innovative solutions to problems in health, finance, education, security, and climate change and have a £1 million to £10 million pre-money valuation, raising £250,000–£5,000,000 of equity investment.

WOMEN'S LEADERSHIP DEVELOPMENT PROGRAM https://www.sbs.ox.ac .uk/programmes/executive-education/online-programmes/oxford -womens-leadership-development-programme

This six-week self-paced online program at Oxford's Saïd Business School is designed to facilitate self-acceptance and self-development to equip women entrepreneurs with the skills to overcome barriers faced by women business owners. It is designed for women who are moving into a senior management or C-suite role and want to break through the glass ceiling.

RISING WOMEN LEADERS PROGRAMME https://www.jbs.cam.ac.uk
/executive-education/open-programmes/leadership/cambridge
-rising-women-leaders-programme/

This three-day program at the University of Cambridge's Judge
Business School is designed for women who are intent on expanding
their professional and personal capabilities. It helps women entrepreneurs develop a clear action path for career advancement and
cultivate a strong, supportive network of peers. Attendees benefit
from a lifelong membership in Cambridge's Wo+Men's Leadership
Center. Participants should be in the early to middle phase of their
careers in management roles, with three to ten years' experience.

European Union

EU PRIZE FOR WOMEN INNOVATORS https://eic.ec.europa.eu/eic-funding
-opportunities/eic-prizes/eu-prize-women-innovators_en

This annual funding opportunity celebrates the women entrepreneurs behind game-changing innovation. Three prizes of €100,000
each are awarded to the most talented women entrepreneurs from
across the EU who have founded a successful company and brought
an innovation to the market. A fourth prize of €50,000 is awarded
to a promising "Rising Innovator" aged thirty or younger. Women
from thirty-five countries applied for the 2020 grant, with companies in advancing health technologies, green technologies, 5G technology, fintech, and more.

ACKNOWLEDGMENTS

This book has been a lifetime in the making. From my earliest experiences as a youth contributing to my father's inventions to my own start-up endeavors as a professional, I developed a passion for problem solving in new and innovative ways—and helping others do the same. Those experiences translated into curricula I developed and taught at Princeton, Columbia, and Yeshiva universities and shared as an adviser to many start-ups, often under the auspices of the University City Sciences Center, the New York University Endless Frontier Lab, and the Columbia University Translational Therapeutics Accelerator. I've also been fortunate to be an innovation practitioner through the many roles I've held in such corporations as Porter-Novelli, Bristol Myers Squibb, Covance (now Labcorp), Cognizant Technology Solutions, IQVIA, and IBM Watson Health. To all the creative and innovative minds I have had the pleasure of working with at all these places—in the classroom, the start-up lab, and the corporate world—thank you for your inventions, your insight, and your inspiration.

I will never be able to repay my literary debt to John Hanc, my cowriter. He enabled this book with his active engagement, partnership, and persistence. Importantly, he made this twelve-month marathon manageable and enjoyable.

I want to thank my research assistant and son, Matt Marchand, for help identifying and interviewing interesting innovators and for his research and writing contributions.

To Myles Thompson and Brian C. Smith, my editors at Columbia University Press, thank you for your belief in the need for an innovation book like this—one of the few on this topic written by a woman—and for your guidance and support throughout this experience.

Thank you to the faculty and students at Columbia Business School for giving me an opportunity to share my knowledge and experiences and for all you have taught me about innovation and entrepreneurship.

I would like to thank each of the innovators featured in the end-of-chapter Innovator in Focus sections, including Aris Persidis, Phil McKinney, Leslie Aisner Novak, Spencer Rascoff, Sylvana Q. Sinha, Laurent Levy, Sarah Apgar, and Dan Navarro. Thank you for sharing your stories, your wisdom, and your tips on innovation. Thank you to Larry Berger and Kari Bjorhus from Ecolab and Jabril Bensedrine from the Triana Group for sharing your case studies on innovation.

Thank you to Jabril Bensedrine, Joanne Moretti, Lynn O'Connor Vos, Amit Rakhit, Lisa Buettner, Chris Laing, Steven Phelan, Cintia Piccina, Tom Maniatis, and Rana Khan for support and endorsement of this book. Many thanks to Anouk Pappers and Deepak Patil for help with content curation and formatting to get the manuscript over the finish line.

Thank you to my husband, Don, for your inspiration, love, and support and for sacrificing many weekends while I wrote this book.

Thank you to my mom, Polly Hudson, for always believing in me, especially as I wrote this book with an aim to memorialize Dad and his unique style of creating and innovating. You brought out the best in Dad. And thank you, Greg Hudson, my "little brother" in the stories about Dad. We learned from the Master Innovator, and you demonstrate his critical thinking skills and entrepreneurial mindset. He would be proud.

To all my family and friends who have supported and encouraged me through the years and during the development of his book, especially my daughter-in-law, Anna Marchand, and my friends Joyce Avedisian, Tracy Harmon Blumenfeld, Avik Roy, and Pamela Yih—thank you. And finally, I'd like to recognize my first grandchild, Nolan Romeo Marchand, who was born during the production of this book. As a member of the next generation of innovators, may you benefit from the experiences, stories, and lessons in *The Innovation Mindset.*

Lorraine Marchand, Yardley, PA, January 2022

NOTES

1. THE FIRST LAW OF INNOVATION: A SUCCESSFUL INNOVATION MUST SOLVE A PROBLEM

1. For those curious about the origin of that quote, the truth is that no one knows for sure, but according to *QuoteInvestigator* an unnamed professor at Yale University said something very similar in 1966.

2. Michael Lawrence Films, *Memory and Imagination*, July 1, 2010, http://www.mlfilms.com/productions.

3. Thomas Wedell-Wedellsborg, "Are You Solving the Right Problems?" *Harvard Business Review*, January–February 2017.

4. Bill Gates, "Exemplars: We're Finally Learning Why Countries Excel at Saving Lives," *GatesNotes*, September 1, 2020, https://www.gatesnotes.com/Health/Exemplars-in-Global-Health.

5. Drake Baer, "Elon Musk Uses This Ancient Critical-Thinking Strategy to Outsmart Everybody Else," *Insider*, January 5, 2015, https://www.businessinsider.com/elon-musk-first-principles-2015-1.

6. See tables in Phil Ball, "The Lightning-Fast Quest for COVID Vaccines—and What It Means for Other Diseases," *Nature*, December 18, 2020, https://www.nature.com/articles/d41586-020-03626-1.

7. U.S. Department of Defense, "Coronavirus: DOD Response," https://www.defense.gov/Explore/Spotlight/Coronavirus/Operation-Warp-Speed/.

4. THE LAW OF ONE HUNDRED CUSTOMERS (THEY CAN'T BE WRONG!)

1. Liz Gannes, "Zuckerberg Tells Investors, 'We Don't Build Services to Make Money,'" All Things D, February 1, 2012, https://allthingsd.com/20120201/zuckerberg-tells-investors-we-dont-build-services-to-make-money/.
2. Boaz Tamir, "Put the 'i' Before the Apple," Lean Post, July 14, 2016, htpps:// www.lean.org/LeanPost/Posting.cfm?LeanPostid=610#_ftn2.

5. LAW-ABIDING INNOVATORS MUST BE READY TO PIVOT AT ANY POINT IN THE PROCESS!

1. "Tag: Al-Anon," Quote Investigator, https://quoteinvestigator.com/tag/al-anon/.
2. See https://www.norulesrules.com.
3. Amy Lamare, "A Brief History of Away: From Suitcases to Scandals," B²: The Business of Business, https://www.businessofbusiness.com/articles/history-of-away-luggage-data/.
4. "An Open Letter from Pfizer Chairman and CEO Albert Bourla," Pfizer, https://www.pfizer.com/news/hot-topics/an_open_letter_from_pfizer_chairman_and_ceo_albert_bourla/.
5. Adi Robertson, "Fading Light: The Story of Magic Leap's Lost Mixed Reality Magnum Opus," The Verge, July 6, 2020, https://www.theverge.com/21311586/magic-leap-studios-last-light-project-mixed-reality-sxsw.
6. Steve Crowe, "Anki Addresses Shutdown, Ongoing Support for Robots," The Robot Report, May 7, 2019, https://www.therobotreport.com/anki-addresses-shutdown-ongoing-support-for-robots/.
7. "Eight Famous (and Staggeringly Successful) Business Pivots," CEO Magazine, April 20, 2020, https://www.theceomagazine.com/business/marketing/famous-and-successful-business-pivots/.

6. DEVELOPING YOUR BUSINESS MODEL AND PLAN

1. James G. Conley, Peter M. Bican, and Holger Ernst, "Value Articulation: A Framework for the Strategic Management of Intellectual Property: The Nespresso Case," June 22, 2013, www.kellogg.northwestern.edu/Faculty/Conley/htm/VA_Nespresso.pdf.

2. Sean Bryant, "How Many Startups Fail and Why?," Investopedia, November 9, 2020, https://www.investopedia.com/articles/personal-finance/040915/how-many-startups-fail-and-why.asp.

3. Bryant, "How Many Startups Fail and Why?"

7. HOW SERIAL ENTREPRENEURS INCREASE THEIR ODDS OF SUCCESS

1. Benjamin Gomes-Casseres, "IBM and Apple: From Rivals to Partners in 30 Years?," *Harvard Business Review*, July 17, 2014, https://Hbr.org/2014/07/ibm-and-apple-from-rivals-to-partners-in-30-years.

2. Marsha Lindsay, "Eight Ways to Ensure Your New-Product Launch Succeeds," Fast Company, April 4, 2012, https://www.fastcompany.com/1829483/8-ways-ensure-your-new-product-launch-succeeds.

3. Bram Krommenhoek, "Why 90% of Startups Fail, and What to Do About It," *The Startup*, April 10, 2018, https://medium.com/swlh/why-90-of-startups-fail-and-what-to-do-about-it-b0af17b65059.

8. COAXING CAPITAL: NO INNOVATION WITHOUT COMMUNICATION

1. "Genomics in Cancer Care Market to Reach USD 39.94 Billion by 2027: Reports and Data," GlobeNewswire, December 15, 2020, https://www.globenewswire.com/en/news-release/2020/12/15/2145491/0/en/Genomics-In-Cancer-Care-Market-to-Reach-USD-39-94-Billion-By-2027-Reports-and-Data.html.

2. "The Origins of Angel Investors," Angel Investors, 2021, www.angel-investors.co.uk/the-origins-of-angel-investors/.

3. Stephen Spinelli, Jr., and Robert J. Adams, Jr., *New Venture Creation: Entrepreneurship for the 21st Century*, 10th ed. (New York: McGraw Hill Education, 2016).

4. Tom Nicholas, *VC: An American History* (Cambridge, MA: Harvard University Press, 2019).

5. Elizabeth Trembath-Reichert, "CU Gives Up Royalty Rights to Lucrative Axel Patents Amid Controversy," *Columbia Spectator*, January 24, 2005, https://www.columbiaspectator.com/2005/01/24/cu-gives-royalty-rights-lucrative-axel-patents-amid-controversy/.

6. Spinelli and Adams, *New Venture Creation*.

9. EXECUTION AND EXIT: MANAGING YOUR INNOVATION, AND IF NECESSARY, MOVING ON

1. Stephen Spinelli, Jr., and Robert J. Adams, Jr., *New Venture Creation: Entrepreneurship for the 21st Century*, 10th ed. (New York: McGraw Hill Education, 2016).

10. UNIQUE CHALLENGES WOMEN INNOVATORS FACE AND WHY

1. Bob Stembridge, "Women in Innovation: Gaining Ground, but Still Far Behind," *Scientific American*, May 3, 2018, https://blogs.scientificamerican.com /voices/women-in-innovation-gaining-ground-but-still-far-behind. See also https://www.aauw.org.

2. Sharon Hadary, "Why Are Women-Owned Firms Smaller Than Men-Owned Ones?," *Wall Street Journal*, May 17, 2010.

3. Ilene H. Lang and Reggie Van Lee, "Institutional Investors Must Help Close the Race and Gender Gaps in Venture Capital," *Harvard Business Review*, August 27, 2020.

4. Matthew Lee and Laura Huang, "Women Entrepreneurs Are More Likely to Get Funding If They Emphasize Their Social Mission," *Harvard Business Review*, March 7, 2018.

5. Lang and Van Lee, "Institutional Investors Must Help."

6. Susan Fourtané, "51 Female Inventors and Inventions That Changed the World," Innovation, July 30, 2018, https://interestingengineering.com/female -inventors-and-their-inventions-that-changed-the-world-and-impacted-the -history-in-a-revolutionary-way.

INDEX

Page numbers in *italics* indicate figures or tables.

curiosity, as child, 2
curiosity, level of, 2, 36, 163
current state, of business of
    customer, 84
customer: feedback from, 67–69,
    74–77, 85–86, 102; launch of
    problem without input from,
    25–26; needs of, 76; not buying
    product, 99–100; problem of,
    16, 17, 75–78; research, 74–77,
    79, 83–90, 122, 131, 231–33;
    understanding of, 103–4, 122
customer-focused culture, 104
customer goal and strategic
    initiative, difference between,
    37–39
Czechoslovakia, 91

Dalai Lama, 49
Dan (from medical device company),
    40
Dara (from presentation of Ray), 73
data, good business decisions and, 18
dating site, origin of YouTube as, 112
Dave (from software testing
    workshop), 55, 56
deadline, of son of business partner
    (molecular diagnostics startup),
    146
deconstruction, of problem, 26,
    30–32
deferment, of judgement, 48–49
defined problem, lack of with
    oxidative stress technology, 25–26
definition, of problem, 29
delay, in demo at workshop, 53–54
delisting, by Amazon, 101
demand for smart deodorant
    dispenser, lack of, 105
demo: of product, 68; at workshop,
    delay of, 53–54
demographic characteristics, mix
    of, 81

deodorant bottle, smart, 105
de-risk situation, plans to, 150,
    154–55, 160
designs of Ray, inspiration for, 74
design thinking, 47
Des Moines, Iowa, 70
detailed financial projections, 131
development: of business plan,
    135–36; of COVID-19 vaccines, 24,
    31–32, 151; of new technology, 149
Dhaka, Bangladesh, 112–13
diabetes patient journey map, 39
diagnosis, of correct problem, 25,
    26–27
diagnostics company, 81
diagnostic test, for oxidative stress,
    13–14, 25–26
different customer, focus on, 100
different results with same process,
    expectation of, 105
difficulty: of cooking healthy food,
    59; of starting business with
    criminal record, 127
digital: ecosystem of Fictiv, 97;
    forums for notetaking, 48;
    tool, for communication with
    physicians, 17; twins, 30
Diners Club, 138
direct-to-customer, 109, 165
disaster recovery plans, of software
    companies, 133
disciplined process, invention as,
    13, 23
discovery, of problem to solve, 16, 17
Discovery Channel, 143
diseases, application of other drugs
    to, 51–52
display, of advertising on Sugar
    Cube, 6
disposal, of sugar, 4–5
disruptive innovation, 10, 15–16
doctor office data collection, new
    solution for, 104